Published by
Gower Publishing Company Ltd
Gower House
Croft Road
Aldershot
Hants GU11 3HR
England

Gower Publishing Company
Old Post Road
Brookfield
Vermont 05036
USA

First edition published 1982

British Library Cataloguing in Publication Data

Marshall, Margaret R. (Margaret Richardson),
    1933–
    An introduction to the world of children's books. —— 2nd ed.
    1. Children's books
    I. Title
    028.5′34
ISBN 0 566 05461 2

Library of Congress Cataloging-in-Publication Data

Marshall, Margaret Richardson.
    An introduction to the world of children's books/
Margaret R. Marshall. —— 2nd ed.
    p.   cm.
    Bibliography: p.
    Includes index.
    1. Children——Books and reading.
    2. Children's literature——History and criticism.
    3. Children's literature——Publishing.
    4. Libraries, Children's.
    I. Title.
    Z1037.A1M374 1988
    028.5′5——dc19

ISBN 0 566 05461 2

Printed and bound in Great Britain by
Biddles Limited, Guildford and King's Lynn

AN INTRODUCTION TO THE WORLD OF CHILDREN'S BOOKS
2nd Edition

Margaret R. Marshall

Gower

Aldershot · Brookfield USA · Hong Kong · Singapore · Sydney

Contents

Introduction

This book is intended for those who are new to the world of children's books or are already in it but need to have an overview or to see their part in perspective.

It is not a small world, though the people in it tend to operate within specialist areas, worlds within worlds. Nor is it concerned only with books, written or illustrated ideas, but also with the psychology, sociology and education of children, their needs and interests and their aesthetic values. The more complex attitudes, values and technical skills of the adults who write, illustrate, publish, sell and promote children's books are also involved.

Coverage in this book excludes the broad range of textbooks and schoolbooks though acknowledgement is made that they too are touching the child's world. In countries that are still developing a literature for children, publishers tend to concentrate on educational texts, perhaps necessary where there is a high level of illiteracy, but a priority which means that children who are technically able to read cannot sustain that skill for lack of enjoyable books for leisure reading.

It is a big step to go from that world to the world of plenty, where the term 'children's book' encompasses a wide range of printed matter in format, content, mother-tongue or foreign language, quality and age range, from toy book to multi-volume series, for ages 0 to teenage, from 'popular' to children's literature with a capital L, and with information books covering nearly every subject.

Many of the books mentioned are British publications but the information about the genre is, in most cases, of

international application. Books for children tend to follow a similar pattern because they satisfy similar needs, worldwide. Practices in publishing, bookselling, librarianship and teaching are also basically similar. But the world is seen differently by children according to the geographical, climatic, political, religious and language factors obtaining in each child's local or national circumstances. The writer and publisher are often similarly affected or circumscribed.

Literacy, education, growth towards knowledge and increased vocabulary, the development of imagination and of insight, these, with the addition of enjoyment, are the benefits of reading for children. But books need promotion and efficient promotion needs knowledge. This book, therefore, is intended to provide basic knowledge, with indications of further readings, for the many adults who are involved with children and who are links in the chain which leads from author to child.

I am one of those links and you, the reader, are the next link in the chain.

Margaret R. Marshall
February, 1988

CHAPTER ONE

Trends in the Children's Book World

Past trends may become the norm in the present but all trends are worthy of notice and the following are the most significant at the end of the 1980s.

Internationalism is the overriding trend, arising from the breaking down of international barriers, the movement of populations, the increase in literacy, the invention of technical processes applicable to book production, the creation of cooperative organizations and large businesses, the awareness of social needs, nationally and internationally, and the spread of other media of communication, leading to greater publicity and possibilities for promotion of children's books.

The effects of this kind of internationalism have led to the spread of children's books across boundaries by means of translation, which in turn has led to the need for a focal point for children's books in each country and the creation of national centres.

Developments in the publishing field are having both adverse and beneficial effects arising from the growth of merged publishing houses. Changes in the visual and subject content of children's books are evident as is the need to recognize the multi-cultural nature of many countries and its integration into books for children.

As the international and local social conditions produce 'voices' speaking up for various needs and demands, so the development of calls for controlling the publication and library availability of some themes and named books has increased.

9

Translations and co-production

The growing internationalism of the children's book world is seen in the spread and interchange of children's books across national boundaries by means of translation. Two influences are apparent – increased awareness of the need for children's books in book-needy countries and the commercial marketing by publishers through co-publishing and co-production.

For many years the small-language European countries have translated English and American books. Norway and the Netherlands, both with excellent indigenous writers, find translation necessary in order to increase the quantity of literature required to provide choice in children's reading. Some European countries have begun to translate English language books into German, the Scandinavian languages, Italian and Spanish. They have also increased the quality and range of their own publications for children, particularly the socialist bloc countries, and some of these works have been translated into English, German and Russian.

In some countries, both developed and developing, there are no children's books written by indigenous authors in the vernacular, and no books translated into the language or languages of the country. These children may read, if they can, the imported books. One example is Benin, formerly Dahomey, in West Africa, where French is the official language and Gung and Fon the major indigenous tongues.

Some countries have a small amount of local publishing for children and a large programme of translation; for example it is common to find in Egypt and Libya, simple books from Britain and Russia translated into Arabic. The Ladybird books are available in several languages, but the author most translated is Enid Blyton, whose books are

available in thirty-two languages. In recent years some book suppliers in the UK and the USA have shipped large quantities of 'early readers' to Middle-Eastern and Asian countries.

The need for translation often lies in the lack of indigenous books which may be the result of political, social or educational factors, or simply, as in small-language countries, too small a market in that language to make publishing a viable concern.

But there is another need for translation, that exemplified in Britain, USA and USSR, all producing a large amount of children's literature annually. This need is for a widening of knowledge and culture, a receiving rather than a giving. So rich has been the children's literature of those countries that there has been no felt need to import much from other countries. Some 'foreign' books have found their way into British children's hearts over the years, some in English language from the USA, such as Louisa May Alcott's *Little Women* and Mark Twain's *Huckleberry Finn*, with more recently, the works of Betsy Byars, Paul Zindel, Virginia Hamilton, Judy Blume and Rosa Guy. From France came Perrault's tales, Babar and Madeline; from Germany Grimm's tales, *Emil* and more recently Christine Nöstlinger's books; from the Scandinavian countries came Hans Christian Andersen's tales, Pippi Longstocking, Mimff, Moomin and more recently, the wealth of teenage novels, and books about children with problems and handicaps; from Netherlands Britain has benefited by the works of Biegel, Bruna, Andreus, Reesink and Rutgers van der Loeff. From Japan have come the works of, for example, Mitsumasa Anno and Satomi Itchikawa.

The American multi-cultural society, the result of years of world-wide immigration, has produced a rich picture of the world in children's books from its immigrant authors, but has also recently attempted to systematically translate

the works of writers who still live in their native lands.

For the first time there is international recognition of the importance of sharing each other's literature.

The method by which such sharing is usually effected is through the foreign rights negotiations between publishers, in which the original publisher of the book sells the right to publish/translate/co-produce to publishers from other countries. Much of this negotiation takes place at the various international book fairs, such as Bologna, Frankfurt and Bratislava. In the 1980s there has been a growth in co-publishing, commonly in picture books, where it is possible both for the colour plates to be printed in large quantities and for the photographic sheets to be available. In order to make the book suitable for another language country, a translated text or a new text can be created and printed with the colour plates by the co-producing publisher.

An example of co-producing by a different method is the Asian Co-Publication Programme, administered by UNESCO and based in Tokyo, where eight children's books have been written and published by the Programme, each using the same illustrations but with different languages. (Details are given in Chapter Four on developing children's literature.)

The translation of children's fiction and non-fiction is another matter. The skill of the translator is now recognized as an art in its own right and rewarded by the IBBY Honour for outstanding translation.

The problems of translating are many, ranging from the technical to the literary and a successful translation depends upon the translator's knowledge not only of the source language but of the social background of its country of origin, the thought and personality of the translator, the need to do a literal translation faithful to the original text, or a free translation particularly where humour or puns are

concerned. Detailed consideration is given to these aspects in two articles in *Bookbird*, the journal issued by IBBY and the International Institute for Children's Literature and Reading Research.[1]

The trend towards translating books originally published in another country provides children with the opportunity to read more widely in every sense, but the trend to co-publishing of picture books has a disadvantage. In order to create a visual and textual content acceptable to a number of nations it may be necessary to minimize distinctive local scenery, facial features and national customs in the illustrations. But the greater availability of children's books and the savings in publishing and production costs are distinct advantages to many countries.

The question of costs and markets is significant in another trend in publishing, the merging of publishing houses.

Publishing and marketing

In the USA and Britain the growth of large conglomerates in publishing, the amalgamation of publishing houses, has put publishing in the hands of the financiers. In the late 1980s large business corporations are successfully bidding for publishing houses both nationally and internationally. The effect on the children's book world is considerable:

● Financial economy/efficiency means short print runs. By producing a reduced quantity of copies initially the warehousing costs and backlist management are reduced and the cash flow increased. For the book buyer the effect is that unless the market demand in the short term is such that a reprint is needed then the book goes out of print. This is one explanation why teachers and others who select from publishers'

13

catalogues or from retrospective bibliographies after even a short time, often find that the books are out of print when they want to order them.

- The emphasis therefore is on the popular readily saleable book at the expense of the less popular or more expensive works, which over a period of time would make a profit. Children's book editors' decisions are thus affected.

- The lucrative paperback market has led a number of hardback publishers to set up their own paperback imprint rather than sell the paperback rights to others. In some cases there is a simultaneous hardback/paperback publication.

  As the hardback market for children's books is largely public libraries, and public library expenditure cuts have affected library book funds in many countries, libraries are increasingly having to economize by buying the paperback editions. It is probable that the hardback publishers, who are predominantly in the USA and Europe, will soon adopt the practice common in some other countries, of publication only in paperback.

- New marketing strategies have opened up the outlets for the sale of children's books, with some publishers negotiating with large multiple stores to sell children's books under the store name, as in Britain's W.H. Smith, Marks and Spencer and Sainsbury stores.

  Bookshops in public libraries and schools are also increasing and the judicious selection of titles for all these kinds of marketing means that large numbers of people who had not been, or would not go, to a bookshop, are being exposed to children's books, particularly those for young children.

- Allied to this expansion of retail outlets is the growth of merchandising by publishers in countries with a

highly developed book trade. Interest in the book is maintained or extended by the creation of toys to accompany the initial publication, or devised later in response to reaction to the book, or as a spin-off from a televised version of the book. From Paddington Bear and Spot to Postman Pat and the Transformers, the publishers hope that the characters become not only a selling attraction but a tangible part of the child's book world.

- The need to find a continuing market has led to a rise in the publication of series in the UK, particularly for the young child and the beginning reader. The trend towards home–school cooperation in reading, with the use of terms like shared reading and paired reading[2] has produced a range of practices and services. The established graded reading schemes, accepted by some as necessary for learning to read are being challenged by others who see 'real' books as both efficient and enjoyable in helping children to learn to read.

Since 1984 publishers' series with a defined reading age/stage have proliferated, for example: Walker Books' *Fun to Read Picture Books* and *Red Nose Readers*; Methuen's *Paired Reading Storybooks*; Collins' *Reading is Fun*; Corgi's *Step into Reading*; Bodley Head's *Beginners*; OUP's *Umbrella Books*; Gollancz's *Share-a-Story* and Ladybird's *Puddle Lane* books having an 'adult' text and a simple text facing.

Within a period of about three years there appeared series for the middle years, for example: Hamish Hamilton's *Cartwheels*, Heinemann's *Banana Books*, Kestrel Vikings' *Kites* and Marilyn Malin's *Toppers*, all attractively packaged and at prices affordable by the child and the library market.

All these series and many information books series blur

the demarcation line between the education market and the trade market. Other series, for example, for teenagers and in the non-fiction subjects are considered later in the relevant chapter but a surge of new series in paperback has added to the range available for teenagers – a significant feature now in many countries.

From 1985 the following teenage series appeared (added to the Fontana Lions, Puffin Plus and Kestrel imprints): the Bodley Head *Paperback Originals*; Women's Press *Livewires*; Virago's *Upstarts* and Hippo's *Cheerleaders*; plus an influx from USA of Bantam's (Transworld in UK) *Sweet Dreams*, *Sweet Valley High* and *Couples* series, each with many titles.

Trends in publishing are charted worldwide in UNESCO's annual statistics and a table is shown in Chapter Five but a comparison of the returns for 1985 and 1986 shows a downturn in, for example, the Philippines and USSR but a greatly increased production of children's books in, for example, Costa Rica, Colombia, Thailand, Australia and New Zealand. Trends in publishing are related to changes in the social and economic climates in each country, but globally, the number of children's book titles continues to increase, the range of books in genres and for ages, stages, languages, interests and needs widens and, as discussed in the chapter on developing literature, there are expectations of indigenous publishing houses helping to produce an indigenous literature in many countries.

National centres

The quantity of children's literature is increasing. Recognition of its importance to children's development is spreading through the range of professionals involved with children and world-wide, there is a surge of interest in creating centres to be the focal point for a nation's children's literature.

This is closely bound up with:

- Producing a literature for children
- Collecting it
- Preserving it
- Documenting it
- Researching it
- Promoting it

Such is the growth of interest that the International Federation of Library Association's Round Table on Children's Literature Documentation Centres is considering ways in which it can encourage and actively support the setting up of new centres in addition to its function as an association of existing centres. Previously called the Round Table of Librarians of Documentation Centres Serving Research in Children's Literature, its name was changed in 1987 and members include a wide range of countries and kinds of organizations, for example:

- The Centre for Children's Books, London, UK
- Children's Literature Center, Library of Congress, Washington, USA
- Children's Literature Research Collections, Walter Library, University of Minnesota, Minneapolis, USA
- Children's Literature Research Service, State Library of South Australia, Adelaide, Australia
- Children's Literature Service, National Library of Canada, Ottawa, Canada
- Internationale Jugendbibliothek, Munich, West Germany
- Dienst Boek en Jeugd, Nederlands Books and Library Centre, The Hague, Netherlands.
- Centro de Documentacion del Banco del Libro, Caracas, Venezuela
- La Joie par les Livres, Paris, France

- Osaka International Institute of Children's Literature, Osaka, Japan
- Schweizerisches Jugendbuch-Institut, Johanna Spyri-Stiftung, Zurich, Switzerland
- Internationale Institut für Jugendliteratur und Leseforschung, Vienna, Austria
- Svenska Barnboksinstitutet, Stockholm, Sweden
- Multi-cultural Children's Research Library and Documentation Centre, Calcutta, India

Descriptions of some of these centres indicate their diverse nature, administratively, yet with basic purposes common to all.

The International Youth Library in Munich has long had the function of collecting and preserving the world's children's books and promoting information about them. Since 1948 when Jella Lepman established the library the aim has been to encourage international understanding through the means of children's and young adults' books. Dr Walter Scherf, a children's literature scholar of international repute, directed the programme from 1956 to 1982, during which time it developed into a world archive of children's books through publishers' donations of about 15,000 titles a year, and with some funding from UNESCO.

In 1983 Dr Andreas Bode was appointed director and the library moved to the renovated castle Blutenburg where the collection now comprises about 600,000 titles in 110 different languages, 270 periodical titles related to children's literature and some special collections. A small staff of specialists administer the major language sections, for instance the English language section oversees those books, the English language newsletter and relevant exhibitions. The IYC is used mainly by national and international researchers in children's literature and related fields.

Other centres have a national function, for example the

Swedish Institute for Children's Books, established in 1967 under the auspices of the city of Stockholm Municipal Library Committee, the Swedish Publishers' Association, the University of Stockholm, the Association of Swedish Authors Juvenile Books section and the Association of Swedish Illustrators, financed by government grants.

Children's books in Swedish and a collection of reference books about children's books form the basis for the information work, the documentation and the publication programme of the institute.

Of similar status and function the *Welsh National Centre for Children's Literature* was set up in 1979, governed by a committee representing various Welsh organizations and funded by a Welsh Arts Council grant and a government grant. The objective is to foster and promote literature in the Welsh language through the collections of books and related materials, liaison, exhibitions, publishing and study facilities. The centre is also responsible for administering the Tir na n-Og Award for the best original book published in Welsh and the best English language book with an authentic Welsh background.

Another method of fulfilling a national function is seen in the *Netherlands Centre for Public Libraries and Literature* (NBLC) whose Department of Children's Books has a large collection. It documents, informs, reviews, researches, exhibits and publishes extensively on children's literature. Funded by a number of relevant library and literary organizations it is also responsible for information and agency service to the country's public libraries for children.

In Venezuela a national function is carried out by a private association, the non-profit making *Banco del Libro* (the Bank of Books), which has a number of children's reading rooms and promotes the need for indigenous publications. Meanwhile it is doing something about the high cost of the books it is necessary to import from Spain,

Mexico and Argentina, by administering a chain of children's bookshops in Caracas and the interior, selling at a lower than market price.

Banco del Libro's international aim is carried out in cooperation with some Venezuelan organizations via the Inter-American Project on Children's Literature (see Chapter Four on developing a children's literature).

One of the centres attached to national libraries is the *Children's Literature Center of the Library of Congress*. This does not house or catalogue a children's book collection but accesses the Library of Congress's enormous, most comprehensive, historic reference collection of American children's books published since the eighteenth century, probably the largest such collection in existence. Established in 1963 as the Children's Book Section it was part of the LC Reference Department with Virginia Haviland as the Librarian. She saw the section's function as 'serving those who serve children'.

The section's name and status changed in 1978 to become one of LC's national programmes. It was named the Children's Literature Center and Sybille A. Jagusch was appointed as Director. Its function is as a reference and referral centre with a basic monograph, serial and pamphlet collection. The center produces a substantial number of bibliographic aids and provides an extensive publishing programme for the benefit of researchers nationally and world-wide. In addition to this center, the Library of Congress serves children who are blind or physically handicapped through its Division for the Blind and Physically Handicapped which has a vast collection of braille, twin-vision and audio books, distributed via a network of regional and state library systems throughout the country.

It is ironic that Britain which produces so much children's literature and has such a developed network of libraries, literary criticism and promotion of children's books, does not have a developed and unified national centre. There are several agencies undertaking the functions between them but without national coordination:

- *The British Library* (the national library) collects British children's books under the legal deposit system, catalogues them and exhibits them occasionally.
- *The National Library of Scotland* and the *National Library of Wales* also have legal deposit arrangements for children's books relevant to those countries. Although children's books are deposited and stored and catalogued they are not housed in such a way as to facilitate access, physically, via the catalogue, or through the British National Bibliography.
- In 1986 Iona Opie offered the Bodleian Library at Oxford the vast collection of children's books that she and Peter Opie had built up over many years. To be known as the *Opie Collection*, this comprehensive picture of children's literature and related fields, possibly the most easily accessible collection in Britain, widens the potential for research workers. Containing about 12,000 bound volumes, 11,000 chapbooks and 4,000 comics and magazines with an estimated value of £1,000,000 the collection of books from the eighteenth and nineteenth centuries will be housed with open access at the Bodleian, subject to the success of the special appeal fund.
- *The Renier Collection* of rare and early and representative children's books is held by the Victoria and Albert Museum in London. Such 'historical' or national collections are largely for preservation purposes.
- *The National Book League* in Scotland has a Children's Book Centre in Glasgow.

Working stock or information accessible to the many professionals and academics who need it is found in a range of 'national' libraries concerned with books for children.

The Children's Book Centre at the Book Trust (formerly the National Book League), a registered charity with help from publishers, librarians and the book trade, is in the process of transition. For many years the centre has been a library with a collection of the last two years' output of children's books in UK, representative samples of other countries' publications, a stock of books about children's books, and an extensive display of periodicals concerned with children's books. There is an annual exhibition of the best children's books and travelling exhibitions. Many bibliographies on themes relevant to children and books have been compiled and published by the centre and information promoted via an enquiry service, a newsletter and by lobbying.

The changes implemented by the Book Trust in 1987 involved the inauguration of the Children's Book Foundation as a division of the Book Trust, funded from within those resources, administered by a director as a non-political and non-commercial organization. Its objectives are seen as:

- To introduce books to children at the earliest possible age
- To establish books and reading at the centre of family life
- To encourage children's leisure reading
- To foster the widest possible use of books through the curriculum
- To sustain the reading habit through adolescence
- To encourage the wider use of libraries
- To identify and initiate appropriate research projects

It intends to take a leadership role in campaigns, research, setting standards, liaison, promoting and supporting books and reading by means of the Children's Book Centre, children's book information services, parental campaigns, using authors, holding book exhibitions, organizing regional events, providing training and demonstration resources and by publishing.

Overall, with the support of relevant government and opposition education spokespeople, the publishing and bookselling bodies, and sponsoring industries, the Children's Book Foundation aims to promote improvements in the British children's book scene and related professions.

The National Textbook Collection is housed in the Institute of Education, London, as a reference and research library of past and current school textbooks and documents.

The National Library for the Handicapped Child is administered as a registered charitable company, funded by public and private donations. It rents accommodation at the Institute of Education in Bedford Way, London. Established in 1985, its aim is to help children whose handicap affects their ability to read and those who have responsibility for them. It acts as a reference library in the following ways:

- Children's books with features that make them suitable for children with partial sight, hearing impairment, mental handicap.
- Books about handicap, reading, teaching handicapped children, children's literature.
- Relevant audio-visual media.
- Computer software.
- Reading-aid equipment and computer hardware for those who need them.
- Library staff who, between them, can read braille, use sign language and speak several languages in addition to library housekeeping proficiency and the skills

necessary for working with children and the adults involved with the children.

- The computer catalogue which uses twenty categories for each children's book in order to identify each characteristic of book format and content.
- The printed catalogue of the library's holdings for sale to other libraries and organizations.
- A small stock of specially selected children's books and guides for adults concerned with special children, for sale by mail or in the library.
- The publication of Handi-Read books for children with special needs, Handi-Read being the logo for the library and the symbol used on books assessed as suitable for special needs.

As the focal point for materials and information in this special field the NLHC serves a wide range of professions and of handicapped children.

Throughout the UK there are special collections of children's literature held by libraries and individuals and these are listed in Lance Salway's pamphlet on special collections.[3]

It can be seen from these examples that children's book institutions with some kind of national function fall into the following categories:

- A special section within a national library
- A children's book specialist within a national or state library
- A section within an education library
- A university institution
- An independent children's book institution or library

Some of the common functions of these centres, whether developing or long-established, include: promoting and supporting both the ideals and the practice of research in children's literature at national and international levels; providing access to and preserving collections of books and related materials; compiling and maintaining bibliographical information; supplying and advising users and enquirers.

The changing content of children's books

Throughout the world many countries have seen a marked change in the physical format of children's books, in the themes writers choose to write about and in attitudes towards both.

Contemporary social issues, initially noticeable in Italian, Danish, Swedish and American books have spread to British, Australian, German and French children's literature. To some extent this is linked with the growth of that genre known as the teenage novel where social, emotional and sexual realism can be found and this is covered in more detail in Chapter Six but books for younger children and much recent non-fiction also cover these themes of contemporary concern.

This has come about partly because of the fact that in many countries children no longer lead the sheltered lives common to earlier generations. Not only are they taught about the wider social, political, cultural and personal aspects of life, but in those countries where television is common much is learned from watching a variety of programmes even in countries where television is a political instrument of the state. There is, too, amongst some writers, publishers and educators the belief that children *should* know about subjects previously taboo, and that the present world has as much right to a place in children's literature as has history, magic and fantasy.

The enrichment of the population by the immigrant communities and the increase in efforts to give recognition to the multi-cultural society found in many countries is leading to a reflection of that society in themes, characters and illustrative content. Similarly the very slow movement towards the improvement of women's status has produced, in recent years, a quantity of action in literary and research areas.[4]

Developments in printing technology and in electronics are opening up possibilities for change in both content and format. The social, educational, political and technological aspects of life affect children's books, creating trends some of which have long-term significance for the world of children's books. A brief discussion of some areas of major significance follows.

Contemporary themes

In the 1980s a growing number of organizations and individuals turned their attention to such themes. In 1983 the conference of the International Research Society of Children's Literature devoted its time to the portrayal of children in children's literature and amongst the papers were some on children's books with children in distressing political situations; neglected children in recent American/ Canadian literature; and refugee children. The Austrian writer Christine Nöstlinger in her acceptance speech for the 1984 Andersen Writer's Medal discussed the writer's dilemma in trying to change society by writing or even helping children to make sense of their social environment:

Should we still be thinking of marks in class, first love, rows with parents ... desire for adventure, dreams and freaking out? Or should we be thinking about Pershings and SS-20's, resources and the Third World? Or about the extinction of species and the survival of mankind? Or about the Third World War, acid rain and lead pollution?[5]

She pondered on whether children in countries where war, oppression, poverty or exploitation prevail – like Chile, Iran, South Africa and Chad – need different books from children in countries where, in general, life is safer and happier. Those and other aspects she called 'the great insolubles' but she warned that writing 'for a small and refined bunch of young thinkers with sensitive souls', plus the seductive effects of television would cause children's literature to shrink 'to what adult literature already is; inaccessible to the majority'.

Robert Leeson takes this a step further, indicating that morality and message can be created:

in the spirit of the book itself and shows the shape of the story, its choices, its changes, its conclusion. If half the battle is in the content, then half the battle is in the form, in the telling, and I believe that the key to acceptance of writing by young people lies in what I call the narrative thread. ... If the readers can make their way safely through the story, as one follows a path through an unfamiliar wood, the journey is everything. Things observed will make their impact on the mind later. But to observe one must get into, and through, the wood.[6]

The English writer Bernard Ashley has written books mainly about children in an inner-city environment, in circumstances that nevertheless speak to children who have not experienced the social context or the emotional setting but who can appreciate the latter because it is possible to feel fear, compassion, joy and sorrow on behalf of, in empathy with, or sympathy with others. One example,

27

Janey, neglected, abused, to some extent amoral, is so created by Bernard Ashley that her needs and relationships enable the reader to identify with the whole situation. He has spoken and written[7] about the ways in which television has created for children a view of society, a widening of realism to take in contemporary culture, which is altering some children's previously limited knowledge of the ways others live, while offering the children who do live in those circumstances the chance to identify. As a headmaster in a London school he captures in his books the reality his school pupils know.

James Watson's *Talking in Whispers*, set in Chile, and *The Freedom Tree* set in the Spanish Civil War, explore characters' essential worth 'in circumstances which are an affront to the essential ingredients of worth'. In a paper given to the British section of IBBY conference in 1986 under its broad theme 'Got the message? Culture, ideology and politics in writing for children', James Watson promoted his passionate belief that writers are part of the global village and cannot escape the daily news and that his still small voice, as a writer, can act as a 'counterweight to the dominant voices that command media channels, by his ability to create pictures in the head'. A sixteen-year-old girl, brought to the book by a teacher's use of it in class, wrote '*Talking in Whispers* was a book which opened my eyes'.[8]

The trend for writers to speak and write about writing on contemporary themes is allied to the trend towards the publication of children's books on ever-widening areas of concern, such as the following.

Child abuse Writers are responding to the increasing revelations of physical and sexual abuse of children in many countries, by attempting the difficult task of warning, without alarm, the child reader. Examples include Oralee

Wachter's *No More Secrets For Me*, Michelle Elliott's *The Willow Street Kids*, David Pithers and Sarah Green's *We Can Say No* and Helen Hollick's *Come and Tell Me*. The Children's Press in USA has a long list of publications covering many aspects of personal and social problems in colourful picture book style with simple language.

Handicap The educational and sociological concern for the handicapped child has led to an increase in the kinds of special book to meet specific needs, for example, large print for children with partial sight, tactile books for blind and print-handicapped children, simple language books for the hearing impaired and for the intellectually handicapped, particularly for the older reader and teenager. The use of non-traditional materials is another feature of this trend, cloth, thermo-plastic and vinyl materials, which are discussed in more detail in the section on books for the less able reader.

The development of libraries and collections of books for handicapped children are also the result of the growing awareness that handicapped children have a right to read. The National Library for the Handicapped Child was established in 1985 in London, to help those who have responsibility for children whose handicap affects reading. The stock, for reference, includes about 7,000 specially selected children's books suitable for such children and is augmented by equipment to help print handicapped readers, computer software, toys and reading aids, tapes, video and films. More detail is given in the section on national centres.

Over a period of three years IBBY compiled a bibliography of books for language retarded children, using lists sent in from many countries.[9] The resulting catalogue and travelling exhibition was successful in increasing awareness of books available for other countries. The books became the basis for a special collection and information service, housed at the Norwegian Institute for Special Education in Oslo with Tordis Orjasaeter as administrator, the IBBY Documentation Centre for Books for Handicapped Children.

Margaret Marshall in Britain was commissioned by the British Library to investigate the need for national coordination of books and libraries for handicapped children, following from her many publications on the subjects. The report of that research was published in 1986, and revealed a vast range of activity with little coordination and less communication between the many professions involved with handicapped children and with books for them.[10]

The same situation appears to be causing concern in other countries, including the USA where, although the Library of Congress's Division for the Blind and Physically Handicapped has a national network of libraries and services, there is no similar provision for the hearing impaired or the mentally handicapped.

In both countries, the legal requirement that all children should be in mainstream education except for the most severely handicapped has been carried out without the provision of the extra or the special resources needed to enable children with disabilities to cope with mainstream education, and without the necessary training of teachers in the special needs of special children in the ordinary school.

On the positive side, children's book organizations, public library services to children, groups concerned with children's books both in the publishing industry and parents' groups, teachers and therapists, have become aware of the need to create, produce and promote books and related materials suitable for children whose handicap affects reading. Lists, exhibitions, in-service courses and public relations activities are all features of the middle to late 1980s in many book-developed countries.

Sexism Eliminating the sexist content of children's books is an aim long held by many in the book-developed countries and one which over the passage of time may well come about in response to the gradual changes in society's opinions and practices with regard to the place of women in society.

While the universality of sexism is proven, not all nations respond to need or to changes in the same way, at the same time or at the same speed, but there is a noticeable trend towards action. Whereas the treatment and characterization of women in children's books is properly part of the content of children's literature, the means of *altering* written and illustrated sexist images to non-sexist images in children's books is strictly in the area of control if not censorship. The term anti-sexist, as with anti-racist or anti-ageist, indicates not only a viewpoint but also suggests that action be undertaken to produce literature free from sexism, that is, non-sexist.

What is sexism? Rosemary Stones describes it as a means of 'discrimination on the basis of gender. In a sexist society choices, benefits and privileges are meted out on the basis of a person's sex rather than on the basis of individual preferences and abilities.'[11] Andree Michel defined the issue as 'practices, prejudices and ideologies that treat one sex as inferior to the other in worth or status'.[12]

It should be noted that sexism is almost always applied to the treatment of women. The negative portrayal of men in children's books may well repay study. Dr Andree Michel's study of sexism in the UNESCO research report *Down with Stereotyping*,[13] looked at examples from children's books and school books in the Arab world, in Asia and the Pacific, China, the Ukraine, Norway, France, Zambia, Peru, Kuwait, Northern America and Western Europe. She looked at prescriptions for elimination, using qualitative and quantitative analysis of aspects such as marital status, level of employment, occupation, activities of female/male characters, domestic tasks, contributing to the education of children, professional activities, political/social/leisure/artistic activities and sports, exploration and adventure, positive and negative emotions, resistance to social pressure, strengths and weaknesses of characters, insinuations and similes and examples from languages where grammar indicates gender as in French, Spanish and Arabic.

Pre-publication action has been evident in a number of ways. Publishers have drawn up statements or guidelines such as McGraw Hill's *Guidelines for Equal Treatment of the Sexes in McGraw-Hill Book Company Publications* in 1974,[14] intended to suggest to its editors and authors the non-sexist attitudes and means of attaining them. In Britain the Publishers Association commissioned a report from the Educational Publishers Council in 1981, entitled *Sex Stereotyping in School and Children's Books*.[15] Organizations and individuals, particularly in the USA, Denmark and Britain, are pursuing the aim, with Rosemary Stones to the forefront in Britain. Her thoughts on the subject were accompanied by a positive list of recommended books, *Pour Out the Cocoa, Janet*, published by the Schools' Council in 1983.[16] The positive selection of non-sexist materials is aided by ILEA's *Anti-Sexist Resources Guide*[17] which in 1984 offered guidance to books, audio-visual materials, posters, organizations, bookshops and exhibitions, mainly in London. Teachers and librarians have devised guidelines for assessing *existing children's books*, both for educational and individual use, many public library authority children's services compiling a policy for internal application.

Numerous articles have appeared in the world's children's literature and librarianship press, much of it abstracted in *Library Literature, Library and Information Abstracts* (LISA) and *Children's Literature Abstracts*.

Workshops and conferences have been held in many countries, including those where the general custom relegates women to inferior status. In 1986 a workshop was held in Uttar Pradesh in India, on the status of women in children's books. During the workshop four hundred children's books in the Indian languages and in English were examined and discussed.

The various methods of eliminating sexism in children's literature are helping to promote greater awareness of the ways in which society conditions attitudes towards the sexes and towards people of different origins. They are concerned also with encouraging the writing and publishing of books with positive treatment, avoiding discrimination, stereotyping and demeaning situations, all of which may also be found in the next aspect.

Multi-cultural content   As with the theme of non-sexism or anti-sexism, so there is a positive and a negative side to the multi-cultural society. There is a trend towards the recognition of multi-ethnic, multi-lingual and multi-cultural contributions to a society, where there may be, simultaneously, evidence of racism, prejudice, discrimination either as a state policy or by authorities and individuals, which may be reflected in the children's literature of the country concerned.

The terminology used to describe a situation which is by no means new, varies from country to country. For centuries there has been a movement of people in and out of most countries, voluntarily or forcibly. In some countries the indigenous peoples have been 'subdued' by the immigrants; a few countries have been successful in immigrant integration; in a few countries individual cultures co-habit uneasily and in some countries separatist groups are actively fighting to retain their identity. Some of the distinctive groups can be defined in the following way and

33

each has an application to literature for the children of each group:

- *Indigenous groups*, for example: American Indians Canadian Indians and Inuit (previously called Eskimos) Australian aborigines
- *the language/religion/culture groups* of tribes in many countries or religious divisions and vernaculars
- *Immigrants*: temporary, such as guest workers, or permanent

Within these divisions in most countries there are basic aspects for consideration in relation to the writing, publishing and reading of books for children. There is a movement towards serious discussion on the following population variables:

- Same language and colour as the majority population
- Same language, different colour
- Different language, same colour
- Different language, different colour
- Different culture
- Different culture/religion plus combination of above

In most countries problems often arise from differing views on assimilation into the 'host' country culture or maintenance of the native culture; from the concentration of ethnic groups in a geographical area; from bi-lingualism; from multi-cultural education and from lack of resources.

Sometimes there is a crisis over cultural identity by young people of second, third or fourth generation, particularly those of a skin colour differing from the majority population. In many countries there is a discrimination on the grounds of race, creed or colour.

A global view puts the subject of multi-culture in perspective, looking at Europe, Africa, Asia and the Americas. After the Second World War there was an influx of people looking for work: mainly from Greece and Turkey in Austria and Germany; Africans from south of the Sahara went to France; Pakistanis and West Indians to the United Kingdom. There was an estimated twelve million immigrant people in Western Europe.

Australia under a planned immigration scheme took in some three million people from Britain, Greece and Yugoslavia, and in recent years has accepted also thousands of Vietnamese refugees and Indonesian immigrants.

The United States of America, probably the most multi-cultural of all countries with about seventeen million immigrants, its Statue of Liberty as a symbol of freedom for the many previously enslaved peoples, receives about 400,000 legal immigrants a year, while Canada has about 100,000 each year.

The five million immigrants to South American countries include Japanese and Europeans.

In the oil-producing countries of the Gulf and Libya, Saudi Arabia and Iran, about three million foreign workers are employed. Immigrants from Tunisia, Egypt and Turkey are in great numbers in Libya, while Pakistan, Egypt, India, South Korea, Bangladesh and the Sudan are major suppliers of immigrant workers to other Asian countries. South Africa has thousands of migrant workers from the surrounding African territories.

A distinction can be made between those who have settled permanently and those who have temporary working status, even though the latter may be long-term. In most cases there are children, who usually become the second generation and whose children often become nationals with a possible culture clash.

Each group has brought something of value to the adopted country in both work and culture and the beneficial effects on society are often subtle and recognized only over a long period of time.

35

The rise in interest in books for minority language and immigrant peoples is thus the result of a number of factors:

- Oppression or war, causing an outflow of refugees to neighbouring or other countries, in some cases producing also forcible removal from the country.
- Poor economic conditions which influence people to go as guest workers or as migrants to other countries.
- The recognition that second- and third-generation children of the original migrants may have identity/language/education/employment problems.
- The move towards wider state control has caused some small-language groups (often with a long history and culture within their own country) to make their presence felt, backing their demands with the human rights argument of the right to their language and to read in their language.

Examples of these trends can be seen in the increased translation into Russian of children's books into the approximately sixty languages of the USSR and satellite states. Elsewhere there is a demand for children's books, for example, in Catalan, Basque, Welsh and Esquimaux, by the inhabitants of those areas.

In USA there is special attention given in books and libraries to Puerto Ricans, Chinese, Europeans and North American Indians.

In Britain multi-culturalism in historical terms is deeply entrenched, with the invasion and settlement by the Romans, then the Normans; then immigration, whether for work or as refugees by the Irish, Poles, Hungarians, Italians, Jews, West Indians, Pakistanis, Bangladeshi, Indians, Chinese, Greeks and, in recent years, Vietnamese.

Pirkko Elliott's research on mother-tongue literacy in London[18] indicated that about 330 mother tongue schools in London cover a range of languages including Polish,

Hungarian, Bengali, Chinese, Hebrew, Greek, Spanish, Italian, Gujerati, Urdu and Turkish. Although most of the children attending speak their mother tongue, few are able to read them. Bi-lingualism appears to extend to oracy rather than literacy.

The growth of dual-language books for children helps to reduce the problem and enables families to read together if the parents are literate in either language.

In Britain the Bodley Head's dual-language picture books were pioneers with editions of Ezra Jack Keats's *The Snowy Day* appearing in 1980 with parallel English and Gujerati or parallel English/Turkish text. In 1987, Watanabe's *How Do I Put it On?* was published as part of a policy decision to consider dual language for every reprint. Methuen has provided texts in Bengali, Punjabi, Urdu and Turkish for the excellent series *Terraced House Books*, by Peter Heaslop.

Individual initiative came to the fore with Jenny Ingham's project on Reading Materials for Minority Groups. Previously a researcher on children's reading habits and interests for the Bradford Book Flood, where there is a high Asian population, she then went to the Middlesex Polytechnic project collecting traditional tales from several countries. As a result of her publication *The Tiger and the Woodpecker* in 1986, a special publishing company Luzac Storytellers came into being with Jenny Ingham editing illustrated dual-language editions. Other small and community publishers have responded to the obvious need, for example, stories from Manta Publishing and picture books from Suhada Press, for under fives 'born in this country of parents from other lands and linguistic backgrounds'.

Simple-language editions with a high illustrative content lend themselves physically to parallel texts and some non-fiction series came onto the market with Franklin Watts adding Gujerati and Urdu to the *People* and *My Class* series. The principle of *designing* picture books in order to facilitate the addition of parallel text or sign language has yet to be practised by mainstream publishers in the UK though many are aware of, and some are working towards, it.

The sale of books with a multi-cultural content is increasing as librarians set up collections or add considerable numbers of such books to the children's library stocks. Two women set up a specialist bookclub, the Letterbox Library, in 1982 to supply non-sexist and multi-cultural books for children.

There is increased availability of children's books about other ethnic and cultural groups, including regional cultures within the United Kingdom. In the 1980s the representation of the multi-racial society in British and American publications moved from the emphasis on the 'problems' of some ethnic or racial aspects to a more positive depiction of perspective, situations, achievements and lifestyles, for example: Marjorie Darke's *Comeback*, where Gail's ambitions are to be a gymnast and to trace her parents; and Jean McGibbon's *Hal* who influences changes in her friends and her locality. Children and teenagers of differing colours and cultures appear frequently in both picture books and non-fiction, moving from the tokenism of the 1970s to an integral part of the book.

The works of black American writers in the 1970s and 1980s have gained a high reputation. Rosa Guy, Julius Lester, Mildred Taylor, Louise Fitzhugh and Virginia Hamilton have produced a body of work recognized as speaking for and about being black. The trend does not yet extend to Britain where there is only a handful of black or Asian writers of books for children.

Part of the multi-cultural range of children's literature is the oral tradition of folk tales and legends. Collections of re-told tales are appearing in many countries, some in versions relevant to the changed times.

One example – a practical way of erasing racism from existing works – is the 'rehabilitation' of Joel Chandler Harris's Uncle Remus stories from the white view of black folk tales to Julius Lester's new retelling of the Brer Rabbit stories in Black English, a reclaim of the stories for black people. He wanted:

> black people to have the experience of the tales, to recognize that they came out of the lives of our ancestors, and that we can take pride in them, learn from them and make them part of our culture again. But I certainly want white people too, to enjoy them, to love them and sense some of the magic that is in black culture.[19]

His book *The Tales of Uncle Remus; the adventures of Brer Rabbit*, published by Bodley Head in 1987 is illustrated by a black artist, Jerry Pinkney who said of his illustrations for the book:

> there is not 'Black Illustration' along the lines of Black English, but I do think there are certain things I'm more sensitive to than, say, a non-black, simply because that's part of my culture . . . it's easy for me to reach back and bring things from my own life, my own childhood, to the work.[20]

In many countries, there is a continuing search for roots and in others a start to setting down in print an oral tradition, both for posterity and as an aid to a literacy programme. (See also Chapter Four on developing literature.) Examples include stories from Canada's Indian and Inuit peoples, American Indians and Australian aborigines and their 'dreamtime'. In India the National Council of Educational Research and Training (NCERT), is now putting into production textbooks and other publications for children in the sixteen constitutionally recognized regional languages, and many of the publications are using traditional stories.

Throughout the world there is growing understanding that it is necessary to make available the oral and literary heritage of each culture, to *all* children.

In multi-cultural countries languages and cultures help to internationalize and cross-fertilize children's literature by increased original material in minority languages; by increased translation of the world's literature; by increased provision of migrant language material and by introducing the adopted country's literature to the immigrant people.

In many countries the demand for multi-cultural books has come from librarians, who see the need for children to have the means of developing their reading skills and interests outside the school textbook, and public librarians are beginning to collect such material for children and young people, to document it and to promote it. In the mid-1980s there was increased action by public library authorities to create a policy and appoint appropriate staff to cater for the needs.

Many British library services, where there are large numbers of ethnic groups, have created one or more specific posts to serve them. The following are examples:

The London Borough of Lambeth advertised for a Librarian (First Languages), describing the job as coordinating and developing library services to people whose 'community language is not English', applicants to have gained experience in inner city multi-racial environments and to have an 'understanding of Lambeth's anti-racist strategy'. Similarly, the Young People's Service Librarian's job description mentions that many of Lambeth's young people 'are black and from a range of other cultural backgrounds'.

Southampton City advertised for a Community Librarian (Ethnic Minority Groups) fluent especially in Punjabi, to select and promote the stock of the Asian languages to the minority ethnic community.

The London Borough of Hackney's Under Fives Librarian is expected to work closely with, amongst others, the Afro-Caribbean and Indo-European sections and to have knowledge of, and preferably speak, one of the languages of the communities in Hackney: Afro-Caribbean, Asian, Greek and Turkish.

In the north of England, Leeds has an Ethnic Communities Librarian responsible for library provision to 'people speaking Indian and Asian languages' and for developing the long-established library service to such communities in the city.

In Scotland, the Glasgow District Libraries hold collections of Asian and Chinese language materials, print and audio, in branch libraries in the areas of the ethnic population. Materials for children include simple reading books in the various mother tongues, folk tales, religious works, history, geography and travel, textbooks for school examinations, and in English, books on the relevant customs, religions, history and travel. Librarians are available to give story hours in Urdu and Punjabi.

Such examples of public library services are to be found in other book-developed countries including USA, USSR, Australia, Denmark, Sweden, Netherlands and West Germany.

While African, Asian and South-East Asian countries have many vernaculars within their state borders, often with no written material in the vernacular, those that have a published literature know that many of their people are illiterate. There is a difference between the small language minority groups in their own country and the small ethnic minority groups in an adopted country in terms of literacy, availability of material and interest in mother tongue reading. However, trends show that the former group is concerned with keeping its language alive by publishing and by use in education, while the latter group is concerned about literacy and the adopted country's language.

After such indications of positive work towards multi-cultural books and library service for children it is unfortunate that the negative side must be indicated – racism.

Racism Racism can be identified in children's books in a number of ways:

- The treatment of people of a race in such a way as to relegate them to secondary or inferior status
- Minority peoples always presented as a 'problem'
- White people shown as having power and making decisions regardless of the black or ethnic group in the story
- Affecting the child's self-image, damaging to self-esteem
- Stereotyping physical characteristics of a race
- Caricatures or misrepresentations in illustrations
- Factual inaccuracies or undue emphasis on the less-developed aspects of a nation in information books

The presence of racist aspects in books for children occurs in all countries and is not confined to the treatment of non-white peoples. Stereotyping of white peoples is also to be found in books emanating from countries where the majority population is not white.

Efforts to eliminate racism from books have increased in the 1980s. In the USA the Council on Inter-racial Books for Children produced in 1976 its *Human and Anti-Human Values in Children's Books; a Content Rating Instrument for*

Educators and Concerned Parents; Guidelines for the Future. To enable selectors to identify racism the guidelines and the journal, *Bulletin*, used a chart of factors against which to check each book. In Britain the National Committee on Racism in Children's Books was set up in 1979 and produces a critical journal *Dragon's Teeth*, with articles and reviews on children's books, materials, classroom and library action against racism.

During the 1980s, the 'future' referred to in the American work, an increasing number of new and long-established children's books have come under scrutiny for jingoism, stereotyping of 'foreigners' and demeaning treatment of non-white characters and greater attention has been paid to textbooks and information books for children and young people.

While the positive aspects of this scrutiny are likely to have a long-term effect on the writer and publisher in pre-publication elimination of racism, some of the negative aspects can be seen in the section on controlling children's literature later in this chapter.

Fantasy gamebooks   The electronic age in technologically developed countries has produced a range of home computers, a vast quantity of computer books not only on how to use the particular machine, but of computer games also. The Dungeons and Dragons cult that sprang from computer games in the early 1980s in USA has spawned game books such as *Talisman of Death* by Steve Jackson and Ian Livingstone, in Puffin's *Fighting Fantasy* series in which adventure, fantasy worlds and science fiction-type scenes and characters abound. Corgi's *Dragon Warriors* series and, for younger readers, *Transformers* gamebooks are examples, as are the *Intergalatic Quests* and, again for younger readers, the *Adventure Packs* from Macdonald Purnell.

Gamebooks are a form of story in numbered sections in which the reader chooses from alternatives the path to be taken towards the eventual outcome. Many contain violent scenes and characters, offer choice of action, but of a mainly violent nature, are written in short sentences, have minimal characterization or depth of plot and have proved to be of considerable interest to many boys who find the action, pace and role-playing participation attractive.

The format of the fantasy gamebooks – paperback, about 350 pages in numbered paragraphs, with black and white line drawings on most pages – requires a fairly high degree of reading ability and stamina, and the availability of alternative action on each page means that the book can be read several times by different routes to the ending.

Boys from seven to upper teenage buy, borrow and swap vast numbers of such books, a proven commercial success for publishers and booksellers but occasioning anxiety in some parents, teachers and children's literature critics, who see the books' popularity as part of the de-sensitizing effect of violence in television and cinema films and uncontrolled video watching at home.

Adults who express their views on gamebooks of this type usually fall into one or other of two positions, polarizing at the end which sees the books as one more indication that young people are increasingly unable to cope with sustained reading and prefer a diet of surface enjoyment and immediate gratification of the base interests, and the opposite end which sees the popularity of the books as a change from the well documented findings that interest in reading declines fast, in teenage boys.

While gamebooks may well be a 1980's cult, they are significant in that they spring from a technological trend, break new ground in page layout and plot construction and combine the trend towards participation, seen in books for the very young child, with the decision-making expected in the period of adolescence – and in the construction of computer programmes.

Controlling the content of children's literature A trend which is being strongly pursued by some people in several countries is the attempt to exclude, delete from, or ban children's books where the content is considered to be sexist, racist, politically unfavourable, obscene, anti-religious, violent or derogatory about particular characterizations or disabilities.

There are two separate lines of discussion:

- There is a positive laudable desire to give humans of every race, colour, creed, sex or political viewpoint, the rightful dignity by *encouraging* writers to write positively on these issues and this has been exemplified in the earlier sections of this chapter. This desire leads in part to the view that it is important to teach children things it is thought to be too late to teach adults.
- There is the negative aspect of intent to control the content of children's books which many, including the present writer, find disturbing. There is an increase in the number and location of people who believe that all books already written should be examined for signs of these issues and banned if considered to be guilty by the banners' criteria. There are those who believe that all writers must adhere to a code of practice which would, for example, require a writer to balance a 'bad' character with a 'good' character or a bad situation with a good situation. There are those who have a politically motivated belief that children's books must be used to show children how oppressed they are by parents and authority and how anarchy can be achieved (this aspect is common to a number of European countries) and there are many countries

where the official line of government requires that children's books conform to a norm of heroism and patriotism, the socialist bloc countries and South Korea being current examples. Add to these, those Roman Catholic and Islamic countries who control literature according to religious tenets, and the amount of 'control' is seen as considerable.

There have developed in several countries pressure groups of both the right and the left, and of women's rights, children's rights, black rights, gay rights, nationalists and others, which seek to influence past, present and future literature for children.

The negative aspects of control include the trend towards a witch hunt – itself a sexist term, of individual books considered to be damaging. In the USA the 1980s have seen an increase in litigation against individuals and authorities, court cases involving children's books and school books, where librarians or school boards have been sued by parents or organizations. In one of many examples a group of Tennessee parents with Christian fundamentalist beliefs objected in 1986 to a series of 'readers' in use in local schools and asked for a ban on the books. They claimed that taken as a whole, the series denigrated Christianity and promoted humanism, feminism, pacifism, world government, vegetarianism, pantheism, scepticism, idol worship, witchcraft, black magic, Hinduism and animism. The books included *The Diary of Anne Frank*, *The Wizard of Oz* and *The Three Bears*. The judgement went in favour of the parents.

In England voices have been raised in print and on television and radio, but not in litigation, against what some considered sexism and witchcraft in Roald Dahl's *The Witches*; charges of racism have been levelled at *Dr Dolittle* and *Biggles* and some of Enid Blyton's books have been edited in the new editions. In 1986, *Jenny Lives with Eric and Martin*,[21] the story of a five-year-old girl spending weekends with her homosexual father and male lover, raised the ire of parents and politicians, as did an accusation of racism against the nursery rhyme *Baa Baa Black Sheep*. One local education authority has appointed 'advisers' whose task is to seek out evidence of racism, sexism and anti-social aspects, including judgement on books in the schools.

The use of swear words in children's books raises objections from some adults, as does the inclusion of sexual inference or description in both fiction and non-fiction, for example, Jane Cousin's *Make it Happy*, a guide to sex and sexuality, which caused unhappiness to some teachers and parents but not to the teenagers for whom it was intended.

There is a need to allow objecting writers' voices to be heard and there is a need for those who find books objectionable to be able to voice those views. The fine line between objecting as an individual or an organization and banning for *everyone* appears to depend on the law of the land concerned. What is deemed to be illegal or what is legal but offensive to some, in published material, varies from country to country, as does the pre-publication control of censorship to be found in countries where the state controls all aspects of culture.

The propagandist didactic approach which seeks to erase the 'unacceptable' history and to allow only the 'acceptable' present and future is a dangerous trend to be countered. Such a trend can lead to censorship locally and possibly nationally, requirement to conform to education or propagandist or religious rules or policies and, at worst, to conform to the socio-political rules of a dictator or an ideology which suppresses anything likely to be critical of, or in opposition to, that ruling power. History is full of such instances, as is the contemporary world.

Pre-censorship and suppression of children's literature is a different process from the selection criteria applied by teachers and librarians when choosing books for inclusion in libraries. Such selection is discussed in Chapter Nine.

Creative literature cannot be written to proclaim a 'message' unless it springs from the writer's imaginative and literary talent, shaping the message as an integral part of the story. For people in the children's book world the message is to treasure freedom to write and to select.

As awareness grows with education and as society itself changes, so there tends to develop as a natural progression, writers and literature that reflect the awareness and the changes.

Visual content and format

There is a widening of the concept of what constitutes a book for children and a recognition that very young children, even babies, can benefit from books, not only 'novelty' books but nursery rhymes, picture story books, alphabet books, counting books and a host of others. Dorothy Butler describes, discusses and advises in the 190 pages of her excellent book *Babies Need Books*.

Developments in colour printing, paper manufacture, computer technology, art forms and publishing policies have made possible the vast growth in what is variously called toy books, novelty books, books for babies, for the very young, for the pre-school child, for the under-fives, or beginning books. The trend is for books designed to be participative, to be touched or manipulated, to provide stimuli for the senses. Though purists may not consider them children's literature they are part of the children's book world and many have won acclaim such as Eric Hill's *Where's Spot?*, Jan Pienkowski's *The Haunted House*,

Virginia Allen Jensen's *What's That?* and Eric Carle's *The Very Hungry Caterpillar.*

The growth of technological machinery to manufacture kinds of paper, and means of shaping it, has enabled illustrators and paper engineers to create an increasingly imaginative range of physical formats, sometimes called toy books or novelty books, with the implication that they are ephemeral, cheap or for small children. Although some examples are, there is a noticeable trend for publishers to use the format for books which are intended to educate and to last, in addition to being enjoyed.

Books for the very young are available in many materials; board, cloth, vinyl, plastic paper and wood. The original pop-up books have led to a highly developed production of books with movable parts, from the very simple such as Richard Fowler's *Touch'n'Go* series of concertina board books, for example, *Let's Make it Go from Side to Side*, to the more complicated Sadie Fields Productions books like *The Plane* which won the 1985 Smarties Prize for Innovation, and the many non-fiction books which now employ the method of explaining actions or changing scenes.

At a purely entertainment level there are many lift-the-flap, turn-the-wheel and scratch-the-page books, the latter requiring the reader to scratch the micro-dot impregnated page to release the smell, and an increasing number of noise books from the simple squeak to the micro-chip musical books such as Hamish Hamilton's *The Snowman* by Raymond Briggs which plays the theme tune from the filmed version of the book.

A book which broke new ground, won awards and pleased both adult and child readers was Allan and Janet Ahlberg's *The Jolly Postman* in which each opening revealed an envelope containing a letter written in the style of the sender and facing a picture relevant to the theme, for example, Goldilocks' letter to the three bears apologizing for her intrusion.

Block or cube books offer another dimension and there are many books shaped like the subject of the book, for example, house, bus or shopping basket. The use of materials to touch is now common, such as fleece in the picture of a sheep, bark on a tree and plastic for a glass jar.

Thermo-plastic inventions have been used to create a tactile surface for pictures, raised surface pictures to feel, and books with detachable object or doll character to be moved about through the theme or story, are obtainable.

The possibilities for technical changes to book format seem endless and the possibilities for the use of such books are important, the main feature being the potential for participation. Involving the child or young person in doing something with the book opens up the use of senses other than, or in addition to, the eyes and the mind, enabling also children who have those senses impaired to benefit from, and enjoy, books.

Librarians and booksellers are displaying and promoting books for the very young to parents, child minders and nursery schools. Some library authorities have appointed Librarians for the Under Fives and in 1985 the Book Marketing Council had a national promotions campaign to highlight the wealth of books in this category.

The increase in the number of books with a format different from the traditional picture books or information books for the young, added to the range of hardback and paperback books of excellent quality in content and design, indicates a world-wide recognition of the need to start young if children are to become literate in the fullest sense.

Audio-visual format

Increased attention to the visual arts is possible through the technological inventions and experiments which have produced magnificent examples of art books, picture strip art, pop-up and paper engineering in recent children's books. But the social influence of television, in those countries where children have access to it plus the effects of the electronic age, are conditioning children to expect visual information and pleasure from other media.

It is perhaps a sign of the trend, at least in Britain, that the promotion of children's books via television is effective both with children and with teachers and librarians. Probably the only country in the world to have such an extensive use of children's books on radio and television, Britain and British children are fortunate to have access to a wide range of popular books, literary children's books and dramatized versions of them.

From an entertainment point of view, very young children can listen to stories on radio in the programme *Playtime* and see and hear on television stories on *You and Me* and *Words and Pictures*. These BBC programmes are notified to schools and public libraries via a regular news-sheet, *Book Track*, which lists the books to be featured in the programmes. The books to be seen and heard in autumn 1987 for instance were as follows:

Lucy and Tom at the Seaside, Hughes, S. (Gollancz, 1976)
Goodnight Owl, Hutchins, P. (Bodley Head) (Penguin, 1975)
The Supermarket Mice, Gordon, M. (Picture Puffins, 1985)
Up Along, Down Along, Wilmer, D. (*Reading is Fun* – Fontana, 1985)
The Elephant and the Bad Baby, Vipont, E. and Briggs, R. (Picture Puffins in association with Hamish Hamilton, 1971)
Going Fishing, Edwards, D. (Fontana, 1979, from a selection of *Listen with Mother Stories*)

The Train, McPhail, D. (Andre Deutsch, 1987)

James and the Model Aeroplane, Blakely, P. and Taniuchi, K. (Adam and Charles Black)

Snuffy and the Fire, Bruna, D. (Methuen, 1970)

A Bear for Christmas, Keller, H. (Julia MacRae Books 1985)

The Magic Porridge Pot (Traditional)

Thomas Tidies His Room, Wolde, G. (Hodder & Stoughton, 1983)

Peter's Chair, Keats, J.E. (Bodley Head, 1984)

Rebekah and the Slide, Parker, C. and Kopper, L. (Dinosaur, 1983)

On the Way Home, Murphy, J. (Macmillan Picturemacs, 1984)

Ben's Gingerbread Man, Daly, W. (Walker Books, 1985)

The Very Busy Spider, Carle, E. (Hamish Hamilton, 1985)

Roger Was a Razor Fish and Other Poems, Bennett, J. and Roffey, M. (Bodley Head, 1980)

Meeting Grandad, Dickinson, M. and Sheikh, Y. (not published)

Happy Birthday, Sam, Hutchins P. (Bodley Head, 1978; Picture Puffin, 1981)

Buzz Buzz Buzz, Barton, B. (Hamilton, 1974; Picture Puffin, 1981)

Dhanji's Spaceship, Crowther, N. Petley Jones, N.

The Tiger Who Came to Tea. Kerr, J. (Collins, 1968; Picture Lion, 1973)

Meg's Eggs, Nicoll, H., Pienkowski, J. (Heinemann, 1972; Picture Puffin, 1975)

Lazy Jack (traditional)

Alex and Roy, Dickinson, M., Firmin, C. (Deutsch, 1981; Scholastic, 1983)

Maisie Middleton, Sowter, N. (Black, 1977; Picture Lion, 1982)

Winklet Goes to School, Ryder, E., Lang, S. (Burke, 1982)

Meg's Veg, Nichol, H., Pienkowski, J. (Heinemann, 1976; Puffin, 1982)

On My Way to School, Berridge, C. (Deutsch, 1976)

The Very Hungry Caterpillar, Carle, E. (Hamish Hamilton, 1970; Puffin Books, 1974)

Butterflies, pop-up book, Tarrant, G. (Heinemann, 1978)

Johnny Cake (traditional)

Each Peach Pear Plum, Ahlberg, J. and A. (Kestrel Books, 1978; Armada Picture Lions, 1980)

The Boy Who Cried Wolf, Ross, T. (Anderson Press, 1985; Beaver Books, 1986)

The Three Bears (traditional)

Forget-me-not, Rogers, P. (Kestrel Books, 1984; Puffin Books, 1986)

Frog and Toad are Friends, Lobel, A. (World's Work, 1971; Puffin Books, 1983)

Kangaroo from Woolomoolloo, Cowley, J. and Mahy, M. (Arnold-Wheaton, 1986)

Mr Cosmo the Conjuror, Ahlberg, A. (Kestrel Books, 1980; Puffin Books, 1980)

Tortoise's Dream, Troughton, J. (Blackie, 1980)

The Cabbage Princess, Le Cain, E. (Faber, 1969)

Mr and Mrs Pig's Evening Out, Rayner, M. (Macmillan, 1976; Piccolo Picture Books, 1978)

The Ugly Duckling, Hans Christian Andersen

Peskybogle, Bowle, J. and *The Let's Join In Storybook* BBC, 1986

Clever Polly and the Stupid Wolf, Storr, C. (Faber, 1979; Penguin and Puffin, 1967)

The Enchanted Palace, Bhattacharya, A. and Basu, C., *Storyteller*

Fairytale Series (Luzac, 1985)

Double Spell, Lunn, J. (Puffin, 1986)

The Haunting, Mahy, M. (J.M. Dent & Sons Ltd, 1982)

Messages, Darke, M. (Puffin, 1985)

Ghostly Companions, Alcock, V. (Fontana, 1985)

Uninvited Ghosts, Lively, P. (Puffin, 1985)

Hearing Things, Eyles, H. (Piccadilly Press, 1987)

Come Danger, Come Darkness, Park, R. (Hodder & Stoughton, 1985)

For older primary school children the BBC radio programmes *Let's Join In*, *Listening and Reading* and *Living Language* offered a further list of books. ITV (Independent Television) also broadcasts programmes for children both through the Schools Broadcasting department and in the general entertainment schedules. For older children the *Middle English 9–13* programme looks at the work of writers and has covered Nina Bawden, Gene Kemp, Betsy Byars, Roger McGough, Janni Howker, Michael Rosen amongst others.

The English Programme for 13–18 similarly discusses writers and poets and has offered to the viewers interviews with Ted Hughes, John Agard and Benjamin Zephaniah.

ITV has a weekly programme for children called *Book Tower* in which a well-known actor recommends children's books with filmed excerpts or readings and participation by children. BBC's daily *Jackanory* uses a personality to sit before the camera and read/tell the story in serial form with stills from the illustrative content of the book. More storytelling comes in signed form with ITV's *Sign a Story* shown on Monday to Friday with two deaf presenters signing the story read by two other people, and sub-titles on the screen.

The visualizing of children's books extends also to the dramatized versions for which British television has a deservedly high reputation. In the last few years many books have been shown in serialized form including:

Box of Delights by John Masefield
Green Knowe by Lucy Boston
The Cuckoo Sister by Vivien Alcock
The Dolls House by Rumer Godden
The Worst Witch by Jill Murphy
That Was Then, This is Now by S.E. Hinton

The Night Swimmers by Betsy Byars
Jack Holborn by Leon Garfield

The televizing of children's books, whether for school work or leisure viewing has repercussions, beneficially, when the children follow up that programme in the library. Public libraries are often inundated with children asking for the book just shown on television.

Another spin-off from television is the television book of the programme, and libraries and bookshops need to stock the book of the film as well as the book of the film of the book. Both BBC and ITV have their own book production and book marketing departments.

The electronic age has seen the advent of cassette players and video recorders and players in the home in the technologically developed countries. Companies producing spoken word cassette tapes and compact discs of children's books are proliferating, some overlapping in the kinds of children's book recorded and some with specialized functions. In Britain companies include the following:

- Chivers Audio Books
- Pickwick's Tell-a-Tale
- Tempo
- Conifer
- ASV
- Tellastory
- BBC
- Listen for Pleasure
- Talking Tape Company
- Anvil
- Caedmon
- Reva Lee

Some companies specialize in complete unabridged recorded readings, for example, Cover to Cover's recording of Robert Westall's *The Machine Gunners* read by James Bolam, Whigmaleerie concentrates on Scottish works, and Side by Side on dual-language books with cassettes. A detailed guide to audio-cassettes of children's books is Rachel Redford's *Hear to Read*.

A similar number of companies produce information cassettes for children and young people. In Britain catalogues of the vast quantity of audio-visual material and the items themselves are available from library supply companies such as T. C. Farries, Chivers Book Sales and Books for Students. Many schools' library services also acquire, catalogue and loan audio-visual materials for school use and most public library authorities in the UK loan cassettes and compact discs in the same way as books. Two of the lending services offering children's book cassettes on a national basis are Calibre, based in Aylesbury, Buckinghamshire, and The National Listening Library at 12 Lant Street, London SE1.

Films and filmstrips using the illustrations from the children's books have long been available from Weston Woods Limited in USA and UK. They now stock video films also in answer to the growing demand from schools, libraries and individuals, as videos become as much a part of the home scene as television. Popular books such as Raymond Briggs's *The Snowman*, Fiona French's *Future Story* and Roald Dahl's *Charlie and the Chocolate Factory* are examples from the many available.

Another trend in the computer age is ironic in that as more and more computers are introduced into offices and homes and factories and as individuals try to master their control, large numbers of books are produced to help them. However, not only are there quantities of books about how to use the computer, but books of computer games, and the spin-off is the advent of gamebooks such as *Dungeons and Dragons* and *Fighting Fantasy series*, the content and format of which break new ground and were considered earlier in this section.

Organizational, technical and commercial aspects appear to respond quite quickly to changes in society, but the writer's and illustrator's response to the social and psychological developments takes longer.

References

1 Anthea Bell. 'Translating humour for children'. *Bookbird*, 2, 1985, pp. 8–13. Wolf Harranth. 'Some reflections on the criticism of translations. *Bookbird*, 2, 1985, pp. 4–8

2 Roger Morgan. *Helping Children Read: the paired reading handbook*. Methuen, 1986

3 Lance Salway. Special Collections of Children's Literature.

4 Andrée Michel. *Down with Stereotypes: eliminating sexism from children's literature and school textbooks*. Unesco, 1986

5 Christine Nöstlinger. Acceptance speech for the 1984 Andersen Writer's Medal. *Bookbird*, 4, 1984 pp. 8–11

6 Robert Leeson. *Reading and Righting*. Collins, 1985, p. 168

7 Bernard Ashley. 'TV reality – the changes and the opportunities'. *Books For Keeps*, March 1987, no. 43, pp. 16–17

8 James Watson. 'Challenging assumptions: ideology and teenage fiction in today's global village'. *International Review of Children's Literature and Librarianship*, vol. 1, no. 3, Winter 1986, pp. 65–71

9 Tordis Orjasaeter. *Books for Language-retarded Children, an annotated bibliography*, compiled by IBBY. Unesco, 1985, Report Study, no. 20

10 Margaret R. Marshall. *Handicapped Children and Books*. BNB Research Fund, 1986

11 Rosemary Stones. *Pour Out the Cocoa, Janet; sexism in children's books*. Longmans, 1983

12 Andrée Michel, op. cit.

13 Andrée Michel, op. cit.

14 McGraw Hill. 'Guidelines for the equal treatment of the sexes', in Michel, op. cit.
15 Educational Publishers Council. *Sex Stereotyping in School and Children's Books*. EPC, 1981
16 Rosemary Stones. op. cit.
17 ILEA Learning Resources Branch. *Anti-sexist Resources Guide*. ILEA, 1984
18 Pirrko Elliott, *Library Needs of Children Attending Self-help Mother-tongue Schools in London*. School of Librarianship, Polytechnic of North London, 1981
19 Stephanie Nettell. 'Rehabilitating that rabbit'. *Books For Keeps*, no. 44, May 1987, pp. 12–13
20 Stephanie Nettell. op. cit.
21 Susan Bosch. *Jenny Lives With Eric and Martin*. Gay Men's Press, 1986

Further reading

Butler, Dorothy. *Babies Need Books*. Penguin, 1980. *Five to Eight*, Bodley Head, 1986
Carrington, Bruce and Short, Geoff. 'Comics, a medium for racism'. *English in Education*, 18 (2), Summer 1984, pp. 10–14
Cianciolo, Patricia J. 'Internationalism of children's literature; trends in translation and dissemination'. *Bookbird*, 1, 1984, pp. 5–14
Costanzo, W. 'Reading interactive fiction; implications of a new literary genre'. *Educational Technology*, June 1986, pp. 31–5
Davies, Anne M. and Hedge, Ann. *Racism in Children's Books*. Writers and Readers, 1985
Donelson, Ken. 'Almost 13 years of book protests – now what?' *School Library Journal*, 31 (7), 1985, pp. 93–8
Elkin, Judith. 'The Books For Keeps Guide to Children's Books for a Multi-cultural Society, 0–7'. *Books For Keeps*, 1986 and ditto *8–12*, published 1985
Hazareesingh, Sandip. 'Racism and cultural identity; an Indian perspective'. *Dragon's Teeth*, 24, 1986, pp. 4–10

Ingham, Jennie. *Telling tales together*. Video and pamphlet on the background to the Reading Materials for Minority Groups Project, Caedmon Trust, 1986

Klein, Gillian. *Reading into racism; bias in children's literature and learning materials*. Routledge, 1985

Leeson, Robert. *Reading and Righting* (see reference 6)

Macleod, Anne S. 'Censorship and children's literature'. *Library Quarterly*, 53 (1), Jan. 1983, pp. 26–38

Patel, Bhadra and Allen, Jane. *A visible presence; black people living and working in Britain today*. London, NBL, 1985, an annotated anti-racist booklist for young adults

Raddon, A. *Exploring cultural diversity; an annotated fiction list*. School Library Association, 1985

Sheridan, E.M. *Sex stereotypes and reading; research and strategies*. Newark, Delaware, International Reading Association, 1982

Stones, Rosemary. *Miss Muffet Fights Back*. Penguin, 1983

Totemeyer, Andree-Jeanne. 'Social criticism in South African children's and youth literature'. *Bookbird*, 2, 1986, pp. 9–21

Trelease, Jim. *The Read-Aloud Handbook*. Penguin, 1984

Tucker, Nicholas. 'Games-books; the best sellers'. *New Society*, 23 May, 1986, pp. 10–12

Tucker, Nicholas. *Suitable for Children? controversies in children's literature*. Sussex University Press, 1976

Waterland, Liz. *Read With Me; an apprenticeship approach to reading*. Thimble Press, 1985

CHAPTER TWO

What is Children's Literature?

Literature for children, whether it is fiction or non-fiction, is part of the larger world of literature and can be written, read, studied, analysed, taught and promoted in the same way as literature for adults, or any other age or subject group.

Children's books can be categorized in a number of ways:

- By format, for example, hardback, paperback, board book, cloth book, pop up.
- By genre or theme in fiction, for example, fairy, school story, animal story, adventure, humour, pony book, short story.
- By broad theme or specific content in non-fiction.
- By age of reader, which can be further sub-divided by reading age, reading stage, interest age, school age/stage.
- By ability or disability of the intended reader, for example, remedial, special needs, 'easy reading'.
- By codes and symbols such as Dewey classification scheme, colour coding according to reading/interest age, colour coding by subject content, pictograms, Kamm code (that is, assigned by reading age/interest age).
- Publisher's series, both fiction and information book.
- Miscellaneous categories such as by language, by popularity, by multi-cultural content, TV tie-ins, 'quality' v. 'trash'.

They can be divided into national categories such as English, American, Indian, African, German, Australian, Scottish, Welsh or Japanese children's literature.

These are all external labels applied to certain texts and/ or illustrations, but what are the factors which have caused the interested adult to pick out from literature in general those books that speak particularly to the minds and interests of children and young people?

1 *Is there a kind of writing specifically suitable for children?*

This raises educational constraints. The term 'suitable' often means different things in different countries. In many Western countries it may mean morally suitable in the sense that certain themes are considered to be taboo in order to protect children from those aspects of adult life thought to be corrupting, unpleasant or sexual. 'Suitable' may also refer to the educational relevance. Perhaps the book may be thought to cover a theme or be written in a style that children cannot understand until a certain stage of mental, physical or reading development has been reached. This is true to some extent.

Writers and publishers are aware that the child's conceptual development, his likely experience of places, people, events, and emotions may all be common to a broad age group as may his stage of reading development, which is mentioned in number 5 of this chapter. It is also true that most books for children and young people are shorter than those for adults and therefore more suitable for the likely concentration span of a maturing reader.

In general, however, 'suitability' is not in the forefront of a writer's mind when writing a novel for children. What the writer wants to say often springs from the subconscious, though the style and layout in which it is put on the page may vary according to the theme and to the broadly intended reader.

Aidan Chambers looked at this question in great detail in his analysis of 'the reader in the book'.[1] There he suggested that a book is 'suitable' for children when the author has written in a way that *includes* the reader, where the meaning is explicit as well as implicit, when the author helps the child reader to negotiate, to develop the ability to receive the text as a literary reader does 'rather than make use of it for non-literary purposes'.

The reported conversation with Alan Garner investigated the writer's views, probes the relationship between child reader, the book and the author and provides an interesting insight into both.

When a story contains the possibility of many meanings, there is room for each reader's interpretation, thus widening the range of potential readership from that commonly accepted as the norm.

But there are many countries where 'suitable' books for children are achieved by requiring them to reflect the political, social or religious outlook of the state. This frequently produces books that can be called didactic, meaning, intended to teach or be instructional. Didacticism is a word frequently found in writings about children's books in many countries, particularly in the early years of English children's literature. But these aspects are looked at in more detail in Chapter Six.

2 *Is there a literature aimed at children and therefore, by implication, not for reading by adults?*

This is even more arguable and makes it necessary to distinguish between books written *for* children and books *read* by children, and between books written for adults and books read by adults. Experience shows that in most countries where children are literate there is no rule which says that children cannot or must not read books supposed to be for adults or vice versa, though from time to time teachers, librarians and organizations attempt to set up barriers.

There are numerous examples of books that are read and enjoyed by adults and children alike, such as *Alice in Wonderland*, *Winnie the Pooh*, the *Narnia* series of C. S. Lewis, Richard Adams's *Watership Down* and Antoine de Saint-Exupery's *The Little Prince*. The illustrated books which straddle any line include Raymond Briggs's *Fungus the Bogeyman* and *When the Wind Blows*, while cartoon books such as Jean Jacques Loup's *The Architect* and Mordillo's *Mordillo's Football* cannot be contained within an age group. All offer greater depths to the adult reader than the child reader, achieved by the greater depth of life experience of the adult.

The reverse of the question can also be studied when looking at the kinds of books used in schools as set books for young people of thirteen to sixteen: 'quality', classic and contemporary literature such as Lee Harper's *To Kill a Mockingbird*, Laurie Lee's *Cider with Rosie*, George Orwell's *Animal Farm*, plus Dickens, Tolstoy, Jane Austen, Ernest Hemingway, Solzhenitsyn and D.H. Lawrence. Is there a literature aimed at adults and therefore not for reading by children?

The myths and legends whether read from books or heard via the storyteller are enjoyed by adults and children in every country.

Some writers say that they write for themselves rather than for an age group of reader, but other writers do have a child or a range of children in mind when they are writing a book, and they try to tailor the concepts, events and the vocabulary for that readership. In both cases some of the resulting books cross the very blurred dividing line between a book for children and a book for adults. The line is usually drawn by publishers who, within their own organization have divisions into adult and children's departments with separate editorial staff. They see the potential market and put the book into adult, teens or children's list and publicize accordingly.

So the author's aim or lack of it does not necessarily create a children's book. Children and adults read across whatever boundaries are made by publishers, librarians, teachers or parents.

3 *Is children's literature a lower level of writing, a second-best training ground for writers who will then progress to writing for adults?*

This suggests that children are less intelligent than adults instead of simply knowing less than adults. Many writers of books write both adult and children's books. Some start with adult fiction or non-fiction and later write a book for children; others start with a children's book and then write for the adult market. Many alternate between the two over the years. Penelope Lively, Peter Dickinson, Ted Hughes, Angela Carter, Rosa Guy, Leon Garfield and Russell Hoban are just a few examples from contemporary children's literature, while examples from the past include Lewis Carroll, Kenneth Grahame and Mark Twain.

Investigation of this feature amongst established writers, past and present, would reveal that the great majority of authors of children's books have also written adult books.

Many writers and illustrators say that children's literature requires much more research, attention to detail and careful writing for the text and the artwork. The many biographies and autobiographies of children's book writers and illustrators, and the articles they write about their craft, bear testimony to this.

There are, of course, in most countries examples of second-rate writing and illustration in which it is obvious that little is expected of the child reader and little offered. Anyone closely connected with children knows that such books are often very popular with children and teenagers, but that point is not relevant to the question posed here.

Simplicity does not mean second-rate. There are many very simple books for young children or older less-able readers which are very well thought through by the author, illustrator, designer and publisher. Equally, there are many lengthy prose works which turn out to be examples of books in which the authors have not given sufficient thought to plot, style, characterization and vocabulary. So the length of the book and the density of the writing do not necessarily mean quality.

4 *Is one of the distinguishing features that the characters in the books are children?*

Some of the best-known characters in literature suggest that this is not so. Cinderella and Sleeping Beauty were past puberty; Big Claus and Little Claus and Ali Baba were adult baddies; Robin Hood, King Arthur, Pandora and Persephone were all adults; in fantasy fiction C.S. Lewis's Aslan, Tolkien's Hobbit, Grahame's Badger, Ratty and Mole are all adults in symbolized form, as are Anansi and Brer Rabbit. Most of Leon Garfield's characters are adult, so are Rosemary Sutcliff's. Mrs Pepperpot, Mary Poppins, Raymond Briggs's Father Christmas and Fungus the Bogeyman are adults, as are Beatrix Potter's Mrs Tiggy-winkle and the people who live in Charles Keeping's *Railway Passage*. Most of the characters in the world's myths and legends are adults.

But there are many books which do have child characters and the good books relate the plot to the child's experience, but there is much 'autobiographical' literature from writers who are able to recreate their childhood and to use those memories as a narrative device. Some of these 'controlled memories' are discussed by Stuart Hannabus in an article, 'The child's eye; a literary viewpoint'.[2] Many writers have spoken of the vivid reality of childhood and writing has opened the gate to previously hidden or previously unremembered experiences and emotions.

Child characters as such are not necessarily a distinctive factor unless shown in relationship to the adult world or adult behaviour patterns; neither is child experience in terms of the so-called 'realistic' description of social setting or patterns of behaviour. This can be limiting to both writer and reader whereas the child's experience of *emotion* tends to be the same as an adult's. It may be much more intense because the child has not yet learned to control the emotions, and the emotion may pass more quickly because new experiences are crowding into a child's life at a fast rate. But books built upon the emotional aspects of the theme can cross national frontiers better than those based on a fixed time or place.

The experience of emotion and the description of social and emotional realism seem to come together most obviously in the genre of fiction known as the teenage novel and this is looked at in more detail in Chapter Six. Though the presence of a child character may not make the book a children's book the author's characterization of the child's emotions is a crucial factor.

5 *What about language as a characteristic of children's literature?*

There is a common belief that for children, language, vocabulary and sentence structure involve writing 'down' by choosing simple words and shortening sentences to aid understanding. In picture books for the young child and in books for the less able reader of any age, this may be necessary even when the pictures give clues to the words. In the recent trend towards paired reading books there are examples of tailoring the language to the reading ability of the child, when each double spread has an 'adult' version of the text on one page with the 'child' version on the facing page. Graded reading schemes used for the teaching of reading exemplify the precise quantification of vocabulary to fit the age or stage of the child reader, though there is a strong body of opinion that 'real' books are more than adequate for the teaching of reading while providing enjoyment also.[3]

The term 'reading age' is usually used by educationists to signify the stage of reading development attained by a child, assessed according to one or other of the many testing procedures available throughout the world. But these and the reading schemes, tend to test the vocabulary comprehension used in *learning* to read rather than in reading, and are designed to enable teachers to monitor pupils' progress. In children's literature, as opposed to books used in graded schemes, the reading age can be determined by a number of factors related to language:

- The likely identification and understanding of written vocabulary, helped in some books by clues from the illustrations.
- The nature of the sentence structure, simple or complex.
- The scope of the subject matter.
- The relevance of theme and style to the reader's experience, that is, what the *reader* brings to the text or picture from his own experience, whether physical, emotional or social. These provide clues to *understanding* the language and therefore to overall comprehension.

These, however, are devices for assessment of a book already written and may be used by, for example, children's book marketing people, by teachers and librarians for their own legitimate purposes. But writers who make concessions to vocabulary or structure unrelated to the theme of the book 'unless it is for a special readership' are likely to produce superficial and undemanding books.

Short simple words and sentences can be rich, as in the first page of Ted Hughes's *The Iron Man*:

> The Iron Man came to the top of the cliff. How far had he walked? Nobody knows. Where had he come from? Nobody knows. How was he made? Nobody knows.

Short simple sentences are effective in many of the myths, legends and folklore tales, as in the story of *How Saynday Got the Sun*, from *North American Legends* edited by Virginia Haviland:

> Then Saynday got busy because he'd finished his thinking. He could begin to do things now.
> 'How far can you run?' he said to Fox.
> 'A long long way', said Fox.
> 'How far can you run?' he said to the Deer.
> 'A short long way', said Deer.
> 'How far can you run?' he said to Magpie.
> 'A long short way', said Magpie.
> 'I can't run very far myself', said Saynday, so I guess I'll have to take it last.'
> Then he lined them all out and told them what to do.

Alan Garner's *Stone Book Quartet*, an example of a book read by young people *and* adults, is written in short sentences, but sentences that contain words which convey a wealth of meaning, a pattern of speech that indicates the regional location of the story and use of language that brings to life the characters and the events. As with *The Iron Man*, the opening sentences of *Stone Book* attract attention:

A bottle of cold tea; bread and half an onion. That was Father's baggin. Mary emptied her apron of stones from the field and wrapped the baggin in a cloth.

In all these examples the simplicity is rich and is helped by repetition of words which give a story rhythm and a narrative quality.

The simplicity is part of the quality of writing and is effective in the context. However, in other books large words and sentences may be needed to convey mood, scene or conversation. Unusual words may create humour, impart information or indicate meaning in the context. Bernard Ashley, Janni Howker, Jan Mark and Roald Dahl use language differently but effectively in their respective books.

There is no one style of writing, language or range of vocabulary that indicates a book for children. However, within the numerous styles throughout the whole range of children's books, the writers who use language not only to convey literal meaning but also to stimulate a wealth of potential child perception, response and insight, are recognized as creators of characteristically *good* children's literature.

6 *Perhaps the subject content is a means of categorizing a book as a children's book?*

But are there subjects which can *only* be put into story form or information book form for children, or can *only* be offered to adults? The whole of human knowledge and experience in any period of time and in any geographical place is open to coverage in children's books and, as indicated, in the chapter on the changing content of children's books, previously taboo themes are being offered by contemporary writers. The books that are suitable for children are those which look at an aspect in a way with which a child, at his stage of knowledge and development can cope, and the 'strong' subjects, the 'sensitive' issues *are* part of contemporary children's literature.

Much of the early didactic literature for children contained deathbed scenes and warnings of a fiery hell that would give today's Western children nightmares, but which were part of the experience of children in the eighteenth century. Robert Leeson in his book *Reading and Righting*,[4] draws attention to the themes in books in times past, indicating the political, religious and social nature of tracts and Sunday School books and the penny dreadfuls and chapbooks, with the differences in moral approach between the popular and the 'establishment' publications. War, hunger and oppression are part of the twentieth-century experience for some children while others know nothing personally of such hardship, a point expanded on by Margaret Meek[5] when taking issue against those who hold the view that the 'cosy' world in some children's books is the 'real' world.

Many of the great themes in story can give awareness, knowledge, and an understanding of things which in real life might be overwhelming. To many children what is real life for them is fantasy for others, depending upon their personal circumstances. So it is the *perspective* which creates a literature for children, the angle from which the theme is viewed through the characters, via the author. Whether the theme involves world issues, morals, emotions, child or adult relationships, peaceful or violent events, realistic or imaginary settings, animals, humans or objects, the angle of vision is what causes a book to catch the interest of a child, the uniting of the mind of the writer with the mind of the child. When the writer recaptures the child-like vision, or as Rosemary Sutcliff describes herself, has a pocket of unlived childhood, or is in tune with contemporary childhood's needs and interests then the result is a book which enables the child to 'see' life and to acquire insight. This causes him not only to say 'That was a good book, have you any more?', but to have the unspoken and subconscious satisfaction of adding to his stature mentally, emotionally and linguistically.

7 *What is children's literature?*

It is the written word which collectively embraces all the features mentioned so far: subject matter, characters and setting, style of writing and use of vocabulary presented from an angle which matches the child's perspective. 'Good' literature is that which also increases his perception. But this body of literature is made up of millions of individual books, each the product of someone's brain, each different from the other, providing for differing languages, differing interests, differing needs and differing levels of reading ability.

However good a book is and however marketed, promoted and recommended, we cannot say that *every* child must read the book, or *every* child will enjoy the book, for a child will not read voluntarily, unless he enjoys the experience or needs the information, any more than adults will, voluntarily, spend time on books which do not engage their minds or hearts.

References

1 Aidan Chambers. 'The reader in the book'. In

Chambers, N. *The Signal Approach to Children's Books*, pp. 250–328

2 Stuart Hannabus. 'The Child's Eye; a literary viewpoint'. *International Review of Children's Literature and Librarianship*, vol. 1, no. 3, Winter 1986, pp. 103–114

3 Liz Waterland. *Read with Me; an apprenticeship approach to reading*. Thimble Press, 1985

4 Robert Leeson. *Reading and Righting*. Collins, 1985

5 Margaret Meek. Review. *International Review of Children's Literature and Librarianship*, vol. 1, no. 3, Winter 1986, pp. 118–19

Further reading

Aiken, Joan. *The Way to Write for Children*. Elm Tree Books, 1982

Byars, Betsy. Spinning straw into gold. *The School Librarian*, vol. 34, no. 1, March 1986, pp. 6–13

Carpenter, Humphrey. *Secret Gardens; the Golden Age of Children's Literature*. Allen & Unwin, 1985

Chambers, Aidan. *Booktalk; occasional writing on literature and children*. Bodley Head, 1985

Cott, Jonathan. *Pipers at the Gates of Dawn; the wisdom of children's literature*. Viking, 1984

Fox, Geoff et al. 'Writers, Critics and Children', articles from *Children's Literature in Education*, Heinemann Educational, 1976

Haviland, Virginia (ed.). *Children's Literature; views and reviews*. Bodley Head, 1973

Kirkpatrick, D.L. *Twentieth-Century Children's Writers*. Macmillan, 1984

Meek, Margaret (ed.). *The Cool Web; the pattern of children's reading*. Bodley Head, 1977

Moss, Elaine. *Part of the Pattern*. Bodley Head, 1986

Shulevitz, Uri. *Writing with Pictures; how to write and illustrate children's books*. Watson-Guptill Publications, 1985 (UK, Phaidon)

Townsend, John Rowe. *Written for Children; an outline of English language children's literature*. Penguin, 1974

Nettell, Stephanie. 'Bringing a sense of joy; an interview with Errol Le Cain'. *Children's Books* (British Book News), Sept. 1986, pp. 2–5

Southall, Ivan. 'Coat of many colours'. *Reading Time*, 100, July 1986, pp. 38–40

CHAPTER THREE

The Development of Children's Literature

Much modern children's literature has its roots in the past, in both form and content; many current attitudes towards children's books are based in the past and in much contemporary sub-literature, or popular literature, there are points of comparison with the 'penny dreadfuls' of earlier times.

That body of literature called the 'classics' is not a once-and-for-all list of great books but a growing body, being added to continually over the years as new books are written, read and acknowledged to be works that stand the test of time.

This is of the essence in a study of the development of children's literature in that literature reflects the time, the relationship of the content of books to the social and cultural time; the technical sophistication of the time as it makes possible methods of book illustration and book production; the religious and educational influences at each period of time affecting literacy; the governmental and political influences of time in the legislative control or promotion of books via publishing, bookselling and libraries.

The following brief outline of development is intended as background information. Those who are interested in the considerable amount of deeper detailed research into the history of children's literature will find recommendations for further reading at the end of the chapter.

It is a fact that what is known throughout the world as children's literature today has its origin in English history,

74

in which a combination of circumstances contributed to the conditions under which a literature best develops.

Every country has its myths, legends and folk tales, passed on orally from generation to generation in times past and today, but the printing of such tales by Caxton in fifteenth-century England provided a basis for development and extension into later centuries. Puritanism had a didactic, moral and religious effect on books and education, exemplified in James Janeway's *A Token for Children*, an exact account of the conversions, holy and exemplary lives, and joyful deaths of several young children. Similarly didactic was John Bunyan's *Pilgrim's Progress*, not written for children but adopted by them for the adventure story rather than the Christian allegory. John Locke, philosopher and educationist had a moral influence on the content of books for children and also sent fairy stories underground. Perrault in France had collected the courtly tales of *Cinderella*, *Sleeping Beauty*, *Red Riding Hood*, *Puss-in-Boots* and many others, and these were widely acclaimed across the Channel, but Locke's disapproval of fairy stories caused them to appear in chapbook form in England, which, as is the case with many things that are disapproved of or banned, gave them a wider market than might otherwise have happened.

Chapbooks, tiny 'paperbacks' were sold by chapmen or pedlars or travelling salesmen, to the same kind of mass market as the modern popular paperback books have today. Locke's disapproval was carried on into the eighteenth century by Mrs Trimmer and the Sunday School movement. Ironically the Sunday School movement, in its function of educating the working population, increased literacy and therefore readers, creating a religious literature to feed their needs, but many of the newly literate adults and young people found the popular literature more attractive.

Though there were many such items adopted by children for reading, the start of the specifically secular literature for children was provided by the printer and bookseller John Newbery (after whom the American children's literature award is named) in 1744. *The Little Pretty Pocket Book*, *History of Little Goody Two Shoes* and *The Lilliputian Magazine* were all aimed at middle-class children and were a mixture of information, moral story and entertainment.

By the turn of the century and throughout the nineteenth century there were changes in society which helped to develop children's literature, the greatest being in education. The Sunday School movement, the growth of the Mechanics Institutes for the education of workers, and the start of compulsory education for children all created a more literate population. This in turn led to an increase in private and organization libraries and in 1850 to the first Public Libraries Act. Towards the end of the nineteenth century compulsory education for children, the invention of lithography, mechanical papermaking and cloth binding coincided to enable the standardized mass production of books, which meant the possibility of greater quantity of any book and the consequent reduction in cost, the possibility of colour illustration and the wider attraction of books to a mass literate population.

Social barriers were breaking down and children were beginning to be seen as human beings in their own right, to be informed and educated but also to be entertained, and writers responded to this freedom by creating a body of literature which has come to be known as the golden age of children's literature, a period which continued up to the 1920s. A few examples of children's books from 1850 to 1932 will serve to justify this description: *Alice in Wonderland*, *Children of the New Forest*, *The Water Babies*, *Tom Brown's Schooldays*, *The Daisy Chain*, *King of the Golden River*, *The Jungle Book*, *At the Back of the*

North Wind, *Treasure Island*, *Lear's Book of Nonsense*, Beatrix Potter's books, *Wind in the Willows*, *Dr Dolittle*, *Winnie the Pooh*, *Peter Pan*, *The Phoenix and the Carpet*, and *The Hobbit*.

These works exemplify the diverse genres. From the largely didactic literature of the early years there developed the adventure story, fantasy, humour, humanized animals, the kind of imaginative literature which is the bonus for those children in every country who have mastered the mechanics of reading and achieved the degree of fluency necessary for the enjoyment of reading.

After the First World War when the social order had changed and international influences were felt, the 1920s and 1930s showed a growth in adventure and family stories with Arthur Ransome's *Swallows and Amazons* and Enid Blyton's *Famous Five* books, Richmal Crompton's *Just William* books and W.E. Johns's *Biggles*, which have maintained their popularity to the present day. In USA the *Bobbsey Twins* and *Tom Swift* were similarly capturing children's interest.

Also in the 1920s and 1930s that truly British institution, the boarding school, was the setting for the genre known as the school story, which achieved enormous popularity in many parts of the world both then and now. Such authors as Angela Brazil, Elsie Oxenham and Eleanor Brent Dyer created schools in which mysteries, challenges and excitement provided wish fulfilment for many girls while authors such as Talbot Baines, Gunby Hadath and Frank Richards entertained the boys with tales of rivalry, adventure and fun in boys' boarding schools.

Most of the authors in this period serialized their stories in the numerous magazines of the time, such as *Magnet*, *Gem*, *Sunny Stories*, *Boys Own*, *Girls Own* and *Aunt Judy's Magazine*, thus reaching a wider readership than book purchasers and library users. For this was the heyday of children's periodicals, whether largely print or largely picture strip as in the comics like *Film Fun*, *Girls Crystal*, *Dandy*, *Beano* and *Mickey Mouse*.

In this period too, official acknowledgement that children's literature could be worthy was seen in the establishment of the Newbery Medal in USA in 1922 and the Carnegie Medal in UK in 1936, both awarded for an outstanding children's book in each year; and the Caldecott Medal from 1938 in USA and the Greenaway Medal from 1955 in UK for outstanding illustrated children's books in each year. For by this time some notable work was coming from illustrators in many countries, the result of developments in colour printing and of the widening market for children's books.

Alongside the expansion of children's fictional reading material came the development of the non-fiction work for children, both individual information books and children's encyclopaedias. A period of recession followed, during the Second World War, after which came another flowering of talent and the development of different kinds of children's books. The works of William Mayne, Lucy M. Boston, Alan Garner, C.S. Lewis, Philippa Pearce, Rosemary Sutcliff, Henry Treece and many others are deemed to be the 'new' classics and were all created in the 1940s to 1960s. Their work covered fantasy, historical novels and family stories and produced a wealth of excellent literature.

By this time publishers in the UK and USA were proliferating to meet the demands of an increasingly large child population, the result of the birth rate expansion after the war. Television was not yet widely available and children needed books for leisure reading and books for school use because one of the results of educational changes legislated by government in UK was a move towards project/topic/child centred learning, which required a wide range of quality of information book.

By the 1960s a solid core of masterly writers was being acclaimed by the critics, librarians and by children. Children were also eagerly reading the work of popular writers such as Enid Blyton, Noel Streatfeild, Malcolm Saville and Richmal Crompton and both child and parent were financially able to consider buying, which led in turn to the start of paperback publishing for children, initiated by the Penguin group in a series called *Puffins*. The Puffin Club, under the leadership of Kaye Webb until 1986, expanded its membership and countless children discovered the magazine, took part in the competitions, sent for the badges and posters, and read the books, which were by the 1980s divided into Picture Puffins, Young Puffins, Puffins and Puffins Plus and Pocket Puffins.

From paperback story books to paperback picture books was a short step facilitated by the developments in printing processes. The 1970s can be categorized as the time at which there was a coming together of certain conditions to produce a new genre of books for young people, the teenage novel. Begun in the 1960s in USA and developing there and in the UK and Sweden in the 1970s, the teenage novel was the result of the following conditions:

- The postwar population bulge had then reached teenage.
- The economic climate which provided well paid employment for teenagers, possibly for the first time in history, meant that money was available to gratify their needs and desires, thus there was a market for specifically teenage literature.
- There was the recognition by writers and publishers that here was a new breed of reader, too old for children's books, not yet emotionally mature enough for many adult books, with a definable set of interests, anxieties and problems.

In the 1970s and early 1980s came serious novels with a teenaged central character, as in Aidan Chambers's *Breaktime* and *Dance on my Grave*, and Jane Gardam's *Bilgewater* and *Summer After the Funeral*. At the same time American writers, Judy Blume, Paul Zindel, Betsy Byars, S.E. Hinton and Robert Cormier were taking British teenagers by storm. British publishers began to cater for the market with Macmillan's *Topliners* series and Bodley Head's *New Adult* books, leading to the noteworthy expansion in 1986–8 of imprints for teenagers, already mentioned in the section on trends. There was an explosion of American paperback series into Britain in the middle of 1980s, creating a considerable quantity of reading matter particularly for teenage girls, with romance series such as *Sweet Dreams* and *Couples*, amounting to hundreds of titles.

Alongside these popular series from both British and American publishers, individual novels continue to thrive from the pens of, for example, Jan Mark, Peter Dickinson, John Rowe Townsend, Margaret Mahy, Robert Westall, Jill Paton Walsh, Janni Howker, Bernard Ashley, Robert Leeson and James Watson.

By the middle 1980s most public libraries had created a teenage library; school libraries could not, financially, keep pace with the demand for teenage books and many booksellers, recognizing that young people *were* buying books, allocated specially labelled shelves to books linked to teenage interests.

In 1986 the Book Marketing Council report by Michael Pountney on *Books in The Teenage World* indicated that the book trade was in urgent need of more information about each category of teenager; what, why and when they read, or why they do not. The BMCC's Teen Read Campaign produced a Top 100 list of books teenagers said they had liked and invited a jury of 12 young people to whittle it down to a Top 21, and this is included in the section on teenage reading in Chapter Eight.

The growth of 'teenage' books and teenagers' interest in reading is a significant and continuing part of the development of children's literature.

The effects of the television age, coupled with improvements in photography, colour printing and the technical possibilities for innovative paper engineering, were some of the factors involved in the expansion of the range of picture books in the 1980s in Britain and the USA.

Some of the major illustrators of the 1960s and 1970s continued to produce good work in the 1980s; for example Mitsumasa Anno, Quentin Blake, Raymond Briggs, Anthony Browne, Dick Bruna, John Burningham, Erroll le Cain, Fiona French, Shirley Hughes, Charles Keeping, Helen Oxenbury, Jan Pienkowski, Maurice Sendak and Brian Wildsmith. The children's book world paid special attention also, in the middle 1980s, to illustrators such as the Ahlbergs, Pamela Allen, Michael Bragg, Michael Foreman, Ron Maris, Jan Ormerod and Gabrielle Vincent.

The traditional view that picture books were for children who could not yet read was giving way to a realization that art speaks to all ages. The picture strip format, used so successfully by Hergé for Tintin, by Uderzo for Asterix books and in Raymond Briggs's equally popular works, began to appear in other books, in whole or in part, in both fiction and non-fiction, even to the picture strip editions of Shakespeare's plays, for example, *Romeo and Juliet* illustrated by Von and published by Michael Joseph.

Books such as Raymond Briggs's *When the Wind Blows*, Fiona French's *Future Story* and *Snow White in New York*, Bob Wilson's *Stanley Bagshaw* books, Charles Keeping's *Sammy Streetsinger* and Roberto Innocenti's *Rose Blanche* are part of a growing range of picture books with interest and messages for young people aged about ten and

81

upwards to adults. They were first accorded status and publicity by Elaine Moss in her *Picture Books for Young People 9–13*, published by the Thimble Press.

The upsurge of paper engineering books with flaps, movable parts, cut-outs and pop-ups, created a special category. A variety of publishers and packagers were noted for such books, such as Dean, Ventura, Purnell, Random House, Blackie, Child's Play, Gallery Five, Viking Kestrel, Heinemann and Methuen.

Described in Chapter One as novelty or toy books, the good examples have become an art form in their own right and some have won awards. The movability device also attracted the makers of information books who saw it as a means of supplying information better than, or in addition to, both text and static picture, in subjects like natural history, human anatomy and transportation. Examples include *The Human Body*, by Jonathan Miller from Cape; Claire Smallman's *Outside-In*, illustrated by Edwina Riddell from Macdonald; Patrick Moore's *The Space Shuttle Action Book* from Arum Press and Ray Marshall and John Bradley's *Watch it work! The Train*, from Viking Kestrel.

Information imparted pictorially became the norm in the middle 1980s with not only an increase in the use of photographs rather than drawings, but a significant growth in the publication of photographic books, that is, the theme treated photographically with captions or a small amount of text, rather than text illustrated by photographs. Both hardback and paperback series and individual information books, for all ages, use this medium.

The development of picture books and books for teenagers was not matched by a growth in books for those in between until the middle of the 1980s, when publishers began to realize that once a child learned to read he would have to make what for many was a leap from picture book to full-length children's novel. For some years Hamish

Hamilton's series *Gazelle* and *Antelope* had held the fort, with Methuen's *Read Aloud*, Collins' *I Can Read* and Abelard Schumann's *Grasshopper* series, but from about 1980 other publishers developed a range of books designed to meet the needs of newly fledged readers, who would not or could not cope with the average style and length of the normal children's book. Julia MacRae's *Blackbirds*, Kestrel's *Kites*, and Kestrel *Read-Alones*, Fontana's *Young Lions*, Corgi's *Young Corgi* series, Hamish Hamilton's *Cartwheels*, Faber's *Fanfares* (orange series for 5–8), followed by in 1986–7, the series for the next stage up with Hamish Hamilton's *Banana Books* and Marilyn Malin's *Toppers*.

Meanwhile mainstream children's books in each genre were being augmented in considerable numbers. The continuing popularity of the adventure stories of Willard Price, Malcolm Saville and the Hardy Boys, Nancy Drew and the Famous Five et al., carried on alongside reading the works of writers who epitomize the breadth and vitality of children's literature in the mid to late 1980s, such as Jean Aiken, Vivien Alcock, Bernard Ashley, Nina Bawden, Nina Beachcroft, Judy Blume, Aidan Chambers, Beverley Cleary, Helen Cresswell, Roald Dahl, Jane Gardam, Alan Garner, Leon Garfield, Janni Howker, Gene Kemp, Robert Leeson, Penelope Lively, Margaret Mahy, Jan Mark, William Mayne, Philippa Pearce, Susan Price, Rosemary Sutcliff, John Rowe Townsend, Jill Paton Walsh, Robert Westall, Barbara Willard, Patricia Wrightson and Diana Wynne Jones.

The development of the social 'voice' in the 1970s and 80s is discussed in detail in Chapter One on trends, but the steady pressure of people like Rosemary Stones and Robert Leeson, and writers such as Leila Berg, Jan Mark, James Watson and the black writers, has borne fruit to the extent that social realism, meaning 'telling it like it is', whether referring to class or race, is an integral part of children's book publishing today right through the age range. Rosemary Stones' efforts for non-sexist and non-racist books include the Children's Rights Workshop, the Children's Book Bulletin, The Other Award, lists such as *Ms Muffin Fights Back*, books such as *Mother Goose Comes to Cable Street* (poems) and an analysis of the theme *Pour Out the Cocoa Janet*, which looked at sexism in children's books.

A quiet campaigner and effective speaker, she has been in the forefront of the movement to have a children's literature that gives due dignity to races and sexes and classes. Different but equally effective was the work of Bob Leeson through his writing on the subject such as *Children's Books and Class Society* and *Reading and Righting* and through his creative writing, whether in *Grange Hill*, *The Third Class Genie* or *It's My Life*.

There was a suggestion in the 1970s that the sociological content was predominant over the literary content, producing what Elaine Moss called 'politikidlit', a term for which there was some justification at that time. But since then the social content has been brought to life by very able writers with perspective and literary talent, noticeable also in the black American writers mentioned in Chapter One who began to speak for the black population, at the same time opening up areas of experience for non-black readers. Julius Lester, Rosa Guy, Mildred Taylor, Louise Fitzhugh, and Virginia Hamilton produced major works to acclaim from readers and critics in many countries.

Black British writers were not so numerous nor so prolific. Poets John Agard of Guyanian origin, Linton Kwesi Johnson from Jamaica and Buchti Emecheta from Nigeria, all based in London, are the few; with writers of Asian origin, Farrukh Dhondy and Rukshana Smith, whose books depict the lives of Asian teenagers in English society.

There is as yet, no body of work voicing the generation born in the UK, which may indicate the difference between historical and contemporary experience of the black American and that of the black or Asian Briton.

Realism in poetry came to the fore in the latter part of the 1980s with volumes of poetry appealing to teenagers and a rise in the output of poets appealing to the middle range, with, in the latter case, humour and accompanied by illustrations to catch the eye, such as Roger McGough and Michael Rosen with titles like *Sky in the Pie* and *When Did you Last Wash Your Feet?* and the numerous anthologies of poetry devoted to humorous verse.

The publication both of anthologies of poetry and illustrated versions of well-known rhymes and poems, has long been a well-intentioned part of many a publisher's list, but recent years have brought many well-selected anthologies, both general and thematic, and an increase in the one poem seen through the eyes of an illustrator. These are looked at in more detail in the section on poetry in Chapter Six.

The influence of television, world events, travel and wider education had opened up the world in all its aspects, creating a mood in which social realism became a major factor in books for children and young people. The number of series aimed at particular age or ability groups greatly increased both in fiction and information books. By the end of the 1980s the combination of educational need and effect, technical developments, social conditions and national and international influences had produced in UK and USA a proliferation of literature for children, ranging from toy books, picture books, cartoon/picture strip, to story books for various reading ages and abilities on almost every imaginable subject, and non-fiction covering most themes to varying depths for varying ages and abilities, all in varying degrees of quality.

This quantity of literature meant a greater choice for children, providing books for every need in a choice of popular, medium and highbrow, and often in a format of paperback or hardback.

Over the years the increasing range made necessary book selection by librarians, and guidance to children, teachers and parents on the suitability and use of books, the display and promotion of children's books, all requiring greater knowledge. This led to the inclusion of children's literature in librarianship and education studies and to the creation of specialist posts in children's and school librarianship, some of which began to be threatened as cuts in public expenditure caused library and education authorities to reduce bookfunds and personnel in the middle to late 1980s.

The quantity of children's literature and the rise in a wider readership and professional interest had led, over the years to a body of literary criticism and analysis from, for example, Margery Fisher, Margaret Meek, Brian Alderson, Aidan Chambers, Elaine Moss, Naomi Lewis, Edward Blishen, Nicholas Tucker and in recent years, Stuart Hannabuss and Neil Philip.

Criticism and analysis in the form of reviews has also increased through review journals, for example *British Book News Children's Books*, *Books for Keeps* and *Books for your Children*, the *Times Literary Supplement* and the *Times Educational Supplement*, plus *Dragon's Teeth*, *Junior Bookshelf* and *Growing Point* and a host of local annotated lists and review journals. The numerous related professional journals also included reviews and longer discussion on books appeared in *Signal* publications, *The International Review of Children's Literature and Librarianship* and critical works on children's literature in general or in particular. Book services developed, such as *The Good Book Guide*, introduced by Bing Taylor and Peter

Braithwaite advised by Elaine Moss, Baker Book Service's little lists *Reading for Enjoyment*, and IFLA's *Children's Literature Abstracts*. The range of such bibliographical aids is indicated in Chapter Ten and in the chapter on publishing and bookselling (Chapter Five). But the intention here is to show the growth of interest in children's books throughout the book trade, as in the Children's Book Circle of the Publishers' Association, the Children's Book Group of the Booksellers Association; the Children's Book Action Group, set up in liaison with the Publishers Association, the Booksellers' Association and the Library Association; interest in schools through the Writers in Schools' programme, the School Library Association; the School Bookshop Association; and the School Libraries' Group of the Library Association; interest in medical and para-medical professions via the use of children's books for various therapies; the pre-school child organizations such as the Play Group Association, and VOLCUF (Voluntary Council of Organizations for the Under Fives); the general public's participation in the Federation of Children's Book Groups. Public librarians through the Youth Libraries' Group of the Library Association and the membership of special organizations connected with children's books have also played a vital part in the development of both the literature and children's interest in it, by activities for children, for parents, for nursery nurses, for teachers and for their own professional and non-professional staff, involving all with the relevant books and related media, with the writers and illustrators and, increasingly, with the publishers and booksellers.

The internationalism of children's books is also evident in the organizations to which many of those mentioned above are members, such as the International Board on Books for Young People (IBBY) a world-wide body with a Secretariat in Switzerland, fifty member nations and for which there is a British Section, c/o the Book Trust in London. British members include publishers, librarians, teachers, writers, booksellers, journalists, illustrators and translators and the section organizes seminars and meetings, publishes a newsletter, pamphlets and booklists, maintains a Third World Book Fund and plays a full part in IBBY's international activities.

The International Federation of Library Associations (IFLA) has several groups concerned with children's literature and librarianship, including the Round Table on Children's Literature Documentation Centres, the Round Table on Library Service to Ethnic and Linguistic Minorities, the School Libraries' Section and the Section on Children's Libraries.

The International Research Society for Children's Literature (IRSCL) meets regularly to discuss and to share research findings. The International Reading Association has for many years had the function of analysing and promoting both reading and literature. The International Institute for Children's Literature and Reading Research in Vienna undertakes research and, with IBBY, produces the quarterly journal *Bookbird*, with articles and information about children's books, writers and events all over the world.

UNICEF's information centre on children's culture maintains an information service on children's books and UNESCO's Regional Book Development Centres are concerned with the need to develop the whole range of books in countries where literature is in the early stages of development.

In any country the development of children's literature reflects that society's developments, not only in the literature's subject content but in style, format and availability.

The broad sociological effects are the result of religious,

educational, psychological and political philosophies and practices. These also have an effect on the development of the book trade, on communication media and travel and on the social status of children. Another factor is the capacity of the language to express adequately in literary form in order to produce children's literature, while further influences upon development include not only the availability of libraries to provide the means of reading but the availability of alternative leisure pursuits which preclude the time or the need for reading.

Historically all these factors appear to have been present in England positively, constructively and beneficially, producing a body of children's literature which is read also by children in many other countries, in English and in translation.

The English conditions were ripe for producing the first golden age of children's literature and contributory to the second golden age, but they created also an established children's book trade which has developed from the early eighteenth century with about six books through to the early twentieth century with hundreds of books, to the present day with approximately three thousand new children's book titles per year in Britain.

Operating within both national and international parameters, British children's book people at the end of the 1980s benefit from the cooperation which now exists between writers, booksellers, librarians, teachers, parents – and the child reader.

Further reading

Alderson, Brian. *Sing a Song For Sixpence; the English picture book tradition and Randolph Caldecott.* C.U.P., 1986

Barr, John. *Illustrated Children's Books*. British Library, 1986

Carpenter, Humphrey. *Secret Gardens; the golden age of children's literature*, Allen and Unwin, 1985

Carpenter, Humphrey and Prichard, Mari. *The Oxford Companion to Children's Literature*. O.U.P., 1984

Darton, F.J. Harvey. *Children's Books in England; five centuries of social life*. 3rd revised edn by Brian Alderson, C.U.P., 1982

Ellis, Alec. *A History of Children's Reading and Literature*. Pergamon, 1968

Hunt, Peter. 'Childist criticism'. *Signal*, no. 43, Jan. 1984, pp. 42–58

Leeson, Robert. *Reading and Righting; past, present and future*. Collins, 1985

Marshall, Margaret R. *Libraries and Literature for Teenagers*. Gower, 1975

Meek, Margaret. *The Cool Web; the pattern of children's reading*. Bodley Head, 1977

Moss, Elaine. *Part of the Pattern*. Bodley Head, 1986

Moss, Elaine. *Picture Books for Young People, 9–13*. Signal Bookguide, Thimble Press, 1981

Ray, Sheila. *The Blyton Phenomenon*. Deutsch, 1982

Salway, Lance. *Reading about Children's Books; an introductory guide to books about children's books*. NBL, 1986

Self, David. Queen Puffin. *Times Educational Supplement*, 14 Nov. 1986, pp. 37 and 38, (Kaye Webb)

Townsend, John Rowe. *Written for Children; an outline of English language children's literature*, 2nd revised edn, Viking Kestrel, 1983

Many other books and articles can be identified by using the abstracting journals and services, for example:

Children's Literature Abstracts
Library and Information Science Abstracts

Library Literature
British Education Index
British Humanities Index

CHAPTER FOUR

Developing a Children's Literature

In many countries there is still a national children's literary history to be made. Developments are slow though knowledge, goodwill and talent exist.

The problems are usually three-fold: a high level of illiteracy, lack of money to produce books of attractive quality and to buy them and the need for books in all the languages of a multi-lingual nation, a situation common to many countries both developed and developing.

Illiteracy is common where education, though it may be compulsory to the age of twelve, is basic and starved of teachers and resources. In many lands children work before going to school, which may be some distance from home and must cope with the climate and social conditions not conducive to consistent and effective learning. Illiterate parents are not able to help their children, either with reading or with money to buy books.

The knowledge that there is no purchasing power in personal or public purses, prevents would-be publishers of children's books from risking the outlay necessary for producing books attractive to children. There is, therefore, little incentive for writers or publishers, apart from creating the textbook 'reader' for school classes. Added to these factors is the problem of producing the books in the languages of the country. In many Third World countries the official language is left from the days of the colonial rule, for example: English in some African countries and in India, French in Algeria, Morocco, Senegal and Zaire,

Portuguese in Brazil and Spanish in Venezuela. In some European countries there are various languages, as in Switzerland where German, French and Italian are spoken, in Yugoslavia with its Serbs and Croats, in the USSR with its many languages. Added to these are the vernaculars spoken, the in-the-home language in many countries, so the quantity of language material in any one country becomes financially prohibitive to publish. Thus, the possibility of a children's book being published in more than one language is a long-term hope. This situation leads to the use of traditional tales and religious stories as subject matter for children's books. In the best instances the rich oral heritage of a country is recorded by folklorists and researchers and becomes the written archive from which writers re-tell and illustrators provide a visual interpretation. In some countries the traditional folktales, heard in the home, in the market place, told by the village story-teller live in the mind of a hearer who is inspired to write it in narrative form for publication.

The gradual progression from oral tale to written tale to original stories is the norm in those countries which have had only imported literature in their language, or have translated literature into the language.

Ministry of Education programmes for the creation of schoolbook material are in progress in several countries to create an indigenous teaching resource where formerly imported textbooks and learning-to-read material had to be used. Some school and library boards undertake their own writing and printing using available reproduction facilities in order to provide the children with relevant backgrounds and experience in their schoolbooks, and in some countries writers' circles have produced the first indigenous stories in small paperback format printed by the local printer and distributed by any means possible.

Bookshops are found in the cities in the Third World

countries and are often well stocked with adult books and with imported textbooks, but have a less well represented stock of children's books, other than the cheaper paperbacks and information book series. Children, and adults wanting to buy for children, living many miles from the city may never see more than a handful of books during their childhood, given the absence of libraries in schools or communities in rural areas. When a fourteen-mile trek on unmade roads over mountains or bush terrain is needed to reach a main road and fifty miles or a sea crossing leads to a town or city with a bookshop, the difficulties become apparent. Though there are children in the Scottish Islands, the American West and the Australian outback who are similarly geographically cut off from bookshops, other means are available which do not obtain in Third World countries.

The problem of restriction on foreign exchange is also a limiting factor on the import of children's books from other countries, and librarians and teachers are unable to order books from abroad even if they have enough local currency because money is not allowed to leave the country. The situation contributes to the dearth of books in those countries.

Schemes set up to help the supply of books vary. Unesco's *Books For All* project was established in 1971, in cooperation with the Children's Libraries Section of the International Federation of Library Associations.[1] The programme recognized that in many countries schools are teaching children to read but they cannot use that skill for lack of books and libraries. It recognized also that teachers and librarians on the spot know best what books are most suitable for local children so the *Books For All* project involves asking book-developed countries for donations of money which are then converted into unum cheques, which are Unesco units of money in coupon form. These are sent to the organizations that have applied for help who then buy books in their own country or from abroad for the children in their community. The bookseller supplies the books, sends the unums with invoice to Unesco headquarters in Paris, which reimburses the bookseller in his own currency. This does not involve local currency leaving the country, enables local booksellers to have the trade, local choice to be made and avoids possible corruption. As with any voluntary organization fund relying on public or private donations there is a waiting list, but many countries have been helped and letters of thanks bear witness to this, for example:

> When your envelope of unums arrived they were opened in the presence of the co-founder of the library and several members of the community. I shared their excitement. For the children it will mean their first experience of selecting a book to look at.
>
> (Liberia)

> My self-help school has no electricity and no running water; the students are mostly from peasant homes and find it difficult to pay fees and impossible to buy reading books.
>
> (Kenya)

> The children will be delighted. They fall on new books as if they are manna from heaven.
>
> (Tonga)

In Britain another body devoted to providing aid and channelling some of it through the *Books For All* scheme, is the *IBBY British Section's Third World Book Fund*,[2] which provides, from voluntary donations, money for selected organizations who have requested help to buy

95

children's books. It also prefers to maintain contact with the assisted body and in one instance was able to hear at first hand about its donation to a community in Peru when a recipient, a priest, came to England on church business.

A scheme operating quite differently, is the Ranfurly-Library Service,[3] which receives donations of books and arranges for them to be shipped to librarians and oganizations in book-needy countries. Reorganization from 1986 reduced the possibility of unsuitable books being sent.

Such schemes are intended to be helpful until such times as the countries requesting aid can be self-sufficient in both monetary and book production terms and are meanwhile much appreciated by the recipients.

The infrastructure of a country's book trade is part of the developing process, involving development of publishing, bookselling, public libraries and book-related activities including literary criticism. All these factors are part of the common stages of development of children's literature in the world today. Some examples are useful for comparative purposes.

Zimbabwe

In Zimbabwe a move towards development was helped by the Zimbabwe Project which came out of an IFLA seminar in 1981 on library work for children and young adults in the developing countries. Supported by the Children's Libraries Section of IFLA and with financial support from the Canadian International Development Agency, the project held a workshop on writing children's books and promoting neighbourhood storytelling and home library groups. Named 'Kudyara Mbeu Yedzidzo', which means 'Sowing the Seed of Education', stress is laid on the need for a written literature for pleasure as well as for cultural reasons, in Shona and Ndebele as well as in English: a

·literature that combats the feelings of inferiority by making children proud of their heritage and their language.

To combat the lure of television in the places where homes have sets and to keep alive the ancient practice of storytelling round the communal fire in many communities, storytelling and home library groups have been established in places where a need was expressed by the local community. They take the form of an adult leading a group of children and other adults with activities such as the reading or dramatizing of stories, reading poems and singing songs and then borrowing books. Shortage of books limits the number of such home libraries, which are dependent on self-help and donations. It is hoped that the library service available in urban areas will be extended by government to mobile and community libraries in both urban and rural areas. Thus the home libraries are a valuable foundation for the present generation of children. Through this pioneer work by Mrs Ellen Waungana the seeds are being sown.

Venezuela

In Venezuela the wealth of oral tales has been transmitted to print since about 1978 with the start of an organized network of public libraries, the creation of the first publishing house for children's books, and the setting up of the Venezuelan Association of Literature for Children and Young People.

Since then efforts have been made to produce a consistent flow of books for children despite the economic problems, supported by lobbying and activity from the Banco del Libro (Bank of Books), a non-profit making private organization, founded in 1960 which has campaigned for recognition of the importance of reading and books for children. Through its publishing, reference and information service, selling of children's books at lower than retail price and its reading rooms for deprived children, in Caracas, it has paved the way for further development. Since 1980 the IBBY section of Venezuela has selected the ten best children's books published in Spanish, including original publishing in Venezuela as well as books from Spain and in translation. The infrastructure is developing ahead of the indigenous literature, largely a result of the quantity of imported books. There are now many people working towards progress in school and public libraries and bibliographical aids and promotion are increasing.

Since 1980 a review of children's literature has been published by a consortium composed of the Banco del Libro, the Venezuelan Section of IBBY, the Inter-American Project of Children's Literature and the Instituto Autonomo of the National Library. Entitled *Parapara*, the journal contains articles about children's literature.

In cooperation with the Regional Centre for Promotion of Books in Latin America and the Caribbean (CERLAC) the Inter American Project for Children's Literature (PILI) has organized a travelling exhibition of children's books and illustrations and Venezuela has taken a major part in this multi-national organization. Its objectives are to seek ways for extending the work already being done in the creation of literature for children and young people, as well as publishing, assessment and research on such books, and to encourage communication channels between all concerned in this field. Publicity, documentation and promotion action is also part of the cooperative work of the project within the Latin American area, as is the programme of financial support to underwrite all this work.

Originating from the Organization of American States and executed by the Venezuelan institutions, Centro de Capitacion Docente El Macaro and the Banco del Libro, the project is pursuing these goals and making steady progress from its inception in 1980.

Vietnam

A different approach is seen in Vietnam where the colonial days had not encouraged the development of a local literature. Since then three major publishing houses have produced between them about a hundred titles in about two million copies. With a clearly defined aim, to prepare children for good citizenship, the books must contain characters who excel in studies and are exemplary in other ways also; patriotism in both historical and contemporary times, moral themes and subjects from school, home and social life, are encouraged in both adult and child writers. Book promotion is undertaken by parents, teachers and librarians and within organizations such as the Young Pioneers' Brigade.

Asian Copublication Programme

Cooperative production of children's literature is in full-scale operation through the Asian Copublication Programme, at the Asian Cultural Centre for Unesco in Tokyo, Japan. Stories written by Asian authors and illustrated by local artists are collected from participating countries and first published in English. Each country then prepares a vernacular edition. For example *Folk Tales Book 1* was produced in the language of sixteen countries: Bengali, Burmese, the languages of India – Hindi, Gujerati, Tamil, Urdu, Marathi, Assamese, Malayalam; the languages of Indonesia (Indonesian, Javanese, Sudanese); in Farsi (Iran), Japanese, Khmer, (Kampuchea) Korean, Laotian, Malay, Nepalese, Pilipino, Chinese, Sinhalese and Thai. The European language editions of the folk tales were in Danish, Faroese, Finnish, Swedish, Norwegian, Portuguese, Spanish, French and the master edition English. The grand total of books in 1982 was around two million copies.

There are countries *not* in the Third World, which have

begun to expand the horizons of the children's book scene and two examples here will indicate the methods they have employed.

Spain

In the 1980s children's book people began to make a concerted effort to improve the state of children's literature after research showed that most children did not own books and 92 per cent said they did not go to public libraries.

The first Children's and Juvenile's Literature Symposium was held in Madrid in 1979 and the Children's and Juvenile's Literature Commission, a section of the Spanish National Book Institution felt it was necessary to find out what the situation was by research into reading habits. Their findings spurred them into coordinating action, using all the aspects of the children's book trade in Spain. A catalogue of Spanish Books for Children was published by the Guild of Spanish Publishers, sponsored by the Institution, and publishers have increased their series of children's books, brought the fiction themes up to date and participate in seminars on children's books.

The Ministry of Culture contributed towards a prize, the 'Lazarillo', for authors and illustrators of children's books, and is providing a library for each new school. It also encourages teachers to attend courses on children's literature and book promotion and organizes exhibitions.

The Biennial Exhibition of Illustrations of Children's Books, an international exhibition held in Barcelona, also offers a prize and holds a contest for the best illustrations published anywhere in the world.

In 1984 there were 1,362 children's books published in Spain in about 21,000 copies, so the quantity of books is increasing and efforts are being made to improve the quality. The Children's Literature Section of the National

Library with its collection of 70,000 volumes functions as both reference centre and for research. A move towards creating research and literary criticism is the current emphasis.

Australia

'Through Folklore to Literature' was the title of a collection of papers given at an IBBY conference in Australia in 1978.[4] Although that is the usual route for most countries it is not followed in this case, the early literature for children in Australia being the kind of books normal in Victorian England.

A large country with the bulk of the fifteen million population settled in the big coastal cities, Australian children read the English and American children's books, and still do, and much of the publishing until the 1970s was typical of the genres available in Europe: family, animal and fantasy. Two books, now classics, exemplify that early period, Ethel Turner's *Seven Little Australians*, published by Ward Lock in 1984 and the *The Magic Pudding* by Norman Lindsay, published by Angus and Robertson in 1918.

The indigenous population has a rich oral tradition of stories of the 'dreamtime'. Though some were collected in print at the end of the nineteenth century and in the 1950s they were not tapped for other stories until the 1970s. Books with an aboriginal background were few, e.g. Frank Davison wrote *Children of the Dark People* in 1936, but in 1960 Patricia Wrightson broke new ground with her *Rocks of Honey*, a story of aboriginal life in the city.

The melting pot of cultures from the background of the immigrants to Australia was a feature of the 1970s when Greek, Italian, Yugoslav, Japanese, Vietnamese people, in addition to English immigrants, began to portray their experiences in literature for children.

Another genre began to interest writers, the novel for teenagers. Hesba Brinsmead's *Pastures of the Blue Crane* in 1964, was the start of a flow of novels depicting the scenes and emotions relevant to the Australian teenager. Perhaps the most significant development was in the picture book field, when in 1970 the first truly Australian picture book was published, *Waltzing Matilda*, followed by about fifteen more in the mid-1970s, growing to nearly two hundred in the 1980s.

Over a period of about twenty-five years a body of writers has achieved international status and acclaim, including Ivan Southall, Patricia Wrightson, Christobel Mattingley, Joan Phipson and Colin Thiele, as have illustrators Pamela Allen, Jan Ormerod, Robert Ingpen, Dick Roughsey and Ron Brooks.

Australia achieved IBBY's highest prize when Patricia Wrightson and Robert Ingpen won the Hans Christian Andersen awards for literature and illustration respectively in 1986.

Recognition of the initially small quantity of indigenous literature set against the vast quantity of other English language children's books available, contributed towards the setting up of the Australian Children's Book Council in 1946, dedicated to the improvement and promotion, of Australian children's books. The Book of the Year Awards in three sections, Book of the Year, Picture Book of the Year and Junior Book of the Year (for the age group just starting on independent reading).

It organizes meetings and workshops and publishes *Reading Time*, which devoted its 100th issue to Australian trends in children's literature.

The Australian Section of IBBY is very active throughout the country and the collection and documentation of children's books increases through the public libraries and the state libraries, such as the *Children's Literature Research Collection* at the State Library of South Australia in Adelaide, which has begun the task of putting onto microfiche the nineteenth-century children's books. The *Thyne Reid Collection* in Sydney is also growing, and in Victoria the Dromkeen homestead collection of children's books begun by the Oldmeadows is now a centre for research and promotion of children's literature, particularly Australian books. Regular reports of research and critical studies of books and surveys appear in the periodical literature and much of this was outlined by Belle Alderson in the 100th issue of *Reading Time*.[5]

Though only about a hundred books were published in 1986 the overall quantity provides a strong national literature and bibliographies and histories are available. Noteworthy is Maurice Saxby's *A History of Australian Children's Literature*.[6]

A young country, with a multi-national population and an indigenous population with a strong story tradition, Australia has the potential for producing a remarkable children's literature.

Conclusion

Unesco's survey, *The Book in Multilingual Countries*,[7] recommends a number of methods of improving book production which could pertain also to the development of children's literature in the following ways:

● Assisting in the creation of books by, for example, paid leave to teacher–writers, cash prizes and awards, tax dispensation on royalties, seminars, workshops, conferences of all concerned with books, research into unwritten languages and conversion of oral traditions into print.

- Production of textbooks relevant to the national philosophy and local needs; standardization of scripts and provision of printing machinery and paper through government subsidies and international finance.
- Removing the various duties, and so on, payable on books and book production materials and increasing the co-production efforts for mass production and picture books.
- Improving the public library system and the national network of libraries, extending book promotion and selling outlets to places where the people congregate; undertaking surveys of reading and marketing.
- Devising a national policy for book development to include a multilingual policy; also the development of the appropriate infrastructure.

There are many book-hungry countries and many people in them who know the needs of the children and the benefits of children's books. They are working towards the development of the kind of children's literature which is often taken for granted in countries with a long tradition of reading, writing and publishing.

References

1 Unesco/IFLA. Books For All Project. Administrator Margaret Marshall, 6a Harmer Green Lane, Digswell, Welwyn, Herts A16 0AD, England
2 IBBY British Section Third World Fund. c/o The Book Trust, Book House, 45 East Hill, Wandsworth, London SE England
3 Ranfurly Library Service. 39–41 Coldharbour Lane, London SE5 9NR, England
4 Saxby, Maurice (ed.). *Through Folklore to Literature; papers presented at the Australian National Section of IBBY Conference on Children's Literature.* Sydney,

1978, IBBY Australia Publications, 1979
5 Alderman, Belle. 'Australian research and studies in children's literature'. *Reading Time*, 100, July 1986, pp. 27–9
6 Saxby, Maurice. *A history of Australian Children's Literature*. 2 vols, Sydney, Wentworth, 1969
7 Hasan, Abul. *The book in multi-lingual countries*. Unesco, 1978, (Report no. 82).

Further Reading

Creative writing and publishing in Africa today; proceedings of the Seminar held in Sierra Leone, 1983. Available from Mrs. Gloria Dillsworth, Chief Librarian, Sierra Leone Library Board, Freetown, Sierra Leone, West Africa

Kalisa, B. L. An interview with noted African children's writer Remi Adedeji. *Bookbird*, 1, 1984, pp. 17–21

Saxby, Maurice. 'The art of Patricia Wrightson and the illustrations of Robert Ingpen'. *Bookbird*, 2, 1986, pp. 4–8 *Unesco Statistical Yearbook*. Annual, Unesco

Bookbird. Quarterly journal of the International Board of Books for Young People and the International Institute of Children's Literature and Reading Research.

Children's Literature Abstracts quarterly abstracting journal issued by Children's Libraries Section of IFLA

CHAPTER FIVE

The Children's Book Publishing Scene

The creation of a book for children follows a pattern of procedure common to most countries; author, publisher, bookseller, reviewer, reader. Many other people may be involved in the means of producing and distributing the book or information about the book, for example:

- Literary agents who, on behalf of the writer or illustrator are responsible for obtaining a publisher for a piece of work and for negotiating the best terms for that work
- Printers and binders
- Publicity and public relations personnel
- Reviewers and review media
- Critics and critical literature in the form of books and journal articles
- Associations and societies concerned with children and books
- Teachers and lecturers in children's literature
- Students of children's literature
- Librarians, libraries and special collections of children's books both national and local
- Researchers and research organizations and collections concerned with the study of children's literature
- Radio, television and press people connected with book programmes and columns
- Commercial companies
- Educational institutions

- Individuals and their interests
- Children as readers

The children's book scene starts with the author or illustrator and some aspects of the work involved are shown in the next chapter. But the relationship between author and publisher can be indicated here.

Author and publisher

There are some specialist children's book publishers but publishing houses tend to have a children's list in addition to their general list and subject specialist lists. There are many publishers who do not include children's books at all, but even within the range of publishers of books for children there are some that specialize in certain kinds or series of children's book, in fiction only or information books only, in hardback or paperback; educational or trade publisher only; books for young children; books aimed at the mass market or upmarket buyers.

In addition to big publishing houses and small specialist children's imprints there are community publishing programmes, small printing companies and vanity publishing (publication paid for by the author or illustrator), producing material for children and young people, as well as government departments and specialist organizations and societies.

As indicated in the previous chapter there are many countries where all books emanate from the state publishing house, for example in China, USSR, and Vietnam and to some extent Tunisia, which gives some state support to children's book publishing.

Although publishers in many book-developed countries receive unsolicited manuscripts of both fiction and non-fiction from hopeful writers, few are accepted for publication.

Often the reason is poor quality of writing, often that the theme has already been covered, and increasingly as costs rise, there is the obvious commercial factor of the need to ensure that the book will sell in sufficient quantity to cover costs or make a profit.

Generally children's books are commissioned from an outline or idea provided by the intending author or illustrator. This may have been offered unsolicited or invited on request from the children's book editor. Children's book editors, whether for fiction or information books, are constantly looking for original ideas and for possible gaps in the literature. When an idea or gap is seen the editor may approach an already published author or, in the case of non-fiction, a person who is knowledgeable in that field, and discuss the possibility of writing such a book.

Books from other countries may be bought for publication in the buyer's edition, and buying the foreign rights is often done at the annual bookfairs such as that at Bologna. Similarly, co-production, particularly of picture books is another means of adding to the publisher's list.

Many already published authors and illustrators have a clause in their previous contract requiring them to offer their next book to the publisher. If author and publisher agree on the need, content and potential market for a book, the publisher draws up a contract which binds the author to delivering a manuscript of a specified length by a specified date and binds the publisher to consider publication on specified financial terms, usually a percentage royalty basis, with special terms for paperback rights, foreign rights, film rights and book club fees, for example. 'Royalty' in this context means a payment to the author for every book sold, usually paid twice a year.

If the terms are that the author is to receive 10 per cent royalty payment on a published book price of £5.00, the breakdown of this price would be fifty pence to the author for each copy sold, the remaining £4.50 going to the publisher's production costs of printing, binding, distribution, publicity, and so on, the percentage given to the bookseller, and a percentage for publisher's profit. Where the book has more than one author and/or an illustrator, the royalty payment will be split between them.

The importance of sales promotion and marketing arrangements is therefore considerable if all concerned are to reap any financial benefit.

The children's book editor works closely with the author and illustrator during the writing/illustrating and when the finished work is submitted may send it to an outside 'reader' for an opinion. This may be a specialist in children's books or a specialist in the subject of the information book.

Meanwhile the production editor is assessing the cost involved in order to arrive at a purchase price and the book is slotted into the production schedule, which is conditioned by a number of factors including how many other books are in progress and what the printer and binder can fit into their schedule.

Publisher and printer

The manuscript will be copy edited for content and errors and marked up for the printer with instructions on typeface, layout, spacing, etc. The graphic designer/art editor has already planned those as part of the total appearance of the book and has organized the jacket design also.

In common with other books, children's books in many countries are given an International Standard Book Number (ISBN) which identifies the publisher and the specific book. The ISBN is usually placed on the back of the title page with the name of the publisher, or at the end of the Cataloguing in Publication data (CIP). Increasingly, particularly on picture books and paperbacks, the ISBN is placed on the back cover near to the bar code, which is the publisher's identification information in optical character recognition (OCR). Orders for that book may be made by ISBN only, though for absolute accuracy it is wise to use author and title also as it is easy to make a mistake with typing or writing a number.

Another piece of information that appears on the verso in many hardback and original paperback books is the Cataloguing in Publication (CIP) data. This cooperative scheme between the British Library and publishers in the UK involves the cataloguing of forthcoming books and the dissemination of the information, in advance of publication, through the print, microform, electronic media and computer tape services nationally and internationally.

The CIP record is coded for automatic processing by MARC (machine readable cataloguing) networks and the entry appears in print in the British National Bibliography (BNB). The book information is supplied by the publisher on the form provided by the CIP office, sent back with proofs or advance information sheet for the CIP office to catalogue the book, and add the Dewey classification number and the Library of Congress classification number. An abbreviated entry is sent back to the publisher for printing in the book.

The usefulness of the CIP data to booksellers and librarians requires that every book should be so processed but at present publishers' participation in the scheme is voluntary. Similar schemes operate in the USA and Australia.

The symbol © indicates that the laws of copyright obtain, whereby this work by an author or other creative artists, is protected against unauthorized reproduction, sale or performance, including storing in a retrieval system or transmitting by any means, electronic, mechanical, photo-copying or recording.

Such protection is intended to give the author and publisher control over their property, which might other-wise be copied and sold anywhere by anybody. The international organizations concerned with ensuring a global adherence to copyright conventions are the World Intellectual Property Organization arising from the original Berne Convention, and the Universal Copyright Convention arising from UNESCO's work. While piracy does occur in some countries there is now a recognition that in some instances, the needs of developing countries require a negotiation of copyright and a special licensing arrangement.

Once all these legal and information aspects are settled the typescript goes to the printer who may print the book by computer typesetting, photosetting, hot metal or other methods depending upon the printer, the country and the availability of technology. Galley proofs or sheets of proof copies will be sent to the editor to check for printer's errors and the editor and author will amend as necessary and return the proofs to the printer. The finished printing is then bound and sent to the distributors. From there copies are sent to reviewers, according to a pre-arranged list, to booksellers and other retailing outlets once the publisher's marketing and publicity personnel have seen the finished book at the sales conference. An attractive and informative book with picture strip description of the whole process is Aliki's *How a Book is Made*[1] intended for children, but helpful also for adults.

In those countries where there is a legal requirement a specified number of copies must be sent to the national library or its equivalent and this is known as legal deposit.

Advance publicity is made in the form of inclusions in the publisher's catalogue of forthcoming publications; notification to the book trade journals; leaflets and posters;

mailing information to libraries, education authorities, overseas agents for the publisher; radio, television and the press; relevant organizations and individuals; and by other promotional activities.

Publishers' catalogues vary considerably in style and amount of information both in text and picture and in guidance to age and ability. Some simply list, others provide annotations for each entry. Almost all print disclaimers to the effect that the age or interest level stated is approximate as children vary in their reading ability and interests. It is expensive to publish and distribute annual catalogues, which usually contain the backlist also and many of the children's book publishers compile Spring and Autumn catalogues to publicize the new publications in those major publishing periods.

From all these, advance orders may be obtained, otherwise most of the sales in library-developed countries arise from purchase by libraries, organizations and individuals via library supply agencies, booksellers, stores and other selling outlets, or, in some countries, directly from the publishing house, the printer, the author or by other retailing methods.

In Britain and a few other countries the author and illustrator may be entitled to a further payment through a system called Public Lending Right. An author or illustrator who registers with the Public Lending Right scheme (PLR) is eligible for an annual payment, proportionate to the number of times that his book has been lent out by a public library during the previous year. After the PLR Act of 1979 the Registrar, John Sumsion, was appointed to administer the scheme with a fund voted by government from which to make the payments. A regularly changed representative set of public libraries was selected to count the loans in their authorities. A ceiling of £5,000 was set for the top and a minimum of £1 as payments and in February 1985 47 authors were eligible for the maximum; 1,680 earned between £100 and £499 for the loaned books and 5,278 authors and illustrators earned up to £99. Some of the children's books which score highest loans are mentioned in the section on reading interests in Chapter Eight.

The children's book as a finished product enters the children's book scene as a result of the work of author, illustrator, children's book editor, the design, financial, publicity and sales departments of the publishing house, the printer, binder and distributor.

Bookseller and purchaser

Booksellers and other retail outlets need to be persuaded to stock the book and their criteria are determined by the kind of buying public they serve, whether mass market, casual purchase, or specialists interested in and knowledgeable about children and books. They bear in mind that, in general, it is adults who buy children's books.

Books are sold subject to the Net Book Agreement by which all booksellers agree to sell the books only at the price fixed by the publishers. However, booksellers may supply public libraries and some others at 10 per cent discount under a scheme known as the library licence. The term non-net applies mainly to schoolbooks, which are usually sold in sets and for which booksellers may offer discounts.

There is a wide range of sales outlets whose decision to stock or not to stock a children's book depends upon factors already mentioned.

Books for children are sold through the following in Britain, and examples of each can be found in other countries also.

Book wholesalers They maintain a warehouse for supply-

113

ing to the majority of bookshops. Hammicks, for example, is one of the wholesalers which provides bookshops with several information aids such as computer printout lists of all its stock and new publications; fiche, media and news and promotion literature, from which the bookseller selects what he wants for his shop, orders it and is supplied from the warehouse.

Bookshops   These can be subdivided as follows:

- *Chain stores* or *multiples* such as W.H. Smith and John Menzies which both have their own children's book buyers and distribution centres for supplying their branches.
- *Independent general bookshops* selling adult and children's books obtained from wholesalers, publisher's representatives' information and in some cases, via an account with a publisher. Stock is often limited by space, confined to paperbacks because hardbacks are considered too expensive by the buying public and the low price of children's books means that the bookseller has to sell many more to make a profit.
- *Specialist children's bookshops* which vary from small one-room shops to large multiple-room premises. The Booksellers' Association in Britain has a list of such specialist retail outlets. In general the bookseller is given about 35 per cent discount on the price by the publisher or wholesaler, from which he must pay his overheads and make a profit. Some bookshops are also schoolbook contractors for local schools or the local education authority.
- *Mobile bookshops*: taking the books to the customers is relatively uncommon in UK, as are book boats, but some permanent and some temporary (for example, for special events) mobile bookshops are successfully operating.

- *School bookshops* are common and the School Book-shop Association was set up to coordinate the work of about six thousand bookshops in primary and secondary schools. Most school bookshops are housed in semi-permanent or moveable lockable shelf units and are staffed voluntarily by teachers or local librarians. Stock is selected in a variety of ways, directly from the local bookshop on a sale or return basis, through a library supplier such as Books For Students or through mail-order bookselling agents. A library licence may entitle the school bookshop to a discount from which the school bookshop is able to make a small profit for school funds or other causes.
- *Public library bookshops* are on the increase where any suitable income generating venture is needed to supplement the decline in local authority book funding. Such bookshops also give an extra service for the book borrower. Some make the bookshop portable for use at talks to Parent Teachers' Association meetings, book fairs and community events.
- *Department stores* have long had book departments but a recent innovation in UK is the retailing of children's books in non-traditional high street stores such as Sainsbury food stores and Marks and Spencer, where books are displayed and sold as a commodity with no attempt at guidance to parents or children, and toy shops like Early Learning and Toys R Us. The convenience, accessibility and non-threatening environment of such stores encourages people to buy the mainly pre-school age range books they stock.[2]
- *Newsagents and neighbourhood shops* and market stalls in many countries hold a nucleus of popular, cheap paperbacks and picture books. In Britain also television-based series, Enid Blyton books, Ladybird books and activity books are the norm and may be found alongside the very wide range of comics.

Book clubs and mail order bookselling   These are common methods of selling in some countries, as is door-to-door bookselling in Japan. Perhaps the best-known book club in Britain is the *Puffin Club* with its newsletter, competitions and promotion of the wide range of Puffin books. Other examples are Heffer's *Bookworm Club* for the 8 to 13s and its *Early Worm Club* for children up to seven years of age. *Books for Children* has a mail order club with monthly magazine and newsletter. *The Letterbox Library* set up in 1983 specializes in non-sexist and multi-cultural books for children and *Scholastic* concentrates on school book club sales.

Book tokens   Book tokens are recognized as a powerful aid to children's bookselling and an incentive to book buying. Retail outlets hold a range of denominations in the form of attractive cards with a stamp to the required value. The book token is sold to the customer who usually gives it as a gift or uses it as a prize. The recipient takes the book token to a bookshop and buys books to the value indicated. Book Tokens Limited is the central organization responsible for the scheme and for supplying the tokens to participating bookshops. The bookseller usually claims reimbursement quarterly for the difference between tokens received and tokens sold. Most booksellers and book people see the scheme as a good way of encouraging children to buy books.

Library suppliers   Public libraries, school and academic libraries are major buyers of large quantities of children's books through the bookselling outlets known as library suppliers. In the UK, examples include Askews, T.C. Farries, Holt Jackson, John Menzies, Morley and Peters. Woodfield and Stanley specialize in children's books and Books For Students in paperback.

Stock is arranged in a variety of ways, some preferring a warehouse stock arrangement in publishers' order, others a showroom display by author for fiction or subject for non-fiction. Catalogues list the full stock and most library suppliers offer an 'approvals' service whereby children's books are sent to library services for children's librarians to view and select from. Visits to the library suppliers are also common for librarians to view and select from stock.

One service which is costly to the library supplier, is the free servicing of each book for many of the library purchasers, servicing in this context meaning putting on the library labels and the classification and cataloguing information. In some cases plastic jacketing is also part of the service.

Publishers depend heavily on the library market for the sale of hardback books so library suppliers provide a necessary bridge between the publishers and the institutional market for children's books.

Discount purchasing Some schools library services offer a discount purchasing scheme for their school libraries, which is not the same scheme as the next item.

Buying consortia Direct purchasing organizations, which are local authority buying consortia offer centralized purchasing of many items needed within the authority, including children's and schoolbooks. The Local Authority Management Services Advisory Committee (LAMSAC) produced a report on the role of the consortia in 1985.

Bookselling is in a state of change occasioned by a number of factors such as computerization. Parts of the British retail book trade uses bar codes, EAN Scanning (European Article Number, now International) and the British Tele-ordering System. But the statistical information that could be obtained and would provide useful information for all concerned with children's books, is not available. Statistics in publishing and bookselling appear to be related solely to accounting rather than to editorial or customer-related aid and needs. Few have a data base big enough to take more than the basic bibliographical information for each book, though W.H. Smith are expanding the classification for their data base and microfiche and some public libraries are able to extract categorized information from their own databases. The absence of detailed statistics means that there is no clear picture of what is published, what is bought and by whom.

The benefits of computerization for ordering, inventory management, book distribution, database material, printed catalogues and lists are under consideration by many in the book trade and experienced by some.

The decline in the schoolbook market towards the end of the 1980s, caused by falling school populations, cuts in local education authority expenditure and the low allocation given by individual schools to their schoolbook and library funds, gave rise to anxiety amongst booksellers who are also school contractors.

John Elsley, a leading bookseller and past President of the Booksellers' Association, in a paper given to the Booksellers' Association conference in 1986, stressed these aspects and their effect on booksellers. He warned of the threat from the increasing power of local authority purchasing officers and the establishment of buying consortia within local authorities. Large publishing conglomerates and large centralized purchasing organizations pose a threat to small publishers and bookselling outlets and any move towards the removal of the Net Book Agreement would lead to a price war with the consequent demise of some.

The growth of non-traditional outlets has begun to tap the non-traditional market. Traditional booksellers are paying more attention to in-shop organization of stock and in-the-community promotion. Special services are offered by some such as the Baker Book Services foreign language stock of children's books in the European languages and much in the Indian languages. The Rainbow Children's Book Service promotes and sells books for under-fives and Rosemary Stones' Bookspace concentrates on selling books with a non-sexist, non-racist and social realism content.

Bookselling in Britain offers a wide choice to the potential buyer at whatever social, financial, educational or interest level but the importance of the children's book is not always recognized. Peter Bagnall of W.H. Smith and Chairman of the Children's Book Action Group, disbanded in 1987, said in reference to the proposed Children's Book Foundation, 'If we underestimate the importance of children's books we put at risk the future of the entire book industry'.

Reviewing

Part of the children's book scene is occupied by the critics of children's books via the reviewing media, and by the literary analysis in literary journals and in books about children's books. Examples of these are given in the chapter on bibliographical aids, and some of the critics are named in Chapter Three.

John Rowe Townsend, amongst others has pointed out that children's books are written by adults, published by adults, reviewed by adults and in general, bought by adults. He and Brian Alderson hold the view that children's book critics should confine themselves to the literary merit of a book rather than offer opinions on 'suitability', popularity, relevance in terms of the potential for creating awareness; looking at the book itself rather than the child who might read it. He suggested that those who were intending to buy the book, or teachers and librarians who were selecting for

119

known needs, were the best judges on its suitability.[3]

This perhaps raises the question of the difference between the purpose of reviews in journals and the more analytical treatment possible in articles, given the greater space to play with.

Review journals are normally used by librarians and teachers for comparative purposes, for catching books that might have slipped through the net of the usual procedures, for non-fiction and specialist subjects, for those working in isolation from book sources or book people, and for expanding knowledge, particularly in the articles in review journals.

The range of review journals indicates the varied nature and needs of the people who read them, as does the categorization used; for example *Books for Keeps* divides its reviews under headings Nursery/Infant, Infant/Junior, Junior/Middle, Middle/Secondary, while the *School Librarian* uses Young Readers, Children Learning to Read, Seven to Eleven, Eleven to Fifteen and Sixteen to Nineteen, in keeping with the intended readership of both journals. *The British Book News Children's Books* arranges reviews under Picture Books, Story Books, Young Fiction and Older Fiction and the non-fiction under broad themes, to suit the broader readership overseas and in the UK.

Practice varies as to the amount of detail given over and above a brief description of the plot or subject content. The evaluative content in terms of literary merit is concise, if present at all, and the 'up to 200 words' allocated to most reviews is barely sufficient for adequately informing the reader who, it is assumed, has not and may not actually see the book before ordering.

The authority of reviewers can be assessed where reviews are signed but some journals pursue a policy of unsigned reviews. The style of reviewing and the format of the journal vary also, from the personal style and restrained format of Margery Fisher's *Growing Point* to the colour and exuberance of both style and format in *Books for Your Children* and *Books For Keeps*, while local authority review media often has to be content with local reproduction facilities for in-house distribution.

Review articles and books of literary criticism of children's books enable the critic to expand on a theme, to be comparative and evaluative, as in *Signal, Approaches to Children's Books, Children's Literature in Education*, the *Hornbook Magazine*, and the many books devoted to the study of, teaching of and reading of children's books.[4]

Most book-developed countries have review journals, children's literature journals and critical works and most are of similar style and content to those available in Britain.

The intending book purchaser may see the book in the bookshop or other selling outlet; or read a review in the review media or literary publication; or be introduced to it through a book club, see it in a publisher's catalogue or at a book fair.

If considering purchase on behalf of others, as for library stock, the selection criteria and clientele's needs and interests will be taken into account and, if appropriate, the book will be bought and eventually read, thus completing the chain of events from author to reader.

But the availability of children's books in any country is affected by a number of factors, some of which are discussed in the chapters on the development of, and trends in, children's literature.

Children's book publishing: the international scene

The publication of children's books depends upon: government policies, political, economic and educational; the state of national literacy; the production and distribution outlets and communication media; the single-language or

121

multi-language conditions; the existence of libraries; the purchasing power of institutions and individuals; and the freedom to read.

All of these must be taken into consideration when looking at statistics for children's book publishing. The following data is reproduced, with permission, from material published in *The UNESCO Statistical Yearbook, 1986* in the sections on the production of children's books (see Table 5.1).

Over a period of five years the ranking of countries according to the highest number of children's books published in the year has changed from UK, USA, Federal Republic of Germany, the USSR, Japan and Korea, to Korea with 5,553 titles published in the year for which the UNESCO figures are available, followed by China, 4,090; USSR 4,055; UK with 3,641; Japan 3,501; USA 2,567; Federal Republic of Germany 2,223; Belgium 1,668; Spain 1,632; Netherlands 1,369; Turkey 1,112; and Denmark 1,017.

Some of the countries in the Table were represented at the UNESCO Regional Workshop for Asian Writers and Editors of Books for Children and Juveniles. This was held in Seoul, Republic of Korea in 1978 and the report was published by the UNESCO Regional Office for Culture and Book Development in Asia, in Pakistan in 1979.

Three areas were covered: the present provision of books and literacy, the kind of training available for writers and editors, and the countries' needs and problems regarding training.

In some of the Asian countries there was evidence of help from various sources. For example in Bangladesh the activities of Bangla Academy, the National Book Centre and National Children's Academy were contributing towards the growth of a children's literature. In Indonesia government aid was granted for the bulk purchase of books

Table 5.1 1986 Statistical Yearbook. Production of children's books: number of titles and copies

Country Pays Pais	Year Annee Ano	Number of Titles Numbre de Titres Numero de Titulos			Number of Copies Nombre d'exemplaires Numero de Ejemplares		
		Books Livres Libros	Pamphlets Brochures Folletos	Total	Books Livres Libros	Pamphlets Brochures Folletos	Total
					(000)	(000)	(000)
AFRICA							
Algeria	1984	13	—	13	...	—	...
Gambia #	1984	10	—	10	...	—	...
Ghana	1983	11	—	11	...	—	...
Madagascar	1984	—	—	—	—	—	—
Mali	1984	...	—	—	...	—	—
Mauritius #	1984	1	1	2	0	0	0
Mozambique	1983	7	—	7	115	—	115
Nigeria	1984	56	...	56	...	...	...
Reunion #	1983	—	2	2	—	...	...
Senegal #	1983	...	...	9	...	...	45
United Republic of Tanzania	1984	—	—	—	—	—	—
Zambia #	1983	11	—	11	...	—	...
AMERICA, NORTH							
Costa Rica	1984	40	...	40	320	...	320
Cuba	1984	67	9	76	5796	510	6306
Nicaragua #	1984	4	...	4	13	...	13
St. Christopher and Nevis	1982	—	—	—	—	—	—
AMERICA, SOUTH							
Argentina	1983	302	...	302	...	...	...
Bolivia #	1982	6	—	6	...	—	...
Chile	1984	60	38	98	...	...	...
Colombia	1984	300	...	300	2100	...	2100
Guyana	1983	—	—	—	—	—	—
Peru	1984	6	4	10	...	...	...
Uruguay	1984	84	44	128	...	...	...

continued

123

Table 5.1 1986 Statistical Yearbook. Production of children's books: number of titles and copies *continued*

Country Pays Pais	Year Annee Ano	Number of Titles Numbre de Titres Numero de Titulos			Number of Copies Nombre d'exemplaires Numero de Ejemplares		
		Books Livres Libros	Pamphlets Brochures Folletos	Total	Books Livres Libros (000)	Pamphlets Brochures Folletos (000)	Total (000)
ASIA							
Brunei Darussalam #	1982	14	—	14	75	—	75
China	1984	4090	...	4090	...	...	907540
Hong Kong	1983	228	250	478	1823	1821	3644
India	1984	544	...	544	...	...	...
Indonesia	1984	196	148	344	...	...	...
Iran, Islamic Republic of	1983	558	—	558	...	—	...
Israel	1982	101	57	158	...	...	1561
Japan	1983	3509	—	3509	52681	—	52681
Korea, Republic of	1984	5553	1629	7182	14793	3733	18526
Malaysia #	1984	270	619	889	1470	2549	4019
Philippines ‡	1984	5	7	12	—	100	100
Singapore	1983	267	64	331	1298	439	1737
Sri Lanka	1983	13	109	122	50	404	454
Syrian Arab Republic #	1983	13	—	13	...	—	...
Thailand	1984	456	—	456	...	—	...
Turkey	1983	1112	—	1112	...	—	...
United Arab Emirates	1983	—	—	—	—	—	—
EUROPE							
Albania	1984	46	16	62	268	170	438
Austria	1984	182	99	281	...	...	...
Belgium	1983	1668	...	1668	...	...	...
Bulgaria	1984	181	58	239	7046	3527	10573
Czechoslovakia	1984	397	383	780	10942	8900	19842
Denmark	1984	1017	...	1017	...	...	...
Finland	1984	201	117	318	...	...	...
German Democratic Republic	1984	437	379	816	11620	12282	23902
Germany Federal Republic of	1984	2223	875	3098	...	...	...
Holy See	1983	—	...	—	—	...	—

Table 5.1 *Continued*

Country Pays Pais	Year Annee Ano	Number of Titles Numbre de Titres Numero de Titulos			Number of Copies Nombre d'exemplaires Numero de Ejemplares		
		Books Livres Libros	Pamphlets Brochures Folletos	Total	Books Livres Libros	Pamphlets Brochures Folletos	Total
					(000)	(000)	(000)
Hungary	1984	283	17	300	13196	700	13896
Ireland	1984	14	2	16	...	...	...
Italy	1984	429	215	644	8593	2847	11440
Luxembourg #	1984	11	1	12	...	...	...
Malta #	1984	4	30	34	...	...	...
Netherlands #	1984	1369	...	1369	...	...	...
Norway	1983	131	73	204	...	...	...
Poland	1984	199	181	380	16993	34357	51350
Portugal	1984	487	...	487	...	...	6704
Spain	1984	1632	2310	3942	21523	22267	43790
Sweden	1984	867	...	867	...	...	...
Switzerland	1984	610	...	610	...	...	...
United Kingdon	1984	3641	789	4430	...	...	...
Yugoslavia	1984	420	178	598	3226	1529	4755
OCEANIA							
Australia ‡	1983	50	58	108	...	...	...
New Zealand	1984	29	103	132	...	...	...
USSR							
USSR	1984	4055	...	4055	...	...	587517
Byelorussian SSR	1984	92	59	151	6980	5170	12150
Ukrainian SSR	1984	244	117	361	19265	30628	49893

Asia
Philippines
‡ Data for copies refer only to first editions

Oceania
Australia
‡ Provisional data

Data for countries shown with this symbol are all first editions. Number of countries and territories presented in this table: 69.

Source: Unesco, *Statistical Yearbook*, 1986

125

for libraries. In Korea the Korean Culture and Art Foundation had plans to produce one hundred volumes of children's books based on the cultural tradition. India had three central government public trusts aiding publication, and the problem of the fourteen languages used in India.

Thailand's writing was strongly influenced by foreign popular stories and the Philippines imported 80 per cent of its children's books in the English language. Here there was a long-term programme for producing children's books, developed by the Children's Literature Association in the Philippines Inc (CLAPI).

Nepal was concentrating on textbooks and had geographical and literacy problems in addition to the problem of a small population.

In Turkey conscious efforts are being made to intensify a publishing programme for pre-school children and to bring the quality of children's book publishing up to an international level. The establishment of awards for children's books and picture books in many countries is helping to raise the standard of book production and to encourage indigenous writers and illustrators.

Concern in the multi-lingual countries has led to recognition that children's books must be published in each of the languages and the Nineteenth Congress of IBBY held in Cyprus in 1984 devoted its attention to Children's Book Production and Distribution in Developing countries. UNESCO took the opportunity of the Bologna Book Fair in 1985 to hold a seminar for publishers in developing countries entitled Book Publishing Management. UNESCO's series of *Studies on Books and Reading* has so far produced studies of the subject in the Arab world, Latin America, Bulgaria, Kenya and China, but the Regional Book Development Councils continue their work on a long-term basis.

One example is the Regional Office for Book Development in Asia and the Pacific which suggested promotion of books for children in that area by means of the compilation of a list of books that might be available to publishers in the developing countries on favourable terms. Ena Noel, from the Australian Section of IBBY was commissioned to select the most suitable books across the age range.

Overall, in countries where publishing is still in its infancy, problems centre on the shortage of printing materials, the system of payment to authors and bulk purchasing by institutions. The need for training for writers and editors is seen to encompass writing, illustrating, production, distribution, research and evaluation; the impact of book reading on children; the relevance of cultural literary values; and age and sex relevance. After these, further training should include psychology, communication, techniques of writing/printing/editing/technology; reading, analysis of language; and the economics of publishing.

These aspects and others relating to countries still to establish children's book publishing have been looked at in the relevant chapter, but many children's book people from those countries meet others from book-developed countries at the book fairs, conferences, and seminars held throughout the world.

Book fairs and seminars

The Bologna Book Fair in Italy attracts over a thousand children's book publishers from over sixty countries, who display their publications and their forthcoming publications, and some of their authors and illustrators. Here there is the opportunity not only to see the world's output of new children's books, but also to bid for the foreign rights or to arrange co-production.

Arranged in pavilions broadly by country or continent

the publishers' stands display to thousands of visitors the latest trends in format, theme or content. In 1987 the first stand for books for handicapped children was displayed, shared by Britain's National Library for the Handicapped Child, Denmark's Valida Foundation and the IBBY research centre at the Statens Spesiallererhogskole in Oslo, Norway.

The Bologna Book Fair Prizes awarded for books exhibited (see section on prizes in Chapter Nine) are selected by an international jury of graphic artists, for the Graphic Prize, and by a jury of children from Bologna elementary schools for the Critici in Erba Prize.

The Biennial of Illustrations Bratislava, is the book fair for illustrators with the exhibition of illustrated books and artwork, seminars on aspects of illustration in children's books and the award of the BIB Golden Apple for outstanding children's book illustration. Held in Czechoslovakia for over twenty years, this fair is, with that in Bologna, an important event in the lives of publishers and other exhibitors.

Similarly at the annual Frankfurt Fair in Germany, publishers attempt to promote their books although this fair includes the whole range of each publisher's output, for adult or child.

Many countries hold a national book fair, for example, the annual Jerusalem Book Fair, the Ife Book Fair in Nigeria, the Harare Book Fair in Zimbabwe and the biennial exhibition held in San Paulo, Brazil.

Several children's literature meetings take place each year, attended by interested people from all parts of the world. Examples include IBBY (International Board on Books for Young People) which has a conference on a children's book theme each year. The Loughborough Conference on Children's Literature meets in a different country each year on an ad hoc basis, the only administrative address being that of the host country's organizers. The International Association for Research in Children's and Youth Literature promotes research into literature and reading for young people and meets for members' discussions.

There is an annual convention of the International Reading Association, the Scandinavian Conference on Reading, the Australian Reading Conference, the Pacific Rim Conference on Children's Literature, the Everychild conference in the USA and the annual congresses of the International Federation of Library Associations and the International Association of School Librarians.

Individual countries hold seminars which are open to all, and at all such international events, publishers, authors, illustrators, graphic designers, librarians, critics and interested individuals can meet to talk about children's books, to negotiate production and promotion arrangements, and to see the ways in which children's books are developing, for the scenery changes in the children's book world.

References

1 Aliki. *How a Book is Made*. London, Bodley Head, 1986

2 Alan Giles. 'The new market for children's books: a closed shop for booksellers?' *The Bookseller*, 26 July 1986, pp. 354, 355, 357–8

3 Townsend, John Rowe. 'Standards of criticism for children's literature'. In Chambers, N. *The Signal Approach to Children's Books*. Kestrel, 1980, pp. 193–207; *and* Robert Leeson. 'To the Toyland Frontier'. ibid pp. 208–216

4 For example: Jennie Ingham. *Books and Reading Development*. Heinemann Educational, 1981; Margaret Meek. *Learning to Read*. Bodley Head, 1982; Cliff Moon and Bridie Raban. *A Question of Reading*.

Macmillan Educational revised edn, 1980; Vera South-gate. *Reading: Teaching for Learning*. Macmillan Educational, 1984

Further reading

Bagnall, Peter. 'Narnia revisited, the future of children's books and of the book trade'. *The Bookseller*, no. 4194, 10 May 1986, pp. 1864–71

Chambers, Nancy (ed.). *The Signal Approach to Children's Books*. Kestrel, 1980

Epstein, Connie. 'A publisher's perspective'. *Hornbook Magazine*, 62 (4), 1986, pp. 490–93

Fox Geoff, et al. *Writers, Critics and Children*. Heinemann Educational, 1976. 'Part two: The critics', pp. 55–173

Hiner, Mark. *Paper Engineering for Pop-up Books and Cards*. Tarquin Publications, 1985

Hodgkin, Marni. 'A personal philosophy of publishing for children'. *Signal*, 46, Jan. 1985, pp. 44–59

Sumsion, John. *Setting up Public Lending Right*, a report to the Advisory Committee. Stockton-on-Tees, Registrar of Public Lending Right, 1984

Roll, Dusan. 'A preview of the Tenth Biennial of Illustration, Bratislava-BIB 85'. *Bookbird*, 1, 1985, pp. 53–6

Sumsion, John. 'Public Lending Right in the UK', in *Writers' and Artists' Year Book*. A. & C. Black, annual, 1987, pp. 431–7

Unesco. *Unesco Statistical Yearbook, 1986*. Unesco, 1987

'Viewpoints on criticism; international perspectives'. *Bookbird*, 3, 1984, pp. 8–18

Walsh, J. P. and Townsend, J. R. 'Writers and critics'. *Hornbook Magazine*, 28(1), 1982, pp. 498–504

Wettern, Arnhild. 'International understanding through children's literature'. *Bookbird*, 1, 1985, pp. 32–5

Writers' and Artists' Year Book, annual directory of information about publishers, journals, legal aspects, trade matters, subject themes, London, A & C. Black

The Bookseller. Weekly journal concerned with publishing and bookselling and advance notice of publications. London, J. Whitaker

Children's Literature Association Quarterly. Journal of the Association with articles concerning publishing and the study of children's literature. USA

CHAPTER SIX

Children's Books – Fiction and Non-fiction

In most countries there are books for children, whether the literature is indigenous or imported, in the vernacular, the national language or another language. These books tend to follow a pattern of theme and structure whatever the country, so this chapter looks at some of those themes and forms, their development and nature and the relationship to children.

Although many of the examples cited are books in the English language, comments made are applicable to books in any language. The information given is intended to enable the interested reader to see some of the aspects common to children's books; to perceive the connection between the examples given and other books in the same genre; to note the aspects found in children's books in most countries or languages, and to follow up the subject by further reading of the critical works about each genre.

The most important preparation and continuation, however, is to read the actual children's books available. Reading for possible library selection, for reviewing, for class use or for storytelling, is one kind of reading but the children's book person who wants to be truly familiar with children's books must read throughout the range as a matter of both professional and personal interest.

The aspects discussed in this chapter are:

● Myths, legends, folk and fairy tales
● Fantasy and ghost

- Animal stories
- Historical stories
- Humour, comics and picture strips
- School stories
- Adventure stories
- Family stories
- Realism
- Books for teenagers
- Poetry
- Plays
- Information books

Myth, legends, folk and fairy

There are numerous different versions of these in the forms of anthologies, collected editions, one-story picture books, illustrated and non-illustrated versions, simplified, translated, or censored.

In most countries there are variations too on themes: the creation theme, variants on Cinderella, the frog prince, the trickster, the magic object to be touched, the dragon, the small but brave man, the use of the number three as in three wishes, three little pigs. In most countries, the traditional tales are passed on orally; in some countries, also in print, and in some additionally by means of drama and film.

Any re-telling of an old myth, legend, folk or fairytale must retain the characteristics of the original if it is to increase the knowledge and insight of the reader or the hearer. But because these stories are essentially oral tales they become different once they are written down, so the best are those which manage to retain the narrative quality in a vigorous colloquial style with the pattern of speech. The best too are also able to reflect the depth of psychological or emotional content which has enabled them

133

to be as relevant to human nature today as they were to previous generations right back to the beginnings of the human race.

Often the illustration of such tales spoils the mental picture which the good textual versions can create in the reader's or hearer's mind, so the best illustrated editions of such tales are those in which the pictures truly illustrate the essence of the text. There are scholarly and classic versions, popular and shallow versions, and writers and publishers are constantly trying to find a suitable way of transmitting the stories that Plato called 'the highest and most natural form of education for young children'.

Myths

The myths are about gods, the origins of evil, of the world, of man's struggle against strange and strong elements and his own human nature. If they are considered as springing from primitive man's emotions and as attempted explanations for the world's existence and man's place in it in story form, we can trace the continuity of elemental emotions, instincts and human nature. This can throw light on our attitudes and beliefs today, which are often difficult to see under layers of sophisticated and civilized protection.

As Alan Garner has said, 'distilled and violent truths' are the basic ingredients of most of the myths. They are truths appealing to contemporary minds as much as to those of other generations and have a thread running through them all of something outside ourselves, or above us, controlling human beings and life, something supernatural, often using men like playthings. These gods achieved their ends by violent means either physical, in tearing up mountains, creating floods, or by intimidation as in the Jason story, or by testing or punishment as with Atlas and Sisyphus, or by violent emotions such as lust, desire, anger, jealousy, fear and love.

Many re-tellings have softened the potential power by omitting the too violent or too adult emotional parts, or by re-phrasing to suggest something less excessive, so many versions are dull because their excitement has gone and left a boring tale about people with unpronounceable names. Illustrations too have toned down the emotions and depict mainly events.

Illustrator Charles Keeping, who believes that the myths are all about human feelings, found that although *God Beneath the Sea* by Leon Garfield and Edward Blishen, was a long book, and the authors could express everything in many words, he had only fifteen drawings through which to give visual expression. He therefore turned from costume or plot depiction, which could date or simply duplicate the words, and attempted to convey emotions in the stories. He had such success that many adults were shocked by the force of his black and white drawings.

Legends and folk tales

As with myths the origins of legends lie in the oral tradition of storytelling about supposed happenings and the actions and exploits of individuals. Just as we may tell a friend about something someone has done, in our own words, so the story got its second and third telling and then was passed on by others who added bits they had heard or used their imaginations to liven up aspects to entertain their listeners. We take legends not as faithfully reported happenings but as stories woven around a character or event.

The legends and folk tales are often attempts over the years to give some explanation, as in the North American legend of How Saynday Got the Sun, or the Papua New Guinea tribal tales of primordial events. Other legends are concerned with heroes, heroines and villains, whether

135

human or animal. In Britain there are King Arthur and Robin Hood; in Scandinavia Balder and Beowulf, and Grettir, Mastermaid; in France Roland; in the USA Pecos Bill and Johnny Appleseed and Brer Rabbit; in parts of Africa and the West Indies there is Anansi the Spiderman; in China there is Monkey; in Ireland Finn McCool; and in Australia Bunyip.

Research shows that tales which initially seem to be exclusive to one area or tribe, often have strong similarities to those of quite different areas or countries. In *Gods and Men*, compiled by John Bailey, Kenneth McLeish and David Spearman, the theme of Creation is told using versions from different cultures. Another section looks at stories of Good and Evil and then at the heroes and prophets in different countries.

The evidence suggests that most legends and folk and fairy tales are founded on one or more of the following themes:

- Weakness and strength
- Bravery and cowardice
- Poverty and riches
- Cleverness and stupidity
- Quest and achievement
- Potential coming to fruition
- Heroes and villains
- Triumph of good over evil

These are exemplified in collections such as Virginia Haviland's *Faber Book of North American Legends*; Grace Hallworth's *Mouth Open, Story Jump Out*, tales from the West Indies; Barbara Leonie Picard's *Hero Tales from the British Isles*; Virginia Hamilton's *The People Would Fly: American black folk tales*; *Tales from the Mabinogian*, the collection from Welsh mythology by Gwyn Thomas and Kevin Crossley-Holland, the myths that inspired Lloyd

Alexander's Prydain novels; *Seasons of Splendour*, Indian stories re-told by Madhur Jaffray with illustrations by Michael Foreman; Catherine Storr's *Great Tales from Long Ago*; and a beautifully illustrated version of *Sir Gawain and the Loathly Lady* by Selina Hastings, decorated by Juan Wjiingaard. The popular myths and legends are told and explained by Richard Barber in his *Companion to World Mythology*, illustrated by Pauline Baynes.

Folklore is widely researched throughout the world and collected by individuals and by libraries. Part of the documentation recently is a two-volume *Katalog zur Volkserzahlung*[1] with 1,135 pages of catalogue entries for publications of and about myths and legends.

Fairy stories

Though some fairy stories are about fairies, elves and pixies, the majority are not, but are concerned with people who are apparently human beings, who find themselves in situations where magic transforms, aids or confounds them. Fairyland can be defined as a world in which enchanted and enchanting things happen, a world which has a place also in the inner mind.

A great deal has been written about fairy stories, describing and analysing, looking for psychological significance, geographical similarity, historical background, imaginative effect on children's minds, and ways of telling, presenting and illustrating fairy stories. A selection of readings covering these topics is given at the end of the chapter.

Most countries have their fairy stories and in most countries the characters are not usually children, though illustrators often depict them as such. Characters in fairy stories tend to be adult, such as Cinderella, Sleeping Beauty and Bluebeard from Perrault's tales; Rapunzel, Snow White and the Dancing Princesses from Grimm's

137

tales; or Andersen's Princess (and the Pea), Tin Soldier, and the Emperor who thought he had new clothes; or Sinbad the Sailor from the *Arabian Nights' Entertainments*. Sometimes the characters are animal as in *The Ugly Duckling* or indefinable as in Tolkien's Hobbit.

So the appeal to children is not identification with the age of the character but with the style and structure of the story and with its inner truth, which in many cases has persisted for a very long time. Western fairy tales are considered to derive from just a few sources. These include:

- Seventeenth-century *1001 Nights* or the *Arabian Nights' Entertainments* which were culled from a sixth-century Arabian manuscript of stories told in the Middle-Eastern palaces.

- Giambattista Basile, the court writer to the Italian princes in the seventeenth century, who is thought to have invented *Cinderella* and *The Sleeping Beauty* and a number of stories of horror and murder.

- Charles Perrault who in the seventeenth century collected stories for telling at the French court, many of which had to be considerably expurgated for later readers.

- The Grimm Brothers, Jakob and Wilhelm, whose first collection of stories in 1812 arose from their work as philologists.

- Hans Christian Andersen of Denmark whose stories were translated into English in 1846.

- Joseph Jacobs of England, who collected English fairy tales from books rather than oral tradition, with examples like *Jack and the Beanstalk*, *Dick Whittington* and *The Three Bears*.

- Andrew Lang in the 1890s who edited many volumes of collected fairy stories, such as *The Blue Fairy Book* and *The Yellow Fairy Book*.

Whatever their origin, and many versions and identical themes appear in many countries' tales, they all contain those features listed under legends and folk tales, and they all have either a happy ending or one in which just retribution is seen. The best tellings or re-tellings, also use narrative flow, from the oral origins, a flow which is perpetuated today by oral telling at mother's knee or in storytelling sessions, in the spoken dialogue in films and televised versions, and, in Britain particularly, in the Christmas pantomimes based on fairy tales.

The structure of the storyline, the vivid description, the economy of words, the clear and simple character studies, are part of the need to get the story across to a listener. The inner truth that retains his interest and leaves him satisfied is demonstrated in the underlying 'moral' in most of the tales; pride in *The Red Shoes* and in *The Emperor's New Clothes*; greed in *Pinocchio*, *Big Claus and Little Claus* and *The Golden Goose*; self-esteem in *The Ugly Duckling*; values of life and death in *The Emperor's Nightingale*; bravery in *The Little Tailor* and *Hansel and Gretel*.

There are thousands of published books of fairy tales throughout the world, some in collected editions but, increasingly, as colour printing and picture-book production improve, there are picture-book re-tellings, of an individual story. In some there is a discrepancy between the theme and the feeling of the story as told in words, and what should be a complementary style of illustration.

Examples of editions where due attention has been paid to the original versions are: *The Brothers Grimm: Popular Folk Tales*, translated by Brian Alderson and illustrated by Michael Foreman, its companion volume, *Hans Andersen; His Classic Fairy Tales*, by Erik Haugaard, also illustrated by Michael Foreman and *Hans Andersen's Fairy Tales*, translated by Naomi Lewis.

Helen Oxenbury's illustrations to Brian Alderson's selection of stories in *The Helen Oxenbury Nursery Story Book* are different from Errol Le Cain's interpretations in Naomi Lewis's *The Snow Queen* picture book. Different again and very popular with parents and children both for text and illustration is Raymond Briggs's large volume, *The Fairy Tale Treasury*.

As already mentioned, Charles Keeping's powerful illustrations complement the strongly worded text of a book of myths, but there is in print a story of *Cinderella* that is told in earthy modern-style language but illustrated in pale silvery, romanticized style. Such lack of sympathy does not enhance the whole effect of the book, nor aid the child reader.

However, the spirit of the fairy tale is magnificently captured in individual ways by artists and book illustrators such as Jri Trnka of Czechoslovakia, Ib Spang Olsen of Denmark, Lilo Fromm and Janosch of Germany, Monika Laimgruber of Switzerland, Maurice Sendak of the USA, Errol Le Cain and Michael Foreman of Britain.

Many fairy stories contain quite horrific events, such as cutting off feet and shoes in *The Red Shoes*, a dead grandmother's body being used to trick someone in *Big Claus and Little Claus*, a child-eating ogre in *Mollie Whuppy*, and Bluebeard's murders of his womenfolk. As in re-tellings of the myths and legends, some versions tone down the violence or omit the more blood-thirsty details. But most tales have a high standard of behaviour and principle and most children safely enjoy the more fearful elements.

Intensive research in this area has been undertaken by many in several countries over a long period of time, particularly by Bettelheim and Chukovsky, and after many years of work, Walter Scherf in his psychoanalysis of *Die Herausforderung des Damons*[2] (the challenge of Demons), the form and function of horror in children's tales, published in German. More accessible to English readers is a brief article by Nicholas Tucker, *Books That Frighten*,[3] in Virginia Haviland's *Children and Literature, Views and Reviews*, in which he looks at the subject in a range of children's reading matter.

The traditional fairy tale, worldwide, allows the reader or the listener to see or hear that time and place are of no concern. The traditional start to the story, 'Once upon a time', is both a stimulater and a pacifier. The fairy story allows the child or adult to follow a clear progression of action and dialogue with no doubt as to who is the good character and who the bad, and with the satisfaction of seeing the former triumph over difficulty with or without magical aid, and the latter getting his just deserts.

But the fairy story does not end with those considered to be traditional. Modern fairy stories exist, including Jay Williams' *The Practical Princess and Other Liberating Fairy Tales*, while Babette Cole devised an up-to-date *Princess Smartypants*. The same ingredients are found in the modern stories as in the old fairy tales and all are set in some enchanted land.

But the child who has loved fairy stories from babyhood may find interest waning round the age of nine, boys sooner than girls. At that age there is often a transition to a stronger liking for what is termed fantasy.

Fantasy

Fantasy is not confined to books. Children and adults fantasize all the time over matters in their own, and other's, lives. They fantasize about their toys or possessions, their relationships, their past and their future lives. Fantasy is an integral part of the thought process. So when Margery Fisher says in *Intent Upon Reading*:[4] 'Fantasy takes known

141

objects and scenes and reshapes them into its own terms', she is speaking not only about books but about a human condition. She says, 'We may properly call those stories fantasy which bring the magic and irrational into our own world'.

Naomi Lewis has said of fantasy: You reach the edge of the probable and then step over, and Asfrid Svensen of the University of Oslo suggested that fantasy demonstrates 'the relativity of all reality ... that reality has scope far beyond our range of vision'.

In an article in the *International Review of Children's Literature and Librarianship*:[5] two characteristics of fantasy were posited as 'highlighting the ordinary by its comparison with the extraordinary' and 'opening a window onto the unknown and the inexplicable'.

A number of inferences can be drawn from that. For example there is the inference that magic from another world enters our 'real' world as in Helen Cresswell's *The Night Watchers*. There is the inference that parts of our world, to which we do not normally go, have magic areas, such as the undersea world in Lucy M. Boston's *The Sea-Egg*, Charles Kingsley's *The Water Babies* or Jules Verne's *Two Thousand Leagues Under the Sea*. We can go to our world in the past via a magic clock in *Tom's Midnight Garden* by Philippa Pearce or by Robert Leeson's *The Time Rope*.

We can see a complete world under the floor in Mary Norton's *The Borrowers*, or under the earth in Raymond Briggs's *Fungus the Bogeyman* and Elizabeth Beresford's *The Wombles*. Or we can be immersed in the fantasy world of Never-Never Land in J. M. Barrie's *Peter Pan* or in *Alice in Wonderland*. Tove Jansson offers a humorous saga of creatures in *Moominland* while Norton Juster takes a child reader to Dictionopolis and Digitopolis in *The Phantom Tollbooth*.

We can travel to mythical worlds created by J. R. R. Tolkien in *The Hobbit* and *The Lord of the Rings*; or the land of Prydain created by Lloyd Alexander in his five-book cycle; to the fantasy places of Alan Garner's *Owl Service*; to the land of *Narnia* with C. S. Lewis in his series, exemplified in *The Lion, The Witch and the Wardrobe*; Ursula le Guin's *A Wizard of Earthsea* and Susan Cooper's books create fantasy worlds brilliantly.

Fantasy can also be seen in the stories of animals and toys who take on human attributes, whether a teddy bear called *Winnie the Pooh*, the woodland life in *Wind in the Willows*, or in the pilgrimage of toys in *The Mouse and His Child*, by Russell Hoban. Similarly Robert C. O'Brien's *Mrs Frisby and the Rats of Nimh* holds up a picture of the 'real' world through the story of rats building a new and better society. Perhaps the best animal fantasy is E. B. White's *Charlotte's Web* in which spider and pig collaborate.

The fantasy of monsters is seen in Maurice Sendak's *Where the Wild Things Are* and in Ted Hughes's *The Iron Man*, both of which use an economy of words yet offer an immense richness of imagery and suspense.

Though part of every period in British children's literature, fantasy was strongly represented in the 1980s after the predominance of realism in the 1970s. Margaret Mahy's *The Haunting*, Diana Wynne Jones's many books, Pat O'Shea's *The Hounds of the Morrigan* are part of that output while the different aspects of fantasy are seen in, for example, Jan Mark's *Out of the Oven*, Jenny Nimmo's *The Snow Spider* and Chris Powling's *The Phantom Carwash*, for a younger age group.

Fantasy in the future world or in another part of space is also represented in the increase in the 1980s. Science fiction builds on present happenings and known objects to project an imaginary world of the future as rooted in reality as those stories that take a mythical setting for the base. Thus

John Christopher, Alan Nourse, Robert Heinlein, present along with Ray Bradbury, H. G. Wells and Isaac Asimov, a picture of this world by the emphases they lay on aspects of another world or our world in the future. In the 1980s came Geraldine Harris's *Warriors of Taan*, Tamara Pierce's *Land of the Goddess*, Robert Westall's scenes in *Futuretrack 5* and the 'Planet Moros' of Douglas Hill. With Monica Hughes, Nicholas Fisk and a host of others, these writers make use of a thought-through interpretation of where today's trends will lead us tomorrow.

At another level fantasy is seen in the game books which became a cult in several countries, particularly with boys. Akin to the space fiction comics and television programmes in terms of depth, themes of conflict, adventure, quest and victory are present but the progression through the plot is decided by the reader. Already described in Chapter 1 as one of the trends in children's books, they use the skeleton of the more literary fantasy, but leave the reader to put on the flesh.

Such books *start* in the improbable rather than 'step over the edge' into unreality. Nevertheless, they are part of the total genre.

Ghosts and witches

The supernatural in children's fiction has long been a favourite theme and is found in books for all ages. From the picture book treatment exemplified in Pam Adams's *Book of Ghosts* published by Childs Play, through the next age group's delight in Shirley Hughes's *It's too Frightening For Me* and Jill Murphy's *The Worst Witch* books, to Vivien Alcock's *The Haunting of Cassie Palmer*, Nina Bawden's *The Witch's Daughter*, Penelope Lively's *The Ghost of Thomas Kempe*, Margaret Mahy's *The Changeover*, and Alison Prince's *The Ghost Within*, the subject of ghosts, witches, strange 'magic' and spine-chilling happenings have kept children and young people glued to the page.

Traditional ghost stories and characters appear in various forms, as in Joan Aiken's *The Kingdom under the Sea*, Aidan Chambers's *Book of Ghosts and Hauntings*, and many other anthologies of ghost stories. Humour is found in for example Gene Kemp's *The Clocktower Ghost* and Helen Cresswell's *Lizzie Dripping*, Margery Norton's *Bedknob and Broomstick* and Barbara Willard's *Spell Me a Witch*.

Towards the end of the 1980s there has been an increasing volume of concern at the expression of supernatural things in books for young people, where the occult and horror and gratuitous violence form a major theme, part of an apparently evil and malevolent force. Coinciding with an increase in interest in the occult generally, the view is held that all books concerned with things 'magic' should be avoided, including the theme of witches and wizards. Time will tell as to whether those concerned to ban the supernatural in books will exercise judgement or call for the removal of all suspected books. Meanwhile throughout the world the theme continues to be published, bought and read as part of mainstream children's literature.

Animal stories

A large proportion of children's books is concerned with animals, birds or insects of one kind or another, possibly on the grounds that they are ageless and timeless. They can be given attributes and faults not acceptable in child characters. They are known to provide the psychological comfort that children find in pets.

Animal stories vary from fantasy humanized animals to the simply informative about animal life. Animals behaving

145

like humans are often a vehicle for a message and some of the earliest stories, such as *Aesop's Fables*, used animals to point a moral, and many of the folk tales have animal heroes or anti-heroes such as Anansi and Monkey.

Books for older readers have humanized animals too, such as the rabbits in *Watership Down* by Richard Adams, the rats of Nimh, or that classic of the twentieth century, *Animal Farm* by George Orwell. At all levels the animals usually behave as equivalent adult humans would or should, so humanized adult animals are acceptable to the child reader where characters shown as adult humans are not. Examples include Beatrix Potter's *Mrs Tiggywinkle*, the characters in *Wind in the Willows*, the spider and the pig in *Charlotte's Web*, *Frog and Toad* by Arnold Lobel and the church mice in Graham Oakley's series of stories.

Stories in which a child forms an affection for an animal are popular with many age groups and are found to be therapeutic for many. Perhaps the vicarious satisfying of a wish for a pet is the reason, providing also a means of having someone or something dependent. Examples include *A Dog So Small*, by Philippa Pearce, a classic in its appeal and quality, in which a small boy longs for a dog. Throughout most of the book he talks and walks with his invented, tiny, imaginary dog and although there is a real dog at the end the reader is satisfied even with the dog so small. In Barry Hines *Kestrel for a Knave*, David a young teenager has an unhappy home and school life and rears a kestrel, lavishing time and love on it.

The appeal of young animals is seen in for example Rumer Godden's *A Kindle of Kittens*, and Ruth Brown's *Our Puppy's Holiday* while a serious novel for older readers involves the quest for the guardian of the city's cats in Robert Westall's *The Cats of Seroster*, and a succession of books from Dick King-Smith reveal him as a master of the anthropomorphic animal story.

Humorous stories about animals are numerous and the young reader of picture books has a wealth to choose from including Mary Rayner's *Mr and Mrs Pig's Evening Out*, Gene Zion's *Harry the Dirty Dog* and Rudyard Kipling's *Just So Stories*.

Arthur, a small dog in a pet shop, tries his hand at imitating all the other animals in the shop in a bid to get himself a home. So appealing was he that the book by Amanda Graham was voted the most popular book of 1985 by members of the Federation of Children's Book Groups.

Stories of real animals often become classics and are read by both adults and children, as these examples show: Henry Williamson's *Tarka the Otter*, Sheila Burnford's *The Incredible Journey*, undertaken by two dogs and a cat in their successful attempt to go four hundred miles back to their Canadian home and Paul Gallico's *Snow Goose*. Real animals are also used in the many photo stories now available.

Popular with many girls, particularly in Britain, USA and Australia, are the 'pony books'. There are large quantities in hardback and paperback and most are the work of a few prolific writers. The early classics, *Black Beauty* by Anna Seton, *The Yearling* by M. Rawlings and Enid Bagnold's *National Velvet*, were forerunners of a spate of pony books written in the 1960s and 1970s at a popular level for the 'horse-mad' girls of twelve upwards. Each of the following writers has written many pony books: Mary Treadgold, Ruby Ferguson, Christine and Diana Pullein-Thompson, Primrose Cumming, Judith M. Berrisford, Monica Edwards, while other writers such as Vian Smith and K. M. Peyton created novels around the theme of horses.

A pony book with a conscience is Linda Yeatman's *Pickles* in which the pony helps 'a disabled girl'. It has all the usual ingredients of a pony book plus the integrated information about riding for the disabled.

147

Girls who may or may not possess a pony read avidly within this genre at around nine to mid-teens, part of the appeal being that need for the child to control something in a life that is otherwise controlled by adults.

Anthropomorphism versus the 'animals shouldn't wear clothes' viewpoint is constantly under discussion, but there is no doubt that the former view enables writers and illustrators to extend the child's horizons, providing a vehicle to say and show what would be difficult if human beings were used.

Beginning with the animal legends of every country, the range of animal books has grown to encompass bird, beast, insect and fish, wild and domesticated, humanized and in its natural state.

Historical stories

Most historical stories are read by the middle-to-older part of the children/young person age and it is probable that three factors are the cause:

- Many children need to be of an age to understand the present before they can appreciate the past.
- Most historical writers for children use the kind of detail, descriptive writing and sentence patterns that demand good reading ability.
- The third factor lies in the age of the main character in the novel. This is usually between twelve and adulthood and the emphasis is often on the adult characters surrounding the child character, thus making the book more attractive to readers within that range than to younger children.

The historical story is in many forms. It can be history in story form, set around an actual historical character or event; it can be an adventure story in historical setting, either pure imagination or a mixture of fact and fiction; it can be time-slip from present to past (and back) or from past to present (and back).

Whichever of these forms the novel takes, the writer has undoubtedly done much research into the events, social customs, costume, practices and principles of the period or country and any period or country is likely to be used by an author if it contains the elements of adventure and human interest necessary for a historical story. For instance some of Rosemary Sutcliff's books are set in Roman Britain, Leon Garfield's in eighteenth-century England and Jill Paton Walsh set *The Emperor's Winding Sheet* in Byzantine times and Mollie Hunter's *The Stronghold* is a story of the early Scottish defence against Scandinavian invaders in the first century.

Laura Ingalls Wilder's books act out the early American settlers activities while Harold Keith's *Rifle for Watie* depicts life in the American Civil War.

The Black Death and time slip are found in Berlie Doherty's *Children of Winter*, and time is slipped into back and forth, past, present and future in Robert Leeson's four-book serial *The Time Rope*. In America the 1986 Scott O'Dell Award for Historical Fiction went to Patricia MacLachan's *Sarah, Plain and Tall* set in the pioneer days on the prairie. It received the Newbery Medal that year also. For a different age group and set in a different period, *Ruth's Story* is Catherine Storr's 32-page book in the *People of the Bible* series from Franklin Watts, with large clear pictures. Exceptionally well illustrated and told is *Rose Blanche*, a picture book by Roberto Innocenti with text by Ian McEwan, showing a German Jewish girl looking at the Second World War as it affected her and her town – a rare example of an historical picture book, and one which has something to say to a wide age range. In different style the strongly felt message against war and justice is powerfully spoken in James Watson's *The Freedom Tree*, a story of the Spanish Civil War, for older readers.

The fact that the majority of historical works for children are based on war or conflict reflects one of the reasons given by many historical writers for choosing the past rather than the present time. The past offers a range of situations in which a child was pitted against his fortune or an enemy and could show bravery, cunning, achievement, loyalty and even love. Many authors feel better able to portray the social history of the past correctly than to understand and correctly define the present, so the two aspects of the subject content and author inclination combine to produce the genre known as the historical novel for children.

Over the years many British writers have contributed to that genre. Geoffrey Trease, Cynthia Harnett, Henry Treece, Leon Garfield, Barbara Willard, Jill Paton Walsh, Rosemary Sutcliff and Hester Burton are names to conjure with in the re-creation of times past.

Analysis shows that most authors give a clue to the period in the first page either by actually giving the date or indicating it by the use of a historical place or a name. Rosemary Sutcliff's *The Light Beyond the Forest* begins:

> On every side, Camelot climbed, roof above coloured roof, up the steep slopes of the hill. About the foot of the hill the river cast its shining silver noose; and at the highest heart of the town rose the palace of King Arthur.

This also exemplifies the style of writing which shows the flavour of the period by the sentence structure and judicious use of vocabulary rather than by imposing the idiom of the period on to a modern style of writing. They typify the kind of historical writing which is firmly in the period where the characters think and act within the limits

150

of their era rather than a present view of past history where the characters are set in a past age but think like some modern character. These books also have something to say to the adult reader.

The responsibility of the illustrator of the historical story is heavy. He must accurately portray the factual aspects of the period while adding the flavour. It is common to find black and white line drawings in the few illustrations to be found in historical books for older readers, but picture story books on an historical theme are rare and tend to be very simple in text and flamboyantly colourful in illustration.

Although many kinds of book and reading interest are common to many countries, the historical novel tends to be found largely in Western countries with a long history of children's book writing, and the books themselves tend to appeal to a small but dedicated percentage of the reading population.

Humour

Whether for adults or children, humour in books takes many forms and produces a variety of responses, from loud laughter to an inner feeling of intellectual amusement.

The most obviously funny forms of literature are the joke books such as *The Old Joke Book* by Janet and Allan Ahlberg (most of whose other books have a strong humorous content in both text and picture).

The nonsense of Edward Lear and of Norman Hunter's Professor Branestawn can also be linked with the books of humorous verse which often include the poems of writers such as Lewis Carroll, Spike Milligan, Ogden Nash and Michael Rosen whose zany humour has endeared him to children in a wide range of stories and books of poems, particularly those with the equally irrepressible illustrations of Quentin Blake.

The 1980s was a period of acceptance that funny verse and humorous stories were liked by children and should be available in school and public libraries. A large number of anthologies appeared, including Beverley Mathias's compilation, *The Hippo Book of Funny Verse*.

After the situation comedy of Dorothy Edwards' *My Naughty Little Sister*, Astrid Lindgren's *Pippi Longstocking*, Richmal Crompton's *Just William* and Mary Rodgers *Freaky Friday*, came Andrew Davies' *Marmalade Atkins*, Helen Cresswell's *Bagthorpes* and Christine Nostlinger's *Conrad*. Substitute children in the form of animals also provide fun as in Michael Bond's *Paddington* books, A. A. Milne's *Winnie the Pooh* and Dick King-Smith's *The Fox Busters*.

The illustrative content of children's books can also convey humour and there are many picutre books in which the subject theme and the pictorial combine to create a 'funny' book. Examples include the Dr Seuss books; the work of the Ahlberg partnership as in *Burglar Bill*; the *Mrs Pepperpot* books by Alf Proysen, illustrated by Bjon Berg; and anything by Quentin Blake.

There is lively humour in John Burningham's *Mr Gumpy's Outing* and Pamela Allen's *Who Sank the Boat?* while Richard Scarry's books are noted for the pages crammed with humorous pictures. One look at the bear in Yasuo Ohtomo's illustrations for Shigeo Wantanabe's books, such as *How Do I Put It On*? raises a smile and the gentle humour in both text and illustrations in Gabrielle Vincent's *Ernest and Celestine* has captivated a wide range.

Anthologies of stories and short stories by single authors are appreciated by children and by adults who read aloud to children. Margaret Mahy's *The Downhill Crocodile Whizz and Other Stories* is an example as is Philippa Pearce's *What the Neighbours Did*.

For young people there is a range of books which can be

read at both the serious and the comic levels, such as Paul
Zindel's *The Pigman* and Betsy Byars' *The Eighteenth
Emergency*, both examples of the art of providing an
underlying comic vein in a serious theme – tragi-comedy,
and both by American authors, who seem to be more adept
at this than writers in other countries.

Adrian Mole burst on the scene with his diary and the
sequel, the *Growing Pains of Adrian Mole*, by Sue
Townsend and in 1987 it was the girl's turn when Eileen
Fairweather's *French Letters: the Life and Loves of Miss
Maxime Harrison* was published in the *Livewire* series from
The Women's Press. Wildly funny letters to her French pen
pal rival Adrian Mole's revelations.

But humour in books may not be appreciated by children
in other countries. Not all humour is cross-national or
translatable. The most common elements are associated
with absurdities, surprise, incongruous situation, exagger-
ation, slapstick, predicaments, taboo, particularly lavatorial
subjects, and verbal humour. It tends to parallel a child's
emotional and verbal development in that it is necessary to
know normality before being able to identify abnormality,
to have some knowledge of language before being able to
appreciate a play on words, puns or verbal humour. Some
experience of life and its situations is necessary in order to
understand when people and their situations are being
parodied or mocked in story or picture.

So humour in children's books tends to start with the
young child's experience of doing or not being allowed to
do 'naughty' things, and develops towards the adult subtle
aspects of irony and satire.

Comics and picture strip books

The pictorial humour in comic books is very popular
throughout the world and the quantity of such material

153

increases both at the most commercial level and at the highest level as an art form.

Comics are usually attractive to look at, easy to read, and on themes similar to those found in books: family life, school, adventure, humour, sport, science fiction, war, romance.

Told in a sequence of narrative pictures with succinct captions or 'balloon' talk they capture the interest of a large proportion of children and young people. The immense popularity of picture strip for both children and adults is due to the following features:

- The pictures, which tend to be informal, fluid, attracting the attention even in black and white; informative in indicating the next step in the visual story progression.
- The contents, which basically conform to the contents of book plots in the elemental themes of love, hate, greed, pride, bravery, cowardice, good and evil, but all starkly simplified by the constraints of the picture-strip format.
- The familiarity of the regular characters and the familiarity of the formula that enables good to triumph over evil, the hero to win in the end and the emphasis on the moral that goodness pays.
- The regularity of the format and its weekly or monthly availability, which provides something to look forward to.
- Comics being the least middle-class of all reading matter for children, cut across social boundaries in both content and readership.
- The inclusion of other items such as puzzles, questions, information snippets and things to do, give a magazine flavour.

Comics are easy to read and never boring, largely

because several technical features aid the ease of reading and of comprehension. The frame surrounding each picture and the balloon surrounding much of the text, enable the eye, the mind and the attention to be concentrated in the required place. Some comics have picture strips which are informative in that they can be followed without the text, others can be found where the text can stand alone without the pictures, but taking the pictures, words and frames together, there is a powerful concentration of aids to comprehension.

Similarly the length of attention needed is short enough to ensure that comprehension is achieved, length being one of the points that children mention in relation to their dislike of book reading.

Some comic strips cause concern about the stereotyped characters, violence in this and other planets, racist/national-ist/sexist prejudices and war, but the 'funnies' represent the safety valve for the relief of tension by mocking parents, teachers, librarians, bullies and authority. That children's lives are such that they enjoy this form of escapism is a problem too large to discuss here but the fact is that children do find tilting at authority a source of amusement and do feel that justice has been done when all is restored to normal at the end. 'Funnies' head the poll in all published and most unpublished surveys of comic book reading.

As comics almost always form part of a larger reading diet or are read by those who are not capable of sustained book reading, the enjoyment of comics need not be denied children.

The picture strip of quality as an art form is discussed in Chapter Seven but is seen here in books such as Hergé's *Tintin* series, Goscinny and Uderzo's *Asterix* and Raymond Briggs's *Father Christmas* and *Fungus the Bogeyman*. Each of these has both textual and pictorial style and wit, requiring much more of the reader than the commercial comic strip, and offering, instead of surface pleasure a depth of satisfaction.

School stories

The boarding or residential school is a particularly British tradition, though many other countries have them. Such a school lends itself to story form because it contains the seeds of adventure, the possibilities of strong and weak characters, authority in the shape of teachers but freedom in the absence of parents; all within the clearly defined framework of a school organization.

The surprising fact about school stories is that though the majority were written in the period 1900 to 1960 girls school stories are not only still popular in the 1980s in Britain but have a wide readership in other countries, particularly in Malaysia and the Pacific areas.

The now less popular boys' school stories range from the documentary/adventure style of Thomas Hughes's *Tom Brown's Schooldays* and Talbot Baines's *Fifth Form at St Dominic's*, to the light-hearted series of Frank Richard's *Billy Bunter* books and Anthony Buckeridge's *Jennings* books. The more modern school stories include those set in day schools rather than boarding schools such as Bernard Ashley's primary school *Dinner Ladies Don't Count* and his *Terry on the Fence*. Alison Prince's *The Doubting Kind*, Jan Mark's *Hairs in the Palm of The Hand* and Jean McGibbon's *Hal* are stories within the framework of a school setting rather than school stories as such, as are Nat Hentoff's *This School is Driving Me Crazy*, Hazel Townson's *Siege at Cobb Street School* or William Mayne's choir school books.

A controversial novel *The Chocolate War*, by Robert Cormier, swings the balance right over to present-day realism in its depiction of a corrupt American school teacher, an extortion racket and one of the boy's attempts to break the vicious circle, and in its sequel *Beyond the Chocolate War*.

Girls' school stories are vast in quantity, ranging from the archetypal Angela Brazil books to the fifty-six titles in the *Chalet School* series by Elenor Brent Dyer, and the numerous titles in the *Abbey School* series by Elsie Oxenham. Enid Blyton's school stories were popular from their beginning in the 1940s and remain so today in three series, *The Naughtiest Girl*, the *St Clare's* and the *Mallory Towers* books.

Nearer the present day, Gene Kemp's *The Turbulent Term of Tyke Tyler* exemplifies the school story set in a more realistic world. But the essence of the appeal of the earlier books lies in the dream fulfilment of being liked, achieving success in sport, hero worshipping the sixth-former or the teacher, or solving a mystery connected with the school or the family.

Many of the plots are repetitive, the characters stereo-typed, the slang outdated; there is little to do with real-life boarding school practice in the educational sense and almost no explicit boy/girl relationships; but the sometimes exotic settings, the evident privilege in the boarding school clientele and the basic relationships depicted in the schoolgirl or schoolboy world, continue to hold interest, particularly for girls.

It seems possible that that kind of school story will disappear as the number of books set in contemporary times increases, though these are more stories in which school plays a large part in the plot but the children are seen in their home and leisure environments also.

An excellent anthology draws together the range of school and of writer in twelve stories. Barbara Ireson's compilation *In a Class of Their Own* exemplifies the changes from traditional to contemporary.

Adventure stories

The word 'adventure' suggests action, suspense, challenge, adversaries, adversities and excitement. When the word is applied to stories it also implies a safe return to normality and covers most children's books in that most of the ingredients can be found in fairy stories, fantasy, historical fiction, school stories, in family stories and other broad categories of fiction.

From earliest times adventure stories have brought interest and excitement to people in many countries in the myths and legends and folk tales; later in stories like *Robinson Crusoe*, *Gulliver's Travels* and *Treasure Island*; and recently in the wealth of modern stories that provide a venturing out of the known into the unknown with all the uncertainty, fear, anticipation and excitement that such a step can bring.

Adventure in the past brings the genre into an overlap with historical fiction and adventure in the future aligns with much science fiction, but the term 'adventure story' is generally applied to the book that depicts a child or gang of children who become involved in a situation where they need to tackle a difficult problem or person, solve a mystery, undertake a journey or right a wrong. This is often done without the presence of parents or authority, though there may be kindly adults around who help where needed. The adversary is often adult and part of the interest for children lies in this fact and in the eventual triumphing over adversary and adversity.

Adventure is a term encompassing experiences in most settings, land, sea, in the air, in space or underground. Armstrong Sperry's *The Boy Who Was Afraid* is a challenge of the sea, as are R. L. Stevenson's *Treasure Island*, and Willard Price's *Underwater Adventure*, *The Dolphin Crossing* by Jill Paton Walsh and *Maroon Boy* by

Robert Leeson. The air is the scene of Ivan Southall's *To the Wild Sky* in which a group of children flying in a light aircraft across Australia have to cope with the situation when the pilot dies in mid-flight. W. E. Johns's *Biggles* books portray an adult pilot in exciting situations. On, or, in, the land, Jules Verne's *Journey to the Centre of the Earth* and Colin Thiele's *Chadwick's Chimney*, the latter a mystery in underground caves in Australia, are part of the genre, as are his *Fire in the Stone* and Joan Aiken's *The Wolves of Willoughby Chase*.

There are many such books for children and many that make from these ingredients an easily absorbed story in which the reader races along with the action. This is the appeal of the phenomenal Enid Blyton books, dozens of which are adventure stories concerning the Famous Five and the Secret Seven in books like *Five on a Treasure Island*, *The Island of Adventure*, *Castle of Adventure*, *Valley of Adventure*, and so on. Her books have been best sellers since the 1940s and are read by children all over the world, despite the very English characters and settings. Similarly, the *Hardy Boys* of American origin have maintained their popularity over the years for much the same reasons of simplicity, action and familiarity because of the quantity.

Adventure stories often centre on school holidays, an obvious choice because not only are children out of their normal school routine but are often also out of their normal setting and are thus conveniently open to the possibility of the unusual.

Some adventure stories involve a mystery or a crime, to be solved by the detective work of the child or group, eventually bringing the criminal to justice. In the 1980s *The Race Against Time* series of books by J. J. Fortune, for example, *Revenge in the Silent Tomb*, and the *Dean Street Mystery* series by Bill Butler, such as *The Spying Machines*, became popular.

159

Some adventures are the result of war and there are many excellent books that treat both war and adventure in a way that grips the reader with suspense. Examples include two in which children journey across Europe to find parents from whom they were separated by war; Ian Serraillier's *The Silver Sword* and Ann Holm's *I Am David*. Meindert de Jong's *House of Sixty Fathers* shows a small boy separated from his family during the Japanese invasion of China in the Second World War. Books that look at the dangers and excitements of a child's life in wartime include Christine Nöstlinger's *Fly Away Home*, set in Vienna in Austria and Robert Westall's *The Machine Gunners* set in Tyneside in northern England, all during the Second World War.

Ivan Southall's novel for older readers, *The Long Night Watch* set on a Pacific island invaded by the Japanese in the Second World War is complemented by Ian Strachan's *Journey of 1000 Miles*, undertaken by a boy in a boat-load of people escaping from Vietnam.

The adventure story seems to translate well across national boundaries and languages, and a foreign setting is not often a barrier to enjoyment. The English child can enjoy Andrew Salkey's *Hurricane*, set in the West Indies; the Jamaican child reads Willard Price's books; the American child can be engrossed in *I Am David* in Europe; while *The Adventures of Tom Sawyer* still pleases British children; and Australia's *Walkabout* by James Vance Marshall has an international readership. Childhood *is* adventure, and challenge and change are part of everyday life for most children in whatever country.

But whether the story adventure is urban, rural, seaborne or airborne it is usually fraught with danger, either actual or potential, involves resourcefulness and sometimes courage. The interplay of characters reveals the strengths and weakness of the group or the individual child, and the ending indicates the successful completion of the journey, the solving of the mystery, the tying up of the threads of the story, the end of the adventure.

Family stories

The trends in family stories reflect the trends in families. The early books on a family theme were of the kind exemplified by Louisa Alcott's *Little Women* where there was a close relationship between parents and each child, a togetherness in thought and action and a comforting feeling that whatever misfortune might befall parent or child, underneath and roundabout was the security of the supportive family.

Whether or not the real children's families were like that, the family story nevertheless provided a satisfying emotional warmth. Similar pictures of family life are seen in Laura Ingalls Wilder's *Little House in the Prairie*, E. Nesbit's *The Railway Children*, Elizabeth Enright's Melendy family in *The Saturdays* and the close-knit family in Joan Lingard's books in Scottish settings, such as *The Clearance*.

But in the 1960s there was a gradual introduction of the idea that not all families were close-knit, nor complete. The possibility of a 'live-in' mother and parental arguments is seen in John Rowe Townsend's *Gumble's Yard*, marital discord in Erich Kastner's *Lottie and Lisa* and William Mayne's *Blue Boat*. Adoption into a family was seen in comforting terms in *Anne of Green Gables* by L. M. Montgomery, still well loved by children.

The disruption of family life is shown in Paula Fox's *How Many Miles to Babylon?*, a black boy's distress when his mother goes into hospital, and in Bernard Ashley's *The Trouble with Donovan Croft*, who is put into foster-care when his mother has to return to Jamaica temporarily from London.

In the 1970s and early 1980s there developed a literature in which the concept of the family appeared to be struggling, particularly in American books such as the works of Judy Blume, Paula Danziger and Paul Zindel, while in Britain mother was seen struggling to keep the family together in books like Tim Kennemore's *Wall of Words* in which mother supports the family while father writes a book, and Ann Fine's *Madame Doubtfire* in which parents are divorced and businesswoman mother becomes involved unwittingly with father in attempts to keep the home and children organized.

Families with a handicapped child appear in increasing quantity as the social recognition of such a situation improves. There are excellent examples of picture-book stories such as Camilla Jessell's *Mark's Wheelchair Adventures* and Freddie Bloom's *The Boy Who Couldn't Hear*. There are books for the young reader such as Susan Burke's *Alexander In Trouble* who amazes himself and his family with what he can do in and out of his wheelchair and Joyce Dunbar's *Mundo and the Weather-Child*. There are books for the older reader in which the family's relationship with a handicapped child is shown to involve each member of the family, as in Eleanor Spence's *The October Child* where the main character is autistic, and Marlene Fanta Shyer's, *Welcome Home Jellybean*, in which a severely mentally handicapped girl comes home from residential care to live with her family, seen through the eyes of her twelve-year-old brother.

Than there are books which depict the discord between parents and child and between brother and sister as part of the natural day-to-day conversation and disagreement of family life, as in Louise Fitzhugh's story *Nobody's Family is Going to Change*, in which eleven-year-old Emma and her black American family hold differing views on what she and her brother should be and do. Family discord is seen too in some teenage novels discussed later, a discord which stems from the fact that teenage is the departure point from dependence to independence, though fictional (and real) parents differ on when and how the vital step is taken.

Happy families do exist in for example Helen Cresswell's *Bagthorpe* books, in Allan Ahlberg's series of small books with the overall title of Happy Families, such as *Mrs Plug the Plumber*, and in Hunter Davies's *Flossie Teacake's Fur Coat*.

Perhaps the masterpiece of 'family' books is Alan Garner's *The Stone Book Quartet* in which the family, their crafts and their lives are depicted in a language and style that recreates the total picture. The author's presentation and the physical format of the book provide one of those rare books, a classic in its own time.

The family story in Western countries has changed from the 'wholeness' of the early books to the treatment of the family as individuals, sometimes in conflict with other individuals in the family; from the standard unit of mother, father, children and often grandparents and extended family, to the family as the child and whoever happens to be sharing his life with him at home. There are exceptions but in general, at the time of writing, modern stories of united family are few, despite modern children's enjoyment of the earlier family stories and their translation to the film screen.

Realism

Arthur Koestler suggests that a distinction between fantasy and reality is a 'late acquisition of rational thought'. The young child who has not yet developed sufficient knowledge and experience to know what is true and what is false or what is real and what is unreal, often finds the two interchangeable and moves happily between them.

For example there are many children who have an 'imaginary' friend who is very 'real' to them, but there are also many adults who get so involved in a television series that they 'believe' the characters are 'real' and send abusive or sympathetic letters, or accost the actors in the street. The inability to make the distinction indicates that many people do not acquire capacity for rational thought as they grow out of childhood.

There is a thin dividing line between fantasy and reality, a point made in Aidan Chambers's *Breaktime* in which both the author and the characters explore that theme. But the realism referred to in this section is not the division of books into those that can be called fantasy and those termed realistic. It is a recognition that reality to which we relate is not necessarily a matter of time, place or character, but of the basic needs we feel. So realism is not always a blow-by-blow description of the everyday reality involved in factual and situation realism, it is also the presence of factors with which the reader can identify emotionally, those that cause the reader to think, 'That's how *I* feel' and which are thus real to him.

Realism can be divided into several areas of which six are listed here:

- *Factual realism*: as in historical novels, stories of other lands, science fiction, career novels, and the coverage of factually important aspects in other forms of children's literature.
- *Situation realism*: where the setting may be in an identifiable location and the characters of an identifiable age and social stratum and where the whole treatment make the situation believable.
- *Emotional realism*: where the psychological, personal

and emotional effect of the facts and the situation must ring true. The way people react to each other emotionally in the story can be a telling comment on a personal relationship in 'real' life even though the reader has not personally experienced it in that particular form.

The depiction of certain emotions are often taboo in children's books. Until recently death was avoided or glossed over, but the death of an animal or an old person is common to children in all countries; death by illness or accident is known to most; the death of people in war is within the experience of all-too-many unfortunate children; and most children know of all of these by television, newspapers or adult conversation, if not by personal experience.

But emotions are concerned also with happy aspects of mind, thought and action and the realistic fictional presentation of love, joy and hope are as valid as that of fear, grief and hate.

- *Social realism*: which tends to be equated with the 'kitchen sink' aspects of life in both adult and children's books. 'Telling it like it is' often refers to topics like drugs, sex, violence, political and adverse social conditions, poverty, racial and class problems, handicaps, and family discord. But social, (in the sense of 'of society') encompasses the brighter sides also of communication, community care, children helping each other, close-knit families, enjoyable school and home activities, leisure pursuits, multi-ethnic projects, children overcoming handicaps.

Society can be as broad as the country in which a child lives or as narrow and localized as the street or the school. The norms may be the same or they may conflict, but both are real to the child in that society.

- *Illustrative realism*: whether in picture book or in the

165

illustrations to story books, realism can be seen in the way the artist portrays the *essence* of a scene, an event, a person, to transmit and extend the feeling of reality obtained from the text. Reality is not always attained by photographic illustration by faithful reproduction in a painting. The true artist perceives the 'real' under the layers of disguise or decoration and is able by simple outline or rich detail to make it real for the reader.

- *Realism for the reading-retarded child*: the use of realistic setting and vocabulary in books for the backward or retarded reader can be supported for a number of reasons, based largely on the technical requirements of learning to read. When we read we are not only identifying the letters and the words as pronounceable and defining the meaning of the words, we are selecting the meaning given to those words by the author, within the context. We are also assigning the meaning which our own experience of the word has given us. The more familiar with the situation described by the word, the better we understand the text. It then becomes easier to find meaning in what we read and we are motivated to do it again, thus gaining practice and increasing reading skill. The handicapped child who for physical or mental reasons is behind in reading ability, or the child who is reading-retarded for social or emotional reasons, tends to have a limited experience. He will find familiarity in stories that describe what he *has* experienced, whether it is physically, geographically or emotionally real. This aids his reading, gives him a feeling of achievement in successfully completing a book or a story, and encourages him to continue to make the effort with books.

Realism in books is a person's relationship with another person, characters, reactions to society, society in manageable proportions. Real life is a form of education and of bibliotherapy. Ann Rutgers van der Loeff has said that real issues in contemporary settings are 'a ripening experience'. This subject is discussed also in the section on the changing content of literature in Chapter One.

Many writers say that they put themselves in their characters' places – what if I found myself in this situation: pregnant as in Gunnel Beckman's *Mia*; uplifted by first love as in Beverley Cleary's *Fifteen*; living in a family affected by unemployment as in Janni Howker's *The Nature of the Beast*; being part of a gang of eleven-year-olds in an urban area, as in Chris Powling's *Daredevils or Scaredycats*; abandoned by your mother and having to make your way across America to your grandmother, as in Cynthia Voigt's *Homecoming*; overcoming a handicap as in *Sweet Frannie*, Susan Sallis's novel of a girl, paraplegic but spirited.

In years gone by children were shielded from the unpleasant issues in life or were amongst them, but now, as never before, many children throughout the world, though living in a small unit of society, are aware of the big issues and indeed may be affected by them. Young people in teenage are particularly aware and vulnerable to both personal and communal issues and this is discussed in the section on teenage books.

But for the average child there is progression towards a larger understanding of society and his place in it, and realistic treatment of themes in children's books can both mirror and aid that progression.

Teenage books

Although other age groups in the years before adulthood are rarely assigned their own literature, because reading

167

age is not always the same as chronological age, there has developed a literature for readers of teenage, either written specifically for the age and the needs of the age or on themes which attract the teenage reader. The attention given to these books and readers in libraries and schools has helped to promote reading amongst young people at a time when reading normally declines.

Teenage can be a vulnerable period in which physiological maturity may not coordinate with social or emotional maturity, and intellectual maturity is a much later and rarer development.

Social conditions in Western countries in the 1960s and 1970s led to a working teenage population with time and money, a ready market for commercial commodities, and an entry into the working adult's life without adults' responsibilities. In addition, many teenagers still in full-time education had parents who were more affluent than in previous periods. This produced a situation not found in many other countries, where the transition from childhood to adulthood was and is, made by means of a ceremony, and although the young people are teenaged chronologically they are either children or adults in their societies. So reading material for teenagers tends to be found in those countries where there is a recognized transition period in which the teenaged person is gradually, legally, socially and emotionally eased into adulthood.

There are available certain kinds of books which can be categorized in the following ways:

- The teenage novel
- Series for teenage readers
- Career stories
- Novels with a teenage character
- Adult fiction preferred by teenage readers

Reading interests are discussed in Chapter Eight where the whole range of needs and preferences are detailed.

The teenage novel

This genre can be defined as fiction written specifically with teenage readers in mind rather than those many adult novels adopted by teenagers. Many teenagers do read adult novels from the early part of teenage and most surveys show that twelve-year-old girls read the light romantic and historical novels and the clear-cut detective stories of writers like Agatha Christie, while boys of thirteen or so are often reading the adventure stories of writers like Ian Fleming and Alistair McLean, Hitchcock thrillers and adult science fiction.

But the teenage novel began in the USA in the 1960s and in Britain and Scandinavia in the 1970s. It has developed to the point where it would be possible to divide it into sub-categories:

- *By age*: suitable for early teenage, middle teenage or young adult.
- *By theme*: love, adventure, protest against war/crime/ adult oppression, coming to terms with failure/success/ death/handicap, accepting that independence brings responsibility and so on.
- *By reading/conceptual ability*: books for the good reader, the able but reluctant reader, the less-able reader.
- *Format*: for example, one-off novels, series, picture books for teenagers.

The teenage novel fills a need for those young people who have grown out of children's books but cannot yet cope with adult books, attracting also those who are able to read but are reluctant to spend time reading. It provides

169

the next stepping-stone for the less-able reader to progress to after the series books for less-able teenagers and is found interesting by those young people who are reading adult books but who enjoy the teenage novel because it is more directly concerned with their interests and age group.

The appeal lies in the fact that the teenage novel has characters of a similar chronological age to the reader, in situations that both conceptually 'speak' to the minds and hearts of the teenager. For instance Gunnel Beckmann's *Mia* is not about a pregnant girl, it is about a girl who realizes that her pregnancy affects her family, her friends, her schooling and her future. Paul Zindel's *The Pigman* is concerned with two teenagers whose practical joke leads them to befriend an old man and to unwittingly destroy him, a novel of a dawning sense of responsibility. Judy Blume's *Forever* holds a strong appeal for young people with its theme of first love and sexual experience and the belief that love would last forever. The feeling of being a loner, a one-off, common to many teenagers, is captured in an anthology edited by Peggy Woodford, *Misfits*, while being black and a teenager is well described in Rosa Guy's many books. Identification with the state of teenage via Sue Townsend's *The Secret Diary of Adrian Mole aged 13¾* was clearly seen in its enthusiastic reception by teenagers and adults and its translation to the television screen and the stage in 1986. Similarly, colloquial speech and humour in Susan Gregory's books, for example, *Kill-a-Louse-Week*, are popular with young teenagers who see themselves in the intimate details of school life, parental and group pressures and their search for identity.

There are hundreds of books with teenage characters, living and working with each other and with adults, finding their way through the challenges, uncertainties, sorrows and joys of adolescence and presenting a wide-screen picture of the whole age range from twelve to twenty in a variety of countries, with sad and happy endings. A literary critic has said that 'a large part of adolescence consists of a magnified awareness of the singularity of one's own situation'. Many of the teenage novels showing individuals in contemporary society in effect provide some counterbalance to that feeling of being the only person this has ever happened to, the only one who feels like this. The teenage novel shows clearly that others have been there before you.

At a time of transition from childhood to adulthood, the teenage novel can be a bridge.

Series and imprints

There are publishers' series for many age groups and subjects, but those for teenagers have increased in recent years. Some put individual titles under a collective heading in order to make it easier for parents, teachers, librarians and readers to pinpoint the books that appeal to the teenage reader. In some cases the books are written specifically for the series, in others the books are already published in hardback but the paperback edition is marketed under a series banner, often by a different publisher. In some there is an age or an ability specification and in others the books are simply those, both fiction and non-fiction for children, teenagers or adults, that are thought to appeal to the teenage reader.

A list of British publishers' teenage series indicates the range and quantity available in 1987:

- Bodley Head: *Paperback originals*
- Deutsch: *Adlib*
- Fontana: *Lions*
- Pan: *Horizons*
- Puffin: *Plus*

- Macmillan: *Topliners*
- Transworld: *Freeway*
- Women's Press: *Livewires*
- Virago: *Upstarts*
- Longman: *Knockouts*
- Kestrel: *Teenage*

These all offer a range of novels with appeal for teenagers across a range of themes. But larger still is the quantity of books in series specializing in romance, providing thousands of titles. Transworld/Bantam have twelve series: *Sweet Dreams*, *Sweet Valley High*, *Caitlin*, *Couples*, *Winners*, *Seniors*, *On Our Own*, *Kelly Blake*, *Sweet Valley Twins*, *All That Glitters*, *Swept Away*, and *Sugar and Spice*.

Add to these Hippo's *Cheerleaders* and Pan's *Heartlines* and there is a vast amount of light romance aimed at young teenagers.

Generally, series for teenagers are packaged in colour covers, with distinctive format and logo and are an identifiable aid to selection, quality and appeal.

Series for the less-able reader are more numerous, particularly in Britain. There are some one hundred and fifty series for the learner reader, with a total of around two thousand titles. Many are graded reading books but there are approximately thirty series specifically aimed at the reading-retarded teenager and sufficiently general to be considered as books rather than reading texts.

The term 'less-able reader' is usual but 'backward,' 'reading-retarded' and 'remedial' are other commonly used terms. The term can be applied to the reader who is a year or more behind the norm for the age, or to the young teenager or adult who has a reading age of less then nine.

In recent years more attention has been paid to this latter group, as in many countries the need for greater literacy has caused educationalists and librarians to press for reading materials suited to the age and interests of the teenager and adult. Many were otherwise condemned to learn from text and pictures intended for the young child, with consequent psychological inhibitions, lack of motivation and of relevance. Whatever the cause of reading retardation, whether physical, emotional, mental or social, first-language or second-language, many countries have large numbers of young people and adults who need books covering both pictorially and textually matters of interest, with simplified controlled vocabulary and with eye-catching and informative illustrations to aid comprehension.

Some examples of enjoyable stories can be found in British series aimed at the less able and in some cases the reluctant, for example:

- Macmillan Educational: *Brighton Books*
- Hutchinson: *Spirals*, *Bulls Eye*
- Longman: *Trendset*
- Methuen: *Jim Hunter Books*
- Macmillan: *Rockets*
- Ginn: *Starpol*
- Nelson: *Getaways*

These and many other publishers' series have teenage or adult characters in situations relevant to many teenagers, while other series for less-able younger children have particular books that would be suitable because they are concerned with topics of interest to all ages, such as animals, information, sport and true stories.

Again, the usefulness of series for teenage and adult less-able readers lies in the fact that they bring together titles which might otherwise be lost amongst the large number of publications available. Such series can save time, provide a body of reading material and, most importantly, can offer the reading-retarded person a chance of success and enjoyment in reading.

The Adult Literacy and Basic Skills Unit produced in 1986 a guide to materials in adult literacy, entitled *Resources*,[6] listing with annotations all the materials available for learning and for pleasure reading.

Career story series

The decline in fictional career stories has two possible explanations: the change in job availability in many countries and in the content and training for those jobs, a factor that dates such novels; and the noticeable increase in the quantity and range of job *information* books aimed at young people, sufficient to create a job library and often shelved as such in school and public libraries.

Fantasy gamebook series

Mentioned as a trend in literature for young people in Chapter One, the publication of gamebooks directed at teenagers increased to a torrent by 1987. The mainly fantasy-land adventures and adversarial content appeal to a wide age range of boys and there is plenty from which to choose, such as:

- Armada: *Solo Fantasy*
- Bantam: *Choose Your Own Adventure*
- Knight: *Way of the Tiger*
- Corgi: *Dragon Warriors, Sagard the Barbarian*
- Puffin: *Cretan Chronicles, Fighting Fantasy, Fantasy Questbook*
- Unicorn: *Fatemaster*
- Magnet: *Forbidden Gateway*
- Target: *Make Your Dreams Come True* (romance/ love)

Science fiction series add to the quantity with for

example, Sphere's *Star Wars* and Corgi's *Star Trek*.

Though few have any depth of plot or characterization – a factor that enables a reader of a more literary work to read and re-read – the gamebooks whole purpose is to allow a choice, and another choice, thus providing the opportunity for re-reading and a different interpretation. The confrontations and violence common to these are part of the cause for interest and accord with the known reading interests of young teenage boys, who may also be reading Alistair MacLean, Ian Fleming and James Herbert, adult novelists known for those two themes.

Adult fiction for teenage readers

As indicated in the chapter on children's reading interests, some children begin to read adult fiction and non-fiction at an early age while keeping up their interest in children's books. Usually adult books chosen in early teenage have a straightforward story with clearly defined characters and action on themes such as adventure, romance, mystery and ghosts.

These themes continue to attract throughout teenage and into adulthood, but for some teenagers the more 'literary' novel begins to offer satisfaction. In the Whitehead survey of Children's Reading Interests,[7] the names of authors of adult books claimed to have been read by the teenagers surveyed included, for example, Asimov, Barstow, Bradbury, Braine, Bronte, Buchan, Chandler, Conrad, Dickens, Drabble, Golding, Graves, Hemingway, Huxley, James, D. H. Lawrence, Somerset Maugham, Mary McCarthy, Henry Miller, Monsarrat, O'Brien, Orwell, Pasternak, Rattigan, Sagan, Sartre, Sayers, Scott, Shute, Simenon, C. P. Snow, Solzhenitsyn, Steinbeck, Thurber, Tolstoy, Waugh, Wells, Wilde, Angus Wilson, Woolf and Zola.

Also named were numerous 'popular' authors such as

Agatha Christie, Catherine Cookson, James Herriot, Alfred Hitchcock, Ian Fleming, Alistair MacLean, Eric Segal and John Wyndham.

Those books still appear on such survey findings lists. In addition many local surveys undertaken by librarians indicate the recent popular authors to be Virginia Andrews, Jackie Collins, James Herbert, Danielle Steel, Stephen King, Dick Francis and Jeffery Archer.

It is clear that those female teenagers who continue to read voluntarily after growing out of children's books, read widely amongst the popular adult literature and magazines, while male teenagers read more non-fiction and are interested in a narrower range of periodicals.

Detailed discussion of the subject of teenage reading is given in Margaret Marshall's *Libraries and Literature for Teenagers*[8] and descriptions and suggestions appear in G. Robert Carlsen's *Books and the Teenage Reader*;[9] a guide for teachers, librarians and parents. But most public libraries in Britain and the USA have regular booklists for teenagers and some countries also have organizations that from time to time produce recommended books such as, Jessica Yates's *Teenager to Young Adult*, published in Britain by the School Library Association,[10] and Margaret Marshall's *The Right Stuff*, published by the Youth Libraries Group of the Library Association in 1987.

There is no doubt that there are teenage readers who read across the very wide range of materials available to them. The well written novel such as Russell Hoban's *The Mouse and His Child*, Alan Garner's *The Stone Book Quartet*, Jannie Howker's short stories in *Badger on the Barge*, Robert O'Brien's *Z for Zachariah*, Robert Westall's *Scarecrows*, Jill Paton Walsh's *A Parcel of Patterns*, Mildred Taylor's *Roll of Thunder* all vary in theme and style but exemplify the quality.

Books for teenagers include all aspects of sexual

orientation, family relationships, school, work, leisure, race, religion, social comment, fantasy, historical and futuristic themes, and humour, presented in a variety of styles from stream of consciousness, straight narrative, picture strip and diary style to letters, split pages and alternating narrators. The progression of the reader from childhood to adulthood in terms of reading matter now allows for motorway speed, meandering through byways, stops in laybys, crossing by means of bridges, possibilities for admiring the view, seeing new vistas and revisiting old scenes. Thus the individual reader has a choice of route and pace towards the destination of mature adult readership.

Poetry

Many children find enjoyment, information, new words, fresh thoughts and the possibility of participation in the rhythm of poetry. As the child grows his awareness can be increased by a turn of phrase, a word, or a poem that encapsulates deep meaning. When the readers' mind grasps the capsule it bursts, to spread the fragrance, the delight, the knowledge and the self-awareness or insight. This can be achieved of course in prose, but the 'special effects' of poetry lie in the sense of rhythm and, when well done, in rhyme; in the poetic imagery; in language that crystallizes thoughts, actions and events.

The length of a poem is appropriate to the concentration span of any reader but the comprehension of the concepts in a poem depend not only upon the ability of the poet to convey them but also upon the kind of mind the reader brings to the poem.

For the very young, nursery rhymes form an introduction to poetry. The rhymes and rhythms, alliteration, humour, the sounds of words, have caused them to remain part of each generation's childhood ever since the early origins of

177

nursery rhymes. Many were social and political comments on events and practices of the day; some were and are baby-handling aids, and all are a means of sharing and communicating between parent and child or other person and child.

While Iona and Peter Opie's *The Oxford Nursery Rhyme Book* is the definitive work with its eight hundred rhymes and six hundred illustrations, the books with greater child appeal include Raymond Briggs's masterly *The Mother Goose Treasury*, with hundreds of rhymes and very effective illustrative content and layout, Helen Oxenbury's *Nursery Rhyme Book* with rhymes selected by Brian Alderson, and Quentin Blake's humorous interpretations in his *Nursery Rhyme Book*. Ballads, epics or narrative poems are popular with the middle age range who enjoy the story and the rhythm of the verse in poems such as Longfellow's *Hiawatha*, Coleridge's *The Rime of the Ancient Mariner*, T. S. Eliot's *Macavity the Mystery Cat* and Clement Moore's *The Night Before Christmas*. There are versions of each of these – illustrated, anthologized or individually published.

Humorous poems are popular throughout the age range as indicated in the section on humour. Further examples include the traditional in T. S. Eliot's *Old Possum's Book of Practical Cats*; the contemporary in Michael Rosen's *Don't Put Mustard in the Custard*; and Colin West's collection with funny pictures, *It's Funny When You Look At It*.

Most anthologies of poetry whether on general or specific themes are the selection of a compiler or editor and thus an individual's personal choice. This can give either a wholeness to the selection because the selector shows clear taste or a clear objective in the choice, or it can make the selection fragmentary and idiosyncratic. When volumes of poetry are considered for library purchase or class use, criteria similar to that used for fiction can be employed: the content (or plot); the language; the style in terms of rhythm and devices; the intended reader in terms of interest, age and ability; the intended use by teacher, storyteller and child.

The range and number of poets included in the anthology can be gauged from the index, contents list or author index and the nature of the poems may be seen in the arrangement into subject sections. The presence of illustration may be a help or a hindrance depending upon whether it is an integral part of the book in quantity, quality and style; whether it is simply there to break up the potentially dull appearance of pages of poetry, or is intended to be page decoration.

Examples of useful anthologies include: Kaye Webb's *I Like This Poem*, an anthology resulting from children's own choice; Louis Untermeyer's *The Golden Treasury of Poetry*; Edward Blishen's *Oxford Book of Poetry For Children*, illustrated by Brian Wildsmith; and Morag Styles's *You'll Love This Stuff, poems from many cultures*. Two anthologies concentrate on the very best: Fiona Waters's *Golden Apples: Poems for Children*; and Herbert Read's selection in *This Way Delight*. But the best anthology is *The Rattle Bag*, compiled by Seamus Heaney and Ted Hughes and offering an inspired selection of old and new poems of value to all ages.

Volumes of poetry by individual poets tend to be less popular but are often packaged in attractive format, offering an aesthetic appeal in addition to the poetic content. Examples include the magnificently illustrated edition of Stevenson's *A Child's Garden of Verses* brought to new life by Michael Foreman's art; Alfred Lord Tennyson's *The Lady of Shalott*, re-created by Charles Keeping's illustrations, and a selection of poems by Walter de la Mare called *The Voice*, enhanced by the illustrations of Catherine Brighton.

Modern poets are also appreciated, particularly John Agard with, for example, *Say It again Granny*; Charles Causley, with his collection of poems *Early in the Morning* and the story poems such as *The Tail of the Trinosaur*. Poets whose works need an older reader are represented in the following examples: Alan Bold, Gareth Owen and Julie O'Callaghan's *Bright Lights Blaze Out*; Mick Gower's *Swings and Roundabouts*; Adrian Henri and Roger McGough's *The Mersey Sound*; Ted Hughes's *Moonbells and Other Poems*, and Brian Patten's *Grave Gossip*.

The subject content in poetry is as varied and interesting as that in fiction and non-fiction, the whole of human knowledge being eligible for poetic inspiration. Thus there is nonsense, fairy, fantasy, adventure, animal, nature, realistic, war, rural, urban, political, satirical, romantic, religious, introspective, philosophical and descriptive poetry that can be read by and read to children throughout the age range.

It is common for many children to lose their enjoyment of poetry as they grow older. It may be that the quantity of other forms of reading material and imaginative experience compete with poetry for the child's attention, or it may be that the *study* of poetry in school leads to the attitude that poetry is a difficult subject, a task rather than an experience.

Children's own poetry

A change in children's creative writing is also seen as children grow older. For some years I have been a member of the panel of judges for the annual W. H. Smith's *Young Writers* Award, and have marvelled at the fresh, original, inspirational poetry of many children in the five to eight age group. The work of children in the nine to twelve range shows the hand of teachers who require a whole class to write a poem on 'snow' or 'my body' or 'the sea', and would-be poets in the thirteen to sixteen age range tend to be derivative and intensely self-conscious, guilty of striving for either stylistic or subject content effect. The truly original and poetic entries are fewer than for the youngest age group. Nevertheless, thousands of entries are received each year and the best are published in book form in *Young Writers*,[11] along with the best prose entries, witnessing to the continuing interest of teachers and children in the literary, intellectual and inspirational facets of poetry.

Librarians and teachers are frequently asked for a particular poem and, unless they are particularly familiar with either the poet's work or the content of anthologies of poetry, they need a finding list for quick access to the poem. Helen Morris's *The New Where's That Poem?*[12] is just such a tool. A much larger and more specialized work is John Mackay Shaw's *Childhood in Poetry*,[13] a five-volume catalogue with biographical and critical annotations of the books of English and American poets comprising the Shaw Childhood in Poetry Collection in the Library of the Florida State University. This work is unlikely to be found in or needed by the average public or academic library but knowledge of its existence is needed in order to direct specialists and researchers to its valuable record of poetry for children.

Plays for children

The development of drama in primary and secondary schools has led to the strengthening of this form of literature in print. A body of scripts now exists for all the age groups and a number of publishers have created drama series, for example:

181

- Ward Lock Educational: *Take Part Starters* and *Take Part Series*.
- Macmillan: *Playreaders* and *Junior Drama Scripts*
- Holt Rinehart and Winston: *Plays Plus Readers*
- Cambridge University Press: *Playmakers* and *Dramaworld*
- Hutchinson: *Spirals*
- Methuen: *Young Drama Series*
- Longman: *Scene Scripts* and *Star Plays*

A useful analysis and critique of plays for young people was produced by Aidan Chambers in 1983 and provides a good starting point for discussion. *Plays (considered as literature as well as theatre) for Young People (from 8–18) To Read and Perform.*[14]

Information books or non-fiction

Factual books written specifically for young people form part of the total range called children's literature. In the chapter on evaluation (Chapter 9) there is an outline of the criteria for selecting information books and a discussion of the importance of looking at the use to which the book may be put in terms of answering questions of varying complexity.

This section is a more general appraisal of non-fiction – general because there are thousands of children's information books and hundreds of adult information books adopted by children and young people. Information can be obtained in a number of different formats which can be listed in the following way:

- Annual reports
- Blueprints
- Books
- Charts

- Clippings or cuttings
- Correspondence
- Graphs
- Kits
- Manuscripts
- Maps
- Music
- Newspapers
- Pamphlets
- Patents
- Periodicals
- Photographs
- Plans
- Reports
- Theses
- Trade catalogues
- Audio-visual media
- Computer software

While recognizing the necessity for each of these as a medium appropriate to information-finding by young people, for the purposes of this book comment is confined to the book format, omitting school textbooks. All textbooks are information books but not all information books are textbooks.

Information books are not usually mere collections of facts but contain fact, concept and attitude and each of these should be examined in order to determine accuracy, vocabulary, scope and author bias or enthusiasm, for there are trends in information books as there are in children's fiction. In recent years emphasis has been laid on the following:

- *Visual appeal*: by the use of varying sizes from pocket book to magazine size; by glossy covers; colour illustration; the development of picture dictionaries and illustrated encyclopaedias; and pop-up and pull-out features.

- *Whole approach*: books of a composite nature presenting situations looking at contributory factors rather than the traditional one-topic book with demarcation between subjects.
- *Research approach*: designed to be used and thus contains index, signposting, captions to pictures, further readings and other aids to ease of use.
- *Series*: these may be designed for age groups, activity use, school project or topic work, individual browsing, basic introductions to themes or in-depth coverage of themes. Whatever the publishers' intentions there are large quantities of series available, differing widely and varying in quality and usefulness even within a series. Each volume in each series needs to be examined rather than making an assumption that the whole series is of equal worth.
- *Subject concern*: the difference between books for younger and books for older children lies in the level of coverage rather than in the choice of theme. There are very simple books on computers or trade unions (Ladybird and Dinosaur publications) for the young reader or the less-able older reader, themes which some years ago would have been considered of no interest or beyond the mental grasp of young children.

Information books may be in the form of a quick reference book or descriptive or discursive book, with the emphasis on text or the emphasis on illustration. Reference books are those to which the reader refers for a particular piece of information and are organized in such a way as to facilitate that search. Atlases, dictionaries, encyclopaedias and yearbooks are examples of this kind of book and it is necessary to check the level of knowledge contained in each, the currency of the information, that is its up-to-dateness, and how to extract the information. Using such reference books involves alphabetical skill, ability to determine the correct keyword, to understand the symbols or codes in atlases and dictionaries, index skill in using heavy type and cross referencing, understanding the way the information is arranged, evaluating the scope of the content and assessing its usefulness to the reader's requirement.

Which of the many available should be selected depends upon the age of the intended users and whether the books are for home, school or library use.

Macmillan's Children's Encyclopaedia in two volumes, plus the *Junior Pears Encyclopaedia* are suitable for a variety of readers and uses.

Chambers Children's Colour Dictionary is admirable for a first dictionary and the range of normal 'adult' dictionaries can be used thereafter.

Wayland's Atlas of the World combines the required pictorial and textual information with great clarity of cartography and print and a wealth of subsidiary information.

Descriptive or discursive books on a theme or number of themes may be useful for leisure reading or for some kinds of schoolwork. Some information books, particularly on the subjects of history or geography, take a documentary approach using original source material, or a human-interest approach, setting the period or place into the context of a real or a fictional child. For example the *History as Evidence* series from Kingfisher, the *Discovering Science* series from Bodley Head and Usborne's *First Science* series, and Bodley Head's *Young Geographer*.

In all the kinds of information book the treatment may be largely pictorial, largely textual or an equal mixture of the two. A glance at many information books reveals the difference between those books in which the pictures

185

inform visually and those in which the pictures are merely decoration for the topic; between those in which the illustrations or photographs are crammed with detail not relevant to the theme and those in which they concentrate on the important features of the topic.

Photo books have already been mentioned under the heading of picture books, where some of the 'first' books for young children are pages of full-colour photographs with or without captions or text. These are mainly intended to provide informative pictures to identify objects or people and to stimulate language by means of encouraging the child to name what is seen and then to talk to himself about it or with the accompanying adult.

Increasingly, information books are appearing in photo book form with explanatory text, the intention here being to offer children in the middle and older sections of the age range, pictorial information from which the reader can pick out specific items according to his requirements while obtaining an overall visual impression from the total illustration. Also available are art books in photographic form and large numbers of activity books in which the reader is shown how to do or make particular things through the various stages depicted in the photographs.

Publishers are beginning to be aware that pictorial information has to be planned and edited in the same way as text, and there are, increasingly, information books in which the illustrations do give information in their own right, via content, the use of colour where appropriate and via the placing of illustrations in relation to the text.

Some useful examples include A. and C. Black's *Stopwatch* series, Longman's *Close Up on Nature* books and Wayland's *Discovering Nature*. Viking Kestrel's pop-up nature books by Cecilia Fitzsimmons enable readers to see butterflies and birds in more realistic outline. Geography lends itself to the pictorial treatment and A. and C. Black's

Beans series of families around the world is helpful as is Wayland's series of that title.

Biography varies between at one extreme, the straight-forward chronological description of people who have influenced the course of events and, at the other extreme, the glossy glamorized depiction of famous people.

Whatever the subject content the books may have a serious or a light-hearted treatment, for a young or an older reader, in pictorial or textual form in descriptive or prescriptive style, with glance or analytical coverage, in quick reference or depth-reading organization, in attractive or dull packaging, in the same way as adult non-fiction.

But it is important for the child reader to have access to this range of treatment so that his varying needs and interests are catered for and so that he has an opportunity not only to be informed factually, but extended, through seeing the author's perception of that branch of knowledge.

There are several countries where information books, as opposed to textbooks, are not readily available. This can be explained in two ways. First the education system in those countries relies heavily on a rigid syllabus, textbooks, teacher-centred learning, and examination, leaving no time and no need for the wide-ranging or specific information books used in, for example, Britain, for topic work, projects, self-learning and assessed work. Thus the lack of an educational market discourages publishers from producing information books.

This in turn creates the second factor for their absence from libraries: that such books are not published in any quantity and few are available in translation, therefore, libraries cannot stock what is not obtainable.

Yet another reason is apparent in some countries where the climate and work and social customs put reading low as a leisure-time priority whether fiction or non-fiction.

As mentioned in the chapter on reading interests,

surveys show that boys read more non-fiction than girls and that for both boys and girls such reading is not the school-subject information but that connected with their hobbies, with sport, animals, transport, nature, science and famous people. Surveys also show that the gifted child often reads voraciously amongst non-fiction rather than fiction. The less-able teenage reader can often cope better with non-fiction on subjects that personally interest him and this fact is used to good effect in much of the material created for literacy programmes.

It is an interesting fact that the non-fiction, children and young people buy in bookshops is almost entirely related to their hobbies or their personal appearance and health, and is usually of the kind that will be read more than once. What children buy and what they borrow are usually quite different, as research undertaken for the Children's Book Action Group indicated (see Margaret R. Marshall's Report on Categorization in Children's Books).[15]

Information books in the school library, the public library and the home are providers of knowledge. Knowledge for school purposes, for personal interest or even knowledge for its own sake, is necessary for the intellectual, social and emotional development of all children.

References

1 Uther, Hans-Jorg. *Katalog zur Volkserzahlung.* 2 vols, Saur, 1987, 3598 10669 6. 1135 pp.

2 Scherf, Walter. *Die Herausforderung des Dämons: form und funktion grausiger Kindermärchen*, Saur, 1986, 3598 10664 5

3 Tucker, Nicholas. 'Books That Frighten', Haviland, *Children and Literature*, pp. 104–9

4 Fisher, Margery. *Intent Upon Reading; a critical*

appraisal of modern fiction for children. Brockhampton, 1964, 0 340 03510 2, 0/P

5 Svensen, Åsfrid. 'Opening windows on to unreality: some elements of the fantasic in Scandinavian children's literature'. *International Review of Children's Literature and Librarianship*, vol. 2 no. 1, Spring 1987, pp. 1–9

6 Adult Literacy and Basic Skills Unit. *Resources.* ALBSU, 1986

7 Whitehead, Frank, ed. *Children and Their Books; a survey of children's reading interests.* Macmillan, 1977

8 Marshall, Margaret R. *Libraries and Literature for Teenagers.* Gower, 1975, 0 233 96604 8.

9 Carlsen, Robert. *Books and the Teenage Reader.* Harper & Row, 1980

10 Yates, Jessica. *Teenager to Young Adult.* Swindon, S. L. A., 1987 and Marshall, Margaret R. *The Right Stuff.* Youth Libraries Group, 1987

11 W. H. Smith, Young Writers Competition. Annual. For Children aged 5 to 16

12 Morris, Helen. *The New Where's That Poem?* Blackwell, 1986

13 Shaw, John Mackay. *Childhood in Poetry.* 5 vol. catalogue, Florida State University Library.

14 Chambers, Aidan. *Plays For Young People to Read and Perform.* Thimble Press, 1982, 0 90335510 8

15 Marshall, Margaret R. *Categorization in Children's Books: research report to the Children's Book Action Group of the Booksellers Association et al.*, 1986

Further reading

Aiken, Joan. 'Interpreting the past'. *Children's Literature in Education*, Summer 1985, pp. 67–83

Aiken, Joan. *The Way to Write For Children.* Elm Tree Books, 1982

Barker, Keith. *In the Realms of Gold; the story of the Carnegie Medal*. Julia MacRae Books/Youth Libraries Group, 1986

Bettelheim, Bruno. *The Uses of Enchantment; the meaning and importance of fairy tales*. Penguin, 1978

Bienstock, June and Anolik, Ruth B. *Careers in Fact and Fiction*. Chicago, American Library Association, 1985

Bratton, J. S. *The Impact of Victorian Children's Fiction*. Croom Helm, 1981

Brogan, Hugh. *The Life of Arthur Ransome*. Cape, 1984

Bull, Angela. *Noel Streatfeild, a Biography*. Collins, 1984

Butler, Dorothy. *Babies Need Books*. Bodley Head, 1980

Butler, Dorothy. *Five to Eight, the vital years of reading*. Bodley Head, 1986

Butler, Francelia et al. (eds). *Children's Literature Annuals*. Modern Language Association, volumes 1980 to date, Yale University Press

Cadogan, Mary and Craig, Patricia. *You're A Brick, Angela; the girls' story 1839–1985*. Gollancz, 1986

Cass, Joan. *Literature and the Young Child*. 2nd edn, Longman, 1984

Chambers, Aidan. *Booktalk*. Bodley Head, 1985

Dahl Roald. *Boy*. Cape, 1984

Darton, F. J. Harvey. *Children's Books in England*, revised by Brian Alderson, C.U.P., 1982

Dickinson, Peter. Fantasy, the need for realism. *Children's Literature in Education*, 17 (1), 1986, pp. 39–51

Ellis, Peter B. and Williams, Piers. *By Jove, Biggles; the Life of Captain W. E. Johns*. W. H. Allen, 1981

Fisher, Margery. *The Bright Face of Danger*. Hodder & Stoughton, 1986

Fisher, Margery. *Classics for Children and Young People*. Thimble Press, 1986

Green, Peter. *Beyond the Wild Wood; the world of Kenneth Grahame, author of the Wind in the Willows*. Webb & Bower, 1982

Harrison, James. 'Reader/listener response to humour in children's books'. *Canadian Children's Literature*, 44, 1986, pp. 25–32

Haviland, Virginia. *Children and Literature; views and reviews*. Bodley Head, 1973

Kirkpatrick, D. L. (ed.). *Twentieth-Century Children's Writers*. Macmillan, 1984

Lane, Margaret. *The Tale of Beatrix Potter; a biography*. revised edn. Warne, 1985

Lanes, Selma. G. *The Art of Maurice Sendak*. Bodley Head, 1981

Mahoney, Bertha E. *Illustrators of Children's Books 1744–1945*. Hornbook, 1947, and subsequent volumes by other authors.

Meek, Margaret. *Learning to Read*. Bodley Head, 1982

Milne, Christopher. *The Enchanted Places*. Eyre Methuen, 1974

Moss, Elaine. *Part of the Pattern*. Bodley Head, 1986

Philip, Neil. *A Fine Anger; a critical introduction to the work of Alan Garner*. Collins, 1981

Quayle, Eric. *Early Children's Books; a collector's guide*. David & Charles, 1983

Quicke, John. *Disability in Modern Children's Fiction*. Croom Helm, 1984

Quigley, Isabel. *The Heirs of Tom Brown; the English school story*. O.U.P, 1984

Ray, Sheila. *The Blyton Phenomenon; the controversy surrounding the world's most successful children's writer*. Deutsch, 1982

Salway, Lance. *Reading about Children's Books; an introductory guide to books about children's literature*. National Book League, 1986

Sutcliff, Rosemary. *Blue Remembered Hills*. (autobiography), Bodley Head, 1983

Townsend, John Rowe. 'Children's author and surviving'. *Books For Your Children*, 20 (3), 1985, pp. 8–9

Townsend, John Rowe. *Written for Children; an outline of English language children's literature*. 2nd revised edn, Viking Kestrel, 1983

Trease, Geoffrey. 'The historical novelist at work', in Fox, Geoff *et al. Writers, Critics and Children*, Heinemann, 1976, pp. 39–51

Tucker, Nicholas. *Suitable for Children?: controversies in children's literature*. Sussex University Press, 1976

Tucker, Nicholas. 'Trends in school stories.' *Children's Literature in Education*, no. 45, Summer 1982

Waterland, Liz. *Read With Me; an apprenticeship approach to reading*. Thimble Press, 1985

Werner, Craig, 'A blind child's view of children's literature'. *Children's Literature in Education*, 12, 1984, pp. 209–216

Whalley, Irene. 'The Cinderella Story 1724–1919'. *Signal Approach to Children's Books*. pp. 140–155

Zipes, Jack (ed.). *Don't Bet on the Prince; contemporary feminist fairy tales in North America and England*. Gower, 1986

Books For Keeps. no. 7, March 1981, issue on humour

Children's Books (British Book News) quarterly journal, every issue.

CHAPTER SEVEN

Illustration and Children's Books

The importance of pictures in the life of human beings is demonstrated from the earliest times. Man has always communicated visually. Cave paintings, sign writing, art, sculpture, film, television and recently holovision, are pictorial forms of communication, expressing messages, concepts, objects, information and imagination. Some written languages in the world are picture-based, such as Japanese and Chinese. Even when we speak we use hand pictures to describe size, shape or emotion, sometimes using these where words cannot adequately express what we want to describe, as with 'circle' or 'spiral', or the visual body language of raised eyebrows, shrug of the shoulders, or 'hands up'.

From birth the sense of sight is stimulated and research has shown that a baby left lying flat in a cot or pram when awake does not learn as quickly as one who is put into a position to see what is going on around. The child carried around on a mother's back thus learns more, earlier, of immediate use in everyday life. Through sight the identifying, classifying and categorizing that enable people to make sense and order begins in babyhood and develops throughout life.

So human beings are accustomed to giving and receiving information both formally and informally by means of sight, vision and pictures. It has been suggested that 90 per cent of what we learn is learned by sight and we tend to remember what we have seen. The old saying 'seeing is believing' is still largely true today, despite the increased knowledge of the scientific intricacies of visual perception and despite recognition that brilliant techniques of photography can deceive the eye.

The child in the technologically developed countries of the world has been used to a high standard of visual presentation of information but the children in other societies were and are not so fortunate. Children in the early days of children's literature in England responded to the woodcuts and engravings in some of the first books for children though such pictures were often decorative rather than strictly related to the story or information. The introduction of colour by hand painting gave rise to the description 'penny plain and tuppence coloured' for marketing purposes, until the invention of colour lithography enabled children's books to be produced with colour printed illustrations. Kate Greenaway's work, commemorated in the annual Kate Greenaway Award for outstanding illustration in children's books in the UK, exemplifies the change from the black and white woodcuts, engravings and drawings to the possibilities for full colour with all that that implies in terms of attraction, imagination, artistic scope, and, particularly to child development, the kinds of information that a colour picture imparts that a black and white picture cannot.

The latest printing and colour printing techniques allow tremendous scope for both artist and book designer in content and format, facilitating most methods from charcoal to water colour, from collage to photography, and computer drawings. High technology enables the book and its pictures to be transmitted to another medium of vision via film as in the films and filmstrips using the picture book's pictures; or via equipment such as epidiascope and other magnifying equipment like Visualtek which magnify the book page on to a screen or visual display unit.

The 'visualizing' of children's book illustration via the television screen in dramatization or straightforward storytelling, as in the BBC's *Jackanory* programme also demonstrates the versatility of, and the importance attached to, the pictorial content of children's books.

Pictorial content is not only that found in picture books but the illustrations used in story books, in information books, in picture reference books, in picture strip and comic books, in paper engineering or pop-up books, because all have a place in the reading diet of children of all ages and all purport to serve a purpose. What is the purpose?

The purpose of illustration can be the following:

- To decorate the pages as part of the total book design
- To enhance the text
- To interpret the text
- To increase visual perception
- To provide visual information
- To aid visual discrimination
- To externalize, pictorially, fears that cannot be expressed in words
- To tell the story (in books without words)

If these purposes are achieved then the result may also include aesthetic appreciation and enjoyment. But the methods by which these are all achieved revolve round factors such as:

- *Graphic style of the artist*: the medium used, for example, line, pencil, oils, collage, full colour; and the originality, vitality, humour and emotional power.
- *Sympathy with the text*: matching the mood/colour/historical period/emotion of the text with line, colour and content emphasis in the illustration.
- *Content*: relates to the single concept per picture or per page or the profusely detailed picture, chosen by the illustrator as suitably representative and descriptive

195

of the textual content, and interpreted in such a way as to accurately portray the text while extending the viewer's knowledge and perception pictorially; how the illustrator makes the pictures tell the story.

- *Relevance to the child's perception and experience*: for example, preferably not abstract art or half shapes for young children.
- *Layout in relationship to the text*: in order to ensure that:

  the illustration is on the page of the text to which it refers

  it is placed logically on that page

  it conforms to the legibility requirements, for example, preferably not overprinted on the text
- *Layout of the book in design terms*: cover, page design, typeface, illustration, endpapers and so on.
- Use of colour where appropriate because colour is an information provider, offering attraction and information, enabling objects and people to be better identified, though black and white pictures are acceptable if they clearly delineate the matter depicted.

As indicated earlier, many kinds of children's book contain illustrations, the most obvious being a picture book.

Picture books

The 32-page picture book is the most usual form and is generally intended for the young child. At the youngest age the picture book may be used by adults for reading to and sharing with the child. The pictures are therefore likely to be more important than the text in that they become a conversation piece with the adult elaborating the text, confirming it, reinforcing it, testing it with the child, usually as a natural part of communication. This is true of the nursery rhyme books in which the words are usually felt rather than understood by the child; the rhythm of the words and the visual interest of the picture being more important. Two examples of the words of nursery rhymes will indicate that a child's comprehension of the meaning is most unlikely, but the rhythm and sound, and probably actions, are paramount:

> See-saw Margery Daw
> Johnny shall have a new master
> He shall have but a penny a day
> Because he can't go any faster.

and

> Moses supposes his toeses are roses
> But Moses supposes erroneously
> For nobody's toeses are posies of roses
> As Moses supposes his toeses to be.

One of the best collections, from an illustration viewpoint, is *The Mother Goose Treasury* of Raymond Briggs, who spent over two years selecting the rhymes, planning the page layout and drawing and painting the illustrations. His perception of both design layout and rhyme content are unequalled as yet. Jack and Jill are given a double spread with an enormous green hill down which it is obviously all too easy to fall, unlike many versions where the reader must wonder how anyone could fall down such a tiny mound. Tom, the piper's son, is seen running away down the page-length street. The illustration for 'Moses supposes his toeses are roses', the essence of the sounds being O, is itself circular and all its contents are round and O-like also. The decision to use black and white for some rhymes and colour for others was appropriate in each case and the whole work forms a satisfying visual experience justifying the Kate Greenaway Award it received.

Nursery rhymes are passed on orally from generation to generation and each generation sees a new crop of nursery rhyme books, either collection of rhymes as the Opie and Briggs and Helen Oxenbury books or individual nursery rhymes such as Maureen Roffey's interpretation of the *Grand Old Duke of York* and the Kestrel pop-up versions, such as Ray Marshall and Korky Paul's *Humpty Dumpty Pop-Up Book*.

The next stage of picture book tends to be counting and alphabet books, most of which are not systematic attempts to instil numeracy and literacy, but attitude formation books which by the use of colour and objects make a start on the process of recognizing letters and numbers. Many fail to provide the clarity of illustration, the familiarity of objects and the repetition needed to lodge in the memory, but some of these can be looked at as picture books rather than as alphabet or counting books, and Brian Wildsmith's *ABC* is the classic example, where strong colours of page and of painting provide a feast for the eyes, making of secondary importance the fact that some of the objects are likely to be unknown to most children as in the 'I for Iguana'. Other examples use different styles as in Robert Crowther's *The Most Amazing Hide and Seek Alphabet Book* which requires the child to lift flaps or pull tags to reveal the letters; Annie Owen's pages of miniature objects repeated in designs of clear precision and colour in *Annie's ABC* and Shirley Hughes's cherubic children in everyday scenes in *Lucy and Tom's ABC*.

The large number of counting books makes it necessary for adults intending to use them with children to distinguish between those which facilitate learning to count and those which are picture books on the theme of number. In the latter category, is William Stobbs's *A Widemouthed Gaping*

Waddling Frog, which may be typical Stobbs's painting but which does not in either text or illustration aid counting.

Eric Carle's *1,2,3 To the Zoo* uses numbers of animals and a small train chugging along the bottom of the page picking up the animals; Susannah Gretz in *Teddybears 1 to 10* puts the fuzzy bears into activities for counting, while Molly Bang, in her *Ten, Nine, Eight* is successful in getting across number by means of father and small child preparing for child's bedtime in a loving secure environment, with the bonus that father and child are black.

Still with a mild 'educative' purpose are those picture books where each page has one object or scene designed to promote identification, recognition and information. These vary from, for instance, the Methuen *Look and See* books which show familiar everyday activities in one photograph per page, such as *Bathtime*; to the peephole picture book of family scenes in Janet and Allan Ahlberg's *Peepo*; Dean Hay's one photograph per page series, for example, *Things in the Kitchen*; to the Methuen Walker board books by Helen Oxenbury with no text, where the pictures say it all on themes such as *Helping* and *Shopping*. Yasua Ohtomo's clear amusing illustrations for Shigeo Watanabe's series of books about a small bear, for example, *How Do I Put It On*, provide information and satisfaction.

More detailed pictures are enjoyed by the young child for browsing and pointing out and in some cases for the humour, for example Peter Spier's books, or in different style the Richard Scarry books, and differently humorous again, the Dr Seuss books and Arnold Lobel's *Frog and Toad*.

The vast majority of children's picture books tell a story in pictures with words that may take up only two or three lines to a page. There is no one style that can identify such a book for a particular age or interest market, the range is enormous. It covers Maurice Sendak's unique style of thought and illustration in his own *Where the Wild Things Are* and *In the Night Kitchen*. Charles Keeping's strong illustration in his many books, for example, *Joseph's Yard*; Ezra Jack Keats's particular collage style in *Snowy Day* and *Peter's Chair*; the distinctive concept in Mitsumasa Anno's extraordinary work, *Anno's Alphabet*. It covers the black and white illustrative style of Wanda Gag used in *Millions of Cats*, the puppet features of Jiri Trnka's work, the water colours of Edward Ardizzone, the clarity of line in the work of Robert McCluskey and Pat Hutchins, the warmth and comfort of Shirley Hughes's work, the picture-strip style of Raymond Briggs and the baroque style of Errol le Cain.

There are hundreds of illustrators throughout the world producing picture books of fine quality and a glance at the Kate Greenaway, Caldecott and Hans Andersen Award lists will indicate the range of styles and nationalities. There is also in some countries, a vast quantity of mass-market picture books. The vast quantity of glossy, brightly coloured picture books often with themes concerning animals, fantasy people and television tie-ins and other books like the range of *Mr Men* books, *Victoria Plum* and *Noddy* stories are aimed at the mass market and appear to reach their target by ready availability in stores, newsagents and supermarkets.

Some mass-market books have trite story lines and garish pictures and are priced to cater for impulse buying. To some extent this has been counteracted by the availability over the last fifteen years of paperback editions of quality picture books, usually photo-reduced from the originals.

In some countries government publishing houses and educational bodies are as yet the only producers of picture books, and these tend to be a formula of cheap, paper-covered, unimaginative, 'educational' content, largely because there are insufficient funds for better-quality production and because there is not a pool of children's book illustrators and designers.

At the present time there is a gulf between that kind of publication and the inspired artistic works of many children's book illustrators in a free market. There is also a difference in price, as many Western publishers are finding in their efforts to keep down the costs of full-colour quality illustration in hard cover.

There are thousands of picture books that tell a story for the child who is not yet competent in reading a longer text, but it is important to recognize that the picture book is a work in its own right not necessarily aimed only at the young child. There is a common belief that the picture book is for young children who cannot read and is thus to be ignored once the child can read. This belief is perpetuated by many teachers who denounce a child who can read, if he chooses to look at a picture book. Similarly librarians who shelve picture books only in kinder-boxes or under labels such as 'for the young child' are doing a disservice to many illustrators and to many children.

There may be a tendency for older children to simply glance at the pictures on the page, that is, to see them rather than look at them, looking involving a more positive, active, conscious approach. When a picture does not engage attention in this way the illustrator has failed at a deep level though the level of surface information and pleasure may be achieved.

Some picture book illustrators purposely pay attention to a conscious process of looking, for example Anthony Browne's *A Walk in the Park* and *Through the Magic Mirror* depict at first glance ordinary scenes but the eye that is looking soon catches the incongruous and each page becomes an exercise in spotting the oddity – a tree trunk like a leg, a park seat with shoes, and an eggcup in a bird's nest.

The graphic brilliance of Mitsumasa Anno's *Alphabet* similarly attracts close inspection of perspective, and there are many picture books in which the reader is specifically invited to spot the objects or consequences. Three different kinds of treatment exemplify this: Janet and Allan Ahlberg's *Each Peach, Pear, Plum* is full of allusions to nursery tales and rhymes to be identified by the reader; *Better Move on Frog*, one of Ron Maris's excellent picture books, takes the reader through the variety of holes encountered by a frog looking for his house, while *The Trek* by Ann Jonas involves a little girl on her way to school seeing all kinds of animals in hidden jungles in the newsagents or the greengrocer's stall, encouraging the reader to look for them also.

There is a distinction to be made between the picture book that is concerned with things obviously related to the very young and the book of pictures and text which speaks to older children and even teenagers and adults. Examples include Fiona French's *Snow White in New York*, a very modern version of the traditional tale in superb full page, detailed, highly stylized award-winning production, with appeal for the older child and teenager who can see the irony and the modern implications. Similarly Michael Foreman's *All the King's Horses* which begins:

In the distant time, on the far-off plateaus of Asia lived a princess. She wasn't the milk-white golden-haired pink little number the way princesses are supposed to be. This was a BIG girl. And dark.

The title refers to the large number of horses acquired by the king as forfeits from all the suitors who failed to beat the princess in a wrestling bout. The big princess is shown tying all the men in knots, the epitome of what the author/illustrator is doing to the traditional fairy tale theme, women's place in society and conventional female romantic aspirations; blatantly sexist in reverse, with a dominant female. Raymond Briggs's *When the Wind Blows*, later made into a radio and film version, is a picture strip laying-it-on-the-line message about the futility of defence against nuclear war, a powerful message affecting the older reader and adult who can see the propaganda and the gullibility for what they are.

In this category of picture books for older children and adults, using picture-strip style, are also Hergé's *Tintin* books, Goscinny and Uderzo's *Asterix* books and Raymond Briggs's *Fungus The Bogeyman*, each of which has adult characters, clever vocabulary and sentence structure and illustrative detail. Though the three illustrators have totally different styles each is master of the picture-strip format as an art form and each offers levels of interest, irony and enjoyment to a very wide age range.

Elaine Moss's booklet *Picture Books for Young People 9–13*, one of the Signal guides,[1] and an article in her autobiography,[2] discusses the attributes of this genre and the potential for the young teenager. Many more such picture books are on the market and their inclusion in teenage libraries and school libraries in Britain is the norm.

There are few specific characteristics of a picture book in that, as in story books, the picture book themes cover fairy, folk and fantasy, animals real and imaginary, social situations in home, school, environment, human relationships within the family and without. A glance at the lists of winners of the world's awards for children's book illustration would reveal that the art defies the setting of limitations on content or method.

The illustrators use vastly differing methods of illustration ranging from black and white, through pastel shades to strong primary colours to glorious technicolour using pencil, water-colour, oils, collage, chalk, scraperboard and a variety of other materials and techniques.

Most picture books are sixteen or thirty-two pages in length and most are, by tradition, intended for the age group that has not yet begun to read any length of text. But increasingly, there are themes and styles that appeal to older children and young adults, and some that are more for collectors than for children.

Children's books with illustrations

The distinction here is that picture books have more illustration than text whereas the illustrated children's book is text accompanied by either line drawings at intervals throughout the book, or as page decoration, or chapter headings or tailpieces, or the occasional colour illustration.

Many surveys show that older children prefer to have little or no illustration in their storybooks other than the cover design. It seems that pictures interfere with the mental image of the character or scene and in some cases indicate an age of character which does not conform to the age of the reader and is therefore possibly an unconscious deterrent to reading the book. This does not apply to books for the child who is just beginning the transfer from picture book to full length story book and most publishers providing books for that age group include illustrations both to give clues to the text and to break up the slabs of print.

Some of the classic story books whether popular or esoteric are remembered for the way in which the illustrations complement and extend the story, as in Shepard's pictures for *Winnie the Pooh* or Tenniel's *Alice in Wonderland*, or Mabel Lucy Attwell's for *The Water Babies*; the illustrations for Richmal Crompton's *William* books and those for Enid Blyton's *Famous Five*, and the pictures in *The Hardy Boys* all contribute to the overall impression of the books in children's minds.

The use of black and white line drawings, often with cross hatching, is on the decline, many such drawings being poorly executed and intended only to break up the page; in other cases designed to add pictorial enhancement but often providing little information.

In the great majority of children's books, the illustrative content goes unremarked, despite the naming of the illustrator or decorator on the title page. The exceptions are notable, as in Ann Strugnell's art work in *North American Legends* edited by Virginia Haviland, or Charles Keeping's explosive illustration in *God Beneath the Sea* by Edward Blishen and Leon Garfield, or Pauline Bayne's numerous works, including her illustrations for the award winning *Dictionary of Chivalry*. Volumes of poetry such as Stevenson's *A Child's Garden of Verses*, may be remembered as 'the one with the Michael Foreman illustration'.

The illustration of non-fiction books is discussed in both the section on information books and the section on selection and evaluation.

Books with unusual physical features

There are available many unusual books for children, unusual in that visual or tactile means are used in addition to print and picture. The trend towards 'novelty' books is discussed in Chapter One in the section on the changing visual content of children's books. The following list indicates the nature of such books:

- Board books
- Concertina
- Rag books and cloth books
- Flaps and tabs

- Half-page
- Cut-out or peep-hole
- Pop-up
- Scratch and sniff
- Overlays and mirrors
- Noise books
- Touch and tell
- Braille
- Movable parts

Although few can be considered children's literature by illustrative literary criteria there are several purposes behind the publication of novelty books which make them useful, valuable and enjoyable to children. The overriding purpose is to facilitate communication and as the child may need to use all his senses with these books, such use is an aid to comprehension.

Board books, for instance – those with stiff card backs and pages – are useful for the young, or handicapped child who has difficulty in turning a normal page, and who may otherwise cause excessive wear and tear. The Bodley Head board books with rounded corners and simple, colourful content; Eric Hill's *Little Spot* shaped board books with an easy-to-hold outline for fingers and thumbs; Collins's series by Richard Scarry and Methuen's Sandra Boynton board books are good examples with multiple titles in their series. Rag or cloth books are often concerned with popular characters such as Walt Disney's, but may fill a need in young and handicapped children. Similarly, concertina books which unfold to a long strip, are of variable quality, the best unfolding to form excellent wall friezes.

The use of flaps and half pages enables some writers and illustrators to provide an extra stimulation to the imagination as in John Goodall's books without words, which employ the device of a half-page flap to extend the action and the scene, and in Ron Maris's *Is Anyone Home?*, half page flaps enable the scene to be changed and anticipation to be engendered in the child reader. Another example is that of a simple book, *Where's Spot* by Eric Hill, a do-it-yourself book about a disappearing puppy. It involves reading the large print questions on each page and opening the door in the picture, lifting the piano lid, the bed flounce, the rug, to see if Spot is there. It is effective in its page engineering, the children can actually 'open' and 'lift' and the story itself has suspense, action and a happy ending.

Books with pull outs and tabs are in abundant supply; as are, for example, concertina books such as Blackie's zig-zag books and Child's Play *Tantrums* series. Books with holes use them in a variety of ways, such as the Ahlbergs's *Peepo* to get a vignette of a scene before turning the page to see the whole scene; Child's Play classics such as *There Was An Old Lady*, where there is a gradual widening of the holes to encompass the growing contents of the lady's stomach, and Eric Carle's *The Very Hungry Caterpillar*, where the holes are made by the caterpillar.

Visual features abound in pop-up books which can vary from poor quality to the award-winning *Haunted House* by Jan Pienkowski. Everything associated with haunted houses is contained within boxes that literally creak, cupboards that open, eyes that move. Those things that cannot be contained spring out at the reader; a spider from the hall ceiling, an octopus from the kitchen sink, a gorilla from the depths of an armchair and a bat from the attic. Odd things happen under the lavatory seat and behind the bed panelling. Pulling the arrow tabs and simply opening the pages cause 'things' to appear. Pienkowski's story and pictures are put into this form, called paper engineering, by Tor Lokvig. Numerous favourite characters appear in pop-up editions as in Arnold Lobel's *The Frog and Toad Pop-Up Book* and *Thomas the Tank Engine Pop-Up Book*. The use of this medium for information books is a worthy development and is growing in both expertise and popularity.

Books with moveable parts are a return to the original toy books of the nineteenth century in concept if not in execution; Richard Fowler's *Slot* books enable the reader to make characters and objects move about the page; John Norris Wood, using die-cut flaps encourages the reader to play *Nature Hide and Seek*.

The ultimate in picture books is the award-winning *The Jolly Postman* by Janet and Alan Ahlberg which incorporates humorous illustrations, an amusing storyline and a selection of letters in envelopes on the page. Delivered by the postman, each letter is appropriate for the recipient, for example, a letter of apology from Goldilocks to the three bears, and a letter from a solicitor to the wolf asking him to stop harassing Red Riding Hood's grandma.

Pictures that stand up on a page have an attraction far beyond the actual content of the picture, as have the books that use overlays and mirrors to create changing visual effects.

There are books which offer sounds also, as in the 'noise' books, in which a squeak or other sound is achieved by pressing the page, or in the books containing a record or disc of words or music related to the text.

The sense of smell is employed when reading the 'scratch and sniff' or 'sniff and tell' books, in which a relevant odour is incorporated in micro-dots in a picture. When scratched the fragrance is released and therefore adds further information for the reader. Random House *Sniffy* books are marketed through Franklin Watts in Britain.

Spongy books in plasticized and waterproofed material are popular for babies, for example Purnell's *Bath Books*. There are innovations in books for the blind and partially sighted, whereby a story is told in printed text and in braille, with raised surface pictures for the child to 'feel'.

'Touch and tell' or 'twin-vision', books are exemplified by Virginia Allen Jensen and Dorcas Woodbury Haller's *What's That?* in which shapes and concepts are 'felt' in embossed pictures as part of the story told in print and braille, and the Royal National Institution for the Blind in Britain is currently trialling braille on a form of plastic sheet inserted into an ordinary children's picture book. This enables the blind child to read an ordinary book with a sighted adult or a blind adult to read a picture book with a sighted child and provides both with the opportunity to read the same books as sighted people. Similarly, the introduction of sign language into the ordinary picture books for children, as in the signed edition of *Where's Spot* enable hearing-impaired children who can read sign language but not spoken language in print, to have access to the same books as every other child.

Touch is also used in the books where the pages have tactile objects in them or on them. The former is exemplified by Methuen's books *Wheels Go Round* and *One Green Frog*, where laminated holes go right through the pages in diminishing sizes, whereas *Soft as a Kitten* by Audean Johnson has a variety of textures to touch and things to smell.

There is in Japan an organization called the Coordinating Committee for the Promotion of Cloth Picture Books, which is concerned with handmade books in which various materials, such as leather, paper, wool, beads, plastic, fur and bark are used for the child to feel. Intended mainly for handicapped children, they have also found a ready interest amongst non-handicapped children in the Tokyo Public Libraries.

The availability of 'toy' books and books of unusual format provides another means of comprehension, learning and enjoyment for many children.

Illustration in children's books uses most of the methods

available to artists, particularly in the picture book format. As the child progresses to short story and then to full-length novel for children the amount of illustration is reduced in quantity and changes from full colour to black and white line drawings. By the time the reader has reached the adult book he will be dependent upon the power of the printed word to evoke mental images.

But the visual image in fiction and information book is a necessary part of reading in most stages of growth to mature readers. It provides information, confirmation, aesthetic pleasure and emotional satisfaction, if the artist has perceived the relationship between the theme and the child.

References

1 Elaine Moss. *Picture Books For Young People 9–13*. Signal Bookguide, Thimble Press, 1981
2 Elaine Moss. *Part of the Pattern*. Bodley Head, 1986

Further reading

Alderson, Brian. *Sing a Song for Sixpence*; *the English picture book tradition and Randolph Caldecott*. C.U.P., 1986
Aliki. *How a Book is Made*. Bodley Head, 1986
Cott, Jonathan (ed.). *Victorian Color Picture Books*. Allen Lane, 1984
Goldsmith, Evelyn. *Research into Illustration; approach and review*. C.U.P., 1984
Hughes, Shirley. Grand designs. *Books For Keeps*, 38, 1986, pp. 6–7
Lanes, Selma G. *The Art of Maurice Sendak*. Bodley Head, 1981

Lima, Carolyn W. *A–Zoo, Subject Access to Children's Picture Books*. Bowker, 2nd revised edn, 1985

Mahoney, Bertha. *Illustrators of Children's Books, 1744–1945*. Then other volumes by different authors. Hornbook, 1947 onwards

Moss, Elaine. 'Picture books then and now'. *Books For Keeps*, 38, 1986

Nettell, Stephanie. 'Bringing a sense of joy; an interview with Errol le Cain.' *Children's Books* (British Book News), Sept. 1986, pp. 2–5

Nettell, Stephanie. Crossing barriers; an interview with Brian Wildsmith. *Children's Books*, March 1987, pp. 2–5

Reeder, Stephanie Owen. 'Sound the drums and clash the symbols; review of Australian picture books'. *Reading Time*, 97, Oct. 1985, pp. 14–23

Shulevitz, Uri. *Writing with Pictures; how to write and illustrate children's books*. New York, Watson-Guptill Publications, 1985

Schulz, Marianne. 'The role of illustration in children's literature'. *Bookbird*, 3, 1985, pp. 15–17

Smyth, Margaret. *Picture Book Index*. AAL Publishing, 1987. *Books for Keeps*. Picture Book Special, no. 38, May 1986, and no. 44, May 1987

CHAPTER EIGHT

The Reading Needs and Interests of Children and Young People

'I chose the book because I like adventure books.'

'The cover looked exciting.'

'I saw it on television.'

These and many other personal statements by children as to why they chose to read a particular book or books provide some clues to the broad preferences in children's reading and clues to their emotions, and educational and intellectual stage. Reasons for choice include the above and a liking for other books by the author, continuing to read through a series; the general appearance of the book which encompasses not only the cover picture but also how 'easy' the book looks in terms of size and density of print and the quantity of illustration.

The collection of accurate information is not easy in that children do not always remember authors and titles of recent reading. They may feel conditioned by the circumstances in which they are asked about books and give answers they think the questioner wants to hear, or they may simply be unable to formulate or articulate the reasons for their choice.

In many countries individual librarians or teachers attempt to find out which books and categories of reading interest children. In some countries large-scale surveys are undertaken to assess national or regional readership and compare possible geographical, sex, age, social status or ability differences. The possibilities are endless and there is a danger of drawing false conclusions if the sample and the methodology are not carefully devised to take account of these factors.

When applied to statistical surveys such factors are called variables, meaning that the findings or significance of the findings may vary according to the age, sex, ability, origin of the children unless these are taken into account in the planning stage of the survey.

Children's reading interests are affected by a number of factors:

- The existence of a range of published books
- The availability of children's books in the home, the school, the library, the bookshop
- The selection made by adults (teachers, librarians, booksellers, parents) on behalf of children
- Time and opportunity to read
- Children's own personal needs and abilities

These need to be noted when studying published surveys of children's reading interests and habits, or when undertaking such surveys. Large-scale surveys are expensive to undertake but provide an indication of the overall preferences and practices in an area or a country. *The Whitehead Report*[1] a survey of a sample eight thousand children in England and Wales in 1971 and published in 1977 as *Children and Their Books*, gave a very detailed questionnaire to the children in the selected schools. The findings revealed a number of apparent preferences, for example, the most widely read books at age ten were listed as *Black Beauty*, *Treasure Island*, *Swiss Family Robinson* and *The Secret Seven*, while the twelve-plus to fourteen-plus age groups indicated a waning interest in school, pony, animals and science and technology books, and a preference for detective, historical, poetry and pets.

An intensive and interesting experiment, known as the Bradford Book Flood, was carried out between 1976 and 1979 and the findings published in Jennie Ingham's *Books and Reading Development*,[2] the report of the project, in 1981.

The saturation of experimental and control schools in Bradford in Yorkshire, with a range of children's books was intended to provide the opportunity to find out whether access to books had any effect on reading skills, attitudes to books and reading interests. The findings are described in detail, analytically and critically and the book is recommended as a source of a variety of information on the subject.

In 1986, *Books in the School Curriculum*,[3] compiled by Florence Davies, provided an in-depth study of the kinds of book involved and the reactions of children and teachers to books in school. A brief summary of the preferences mentioned shows that the following themes were found to be of interest to children of thirteen to fifteen: animals, war, science, love, true stories, history, views of the future, America, transport, school, hospitals, countryside and football.

Many surveys of teenage reading interests are carried out by librarians and teachers for their local purposes and it is important to note that in the USA and Britain the findings are very similar, regardless of the geographical locality in each country. Jean Bird's study of the Bookmaster Scheme in Westminster Public Library, *Young Teenage Reading Habits*,[4] produces similar findings to the Waltham Forest report on *Teenagers and Libraries*[5] within the London Borough of Waltham Forest Libraries Department; and June Dunster's survey in her area of Dorset County Library Service, also found that *Early Teenage Reading*[6] included not only children's books, but the teenage novel and a wide range of adult novels. Some examples from the adult list will indicate the commonality of Dorset teenage reading interests with those of most others in British public libraries:

Alistair MacLean, Agatha Christie, Dick Francis, Catherine Cookson, Virginia Andrews, Ian Fleming, Douglas Adams, Arthur Clarke, Harold Robbins, Sven Hassell, James Herbert and adult film tie-ins.

At the other end of the age range, popular books for very young children have been identified through the Public Lending Right Scheme, by which books borrowed from public libraries are recorded in order to make payment to their authors. The loans analysis for 1982–3 showed that of the hundred children's books which scored the highest loans only ten were not picture books. the Ahlbergs's books topped the list and other authors or illustrators included Val Biro, Dick Bruna, John Burningham, John Cunliffe, Roald Dahl, Goscinny's *Asterix* Books, Shirley Hughes, Pat Hutchins and Dr Seuss.

Such a list does not necessarily indicate preference on the part of the child, rather a preference exhibited by the parent, who may well have borrowed the book on behalf of the child or led the child to the appropriate book.

Preferences in book buying are clear, often characterized by the fact that the choice is probably not available in the school or public library, or in the case of non-fiction, has an obvious use to the owner over a period of time and is not bought to read once only.

Booksellers say that although parents, and other adults buying for children, tend to buy the 'good' or literary work, children buying for themselves choose joke and puzzle books, cartoon books like Garfield and *Asterix*, *Fighting Fantasy* and other game books.

The detailed criteria for selecting books to fit children's needs and interests are given in Chapter Nine but what follows here is an outline of the interests expressed by children, as shown in surveys of children's reading interests, local, national, large and small.

Outline of stages of reading interest

Beginning in early childhood there is a preference for books that allow the child to participate while the parent or other person is reading aloud. For instance, nursery rhymes, folk rhymes, simple fairy stories, song books, finger-play or action books, simple picture books with stories set in everyday life, tales concerned with animals or toys, all please the child because he can make noises, do the actions, point to the objects and characters in the pictures and repeat the words read aloud. The basic reason for this preference is not only the actual book, but also the fact that at that age the child is *sharing* the book with an adult or older child and the book is a stimulus to communication and a means of enjoying the attention of the person who is reading to him. In the section on selection criteria more detail is given about picture books for the young but here the concern is with the child's preference rather than the adult's assessment of what is needed or useful.

The next stage in most countries is from ages five to eight when children are just learning to read, but may not yet be capable of reading a full-length children's book and prefer books with pictures partly because they can give a clue to the text and partly from the sheer enjoyment of the visual story. At this stage too there is a preference for fairy and folk tales in various forms, some in picture-book form, some in illustrated re-tellings and some in collections of tales. This choice develops from the oral tradition, and, in some countries where there is little published material, there still exists the tradition of family community story-telling for all age groups. Books of folk and fairy tales are a link between what is already known orally and the same thing in printed form, thus providing familiarity. As with all reading, familiarity with the subject content makes the reading easier and more comprehensible, and an episodic approach carries the reader along. Other benefits are discussed in Chapter Eleven.

At this age also there is generally an interest in animal stories, both real and humanized, reflecting the fact that many children develop a strong feeling for their pet animals and their toy animals and project on to these their own joys and frustrations. Situation humour becomes popular as the children develop an understanding of what is normal and what is not. All research shows that each year in a child's growth sees a decline in interest in imaginative literature in favour of more realistic. What constitutes realism has already been discussed earlier in the book.

The Baker 'Top 50 Hardbacks' each year are selected in a popularity poll of book purchase and the fiction list for 1986 included a cross-section of books for the middle age range, for example, Dick King-Smith's *Saddlebottom*, Shirley Hughes's *Chips and Jessie*, Ted Hughes's *The Iron Man*, Bernard Ashley's *Running Scared*, Gene Kemp's *Jason Bodger and Priory Ghost* and Sheila Lavelle's *Holiday With the Fiend*.

Adventure stories too feature high on any list of preferences at the top end of this age range and continuing into the next period, the nine to thirteen group. It is in this middle period of childhood that many children find pleasure in the stories of children having adventures without their parents, solving mysteries, catching criminals, overcoming difficulties, coping in an adult world; books which liberate the children's own feelings of being restricted by parental and authority's control. Such wishful thinking and desire for thrills on the part of children is one of the reasons why there is such immense interest in series such as the American *Hardy Boys* and the *Bobbsey Twins* and in Britain's Enid Blyton books featuring the *Famous Five* and the *Secret Seven*, all of which are still read eagerly in many countries by thousands of children regardless of age or ability.

The analysis of Enid Blyton's books in Davies's *Books in the School Curriculum* (pp. 30–33), examining the reasons for the popularity of the books suggests that security and predictability, excitement and adventure, the absence of adults, the possibility to continue through a set of books and the constant recommendation of other children were pointers, as was the fact that in Enid Blyton's books, as in many other popular author's books there is immediate action and characters on which children could project their own images.

Other countries have their examples of popular series for both boys and girls and most countries have produced individual titles which show children meeting challenges, getting into difficulties, achieving success or glory and, usually, returning to the safety of home and family at the end.

In many countries children in the eight to thirteen range are already showing the distinct difference between boys' and girls' reading preferences. At this age girls are interested in school stories, horse stories, animals, works of fantasy and imagination, historical stories and nature books, while the boys prefer adventure stories, funny books and have a strong and growing preference for non-fiction in the form of books on technical and scientific subjects and hobbies such as sport, birds and stamp collecting. In the fourteen-plus age range young people in many countries read less than ever and boys read less than girls. When boys do read they read considerably more non-fiction than fiction, whereas girls read more fiction than non-fiction.

There are many countries where young people of fourteen have finished school education and will not have achieved a level of literacy that enables them to read fluently enough to enjoy books.

In the countries where teenagers can and do have books available to them, there are striking common preferences. The girls put romance first, then humorous stories, followed by historical novels and ghost stories while teenage boys prefer humorous books, war, adult adventure, mystery and science fiction. One reason for differences may be that the leading characters in war and romance are of the opposite sex and identification is a high priority at teen age. Another possibility is the fact that boys prefer realistic action and situation whereas for girls, realism centres on people.

In 1986 the Book Marketing Council in Britain promoted books for teenagers through a Teen Read Campaign. A Teen Read jury of twelve young people selected a long list of one hundred books and then whittled it down to a shorter list of twenty-one. The result supports the general indications of teenage reading interests gained from everyday sources and the list in alphabetical order is reproduced here to put flesh on the bones of the theory.

Across the Barricades: Joan Lingard
Adrian Mole: Sue Townsend
Batteries Not Included: Seth McEvoy
Breaking Up: Norma Klein
Buddy: Nigel Hinton
Caitlin Trilogy: Joanna Campbell
The Change Over: Margaret Mahy
Children of the Dust: Louise Lawrence
Dark is Rising: Susan Cooper
First Term at Trebizon: Anne Digby
Forever: Judy Blume

Goodnight Mr Tom: Michelle Magorian
The Hitchhiker's Guide to the Galaxy: Douglas Adams
It's My Life: Robert Leeson
Lord of the Rings: J. R. R. Tolkien
Malibu Summer: Kate William
Spitting Image: Lloyd, Fluck and Law
Stranger with My Face: Lois Duncan
Tex: S. E. Hinton
When the Wind Blows: Raymond Briggs.

Non-fiction

Preferences in non-fiction may be determined by more than simply a desire for entertainment.

Children want or need information books for:

- Individual interest, at home and at school
- Reference: finding specific information
- Project or schoolwork

When children read non-fiction they want information in terms of facts, concepts or attitudes and they need an understanding of that information in the context of *purpose* for which they are reading the book. Many of the more successful information books are those which attempt to place the information in the reader's context, subtly.

Facts on their own can be useful and these tend to be found in the quick-reference books like dictionaries, directories and encyclopaedias, but the important element in reading information books lies not only in the information gained but in the thought process involved in understanding the information and then in making use of it.

In the non-fiction fields the preferences are for the natural sciences (animals, birds, biology), practical subjects, geographical and historical books, social science themes, arts and crafts and sex.

Within each of the fiction themes there is a wide variation in quality amongst the books read. Describing children's reading preferences for subject matter does not imply that they read only quality books in these subjects and one of the aims of teachers and librarians, in countries where children and young people are literate and have a choice of reading materials, is to lead the reader to the well-written book on the preferred theme.

In all the surveys of reading interests the difference between those of boys and those of girls is striking, even in countries where there are attempts to change sex discrimination in the ways children are reared. There are some factors which may influence the differences: biological, family upbringing, social conditioning, educational requirements; but there is not yet a clear reason for the different reading preferences. It is also noticeable that in many countries the boys who do read voluntarily at fourteen-plus (and in some cases at twelve-plus) are interested in *adult* adventure, mystery and science fiction books, and that large numbers of teenage girls from twelve-plus read quantities of adult romantic and historical fiction.

Physical criteria

In addition to interest in subject themes, both fictional and non-fictional, there are preferences for certain physical characteristics of the book. Surveys indicate that from the age of about twelve young people show a clear preference for the paperback or pocketbook edition of a book, rather than the hardback. This is likely to be the result of a number of factors.

- *Cover (or jacket) attraction*: the cover of a paperback is usually different from that of the hardback edition and is designed to appeal to the mass market and casual buyer.

221

- *The size*: a small size makes it look less daunting, easier to read in terms of apparent length, and easier to handle for carrying in bag or pocket.
- *Appearance*: it does not look like a school book and is therefore psychologically more likely to be enjoyable.
- *Cost*: it is cheaper than a hardback edition and therefore it is possible for the reader to enjoy the pleasure of ownership.
- *Availability*: it is more likely to be found in newsagents, stores, supermarkets, market stalls, bookshops and school bookshops.

Given a choice, other physical factors for which most children show preference in books are the external appearance, the presence of illustration, well laid-out text and reasonable print size. There is no doubt that the popular books are less complex than the books that win literary awards and popularity normally equates with 'easier to read'.

It has been noted in many countries that when children select books from the shelves they look first at the title and if it is intriguing enough they take the book off the shelf; glance at the cover of the book; flick through the pages to see how difficult the text looks in terms of legibility and in difficulty of vocabulary; look at some of the illustrations if there are any; read the 'blurb' to see what the book is about; and then either select or reject it.

This is not so for paperback selection by teenagers, preference there being for interesting cover, intriguing title, narrative style, set in contemporary times, high on physical action and with one main character.

Children's reading needs

Individuals have individual preferences in books though

there may be textbooks which children *must* read for school or examination purposes. The development of critical faculties and personal taste are part of the whole reading process and just as people have likes and dislikes about food so there is taste and distaste in reading, whether child or adult. But interest or preference is not necessarily the same as need.

There are at least three categories of 'need' in relationship to books:

- A child may 'need' a book in order to get information for a specific school essay or project or in order to find out about a hobby, 'need' here meaning actual physical access to the required book.
- The second area of need is more likely to be subconscious and refers to what happens to the mind of the reader when he is reading. This kind of need is usually recognized by the adult responsible for children's reading and results in broad statements like, young children 'need' a happy ending to their stories because they are not sufficiently mature to cope with unhappy endings; or because each Western teenager tends to think that he or she is alone in the suffering or distress facing him, teenagers 'need' books which enable them to see, firstly that others have been there before them, and secondly, that the problem or distress was resolved, or at least coped with, if only in the way shown in the story.
- Broad statements can be made about a third category of need, that is the need which adults impose or require to be satisfied, as in children 'need' books which are well written so that they are introduced to good language and sentence structure, or children 'need' books which present them with an acceptable view of their country/moral issue/death/sex/politics/

religion/adults, acceptable in terms of the school or the parents or the state; or, children who are slow learners need books with simplified language and lots of pictures.

The difference between these three areas of reading 'need' and that of reading 'interest' is seen in a child's simple statement, 'I like books about . . .' in other words, books about his own particular interest.

Now there is a wealth of analytical discussion on what reading is for, and what happens to the mind as a result of reading fiction. The reading list at the end of the book recommends some books which lead further on this theme, but basically there is often a link between the second kind of 'need' and reading 'interest'. A child may show a preference for, a taste for, an interest in, certain kinds of book *because* they satisfy a subconscious need in him. There are obviously too many such links to categorize but when a child says, 'That was a good book!', some need in him was satisfied and he is likely to be interested then in more of the same.

This feeling is sometimes called *therapeutic* in the sense that it has a curative power, or *cathartic*, meaning cleansing or purifying. Over a short period of time there has developed the science of bibliotherapy, which is the practice of using certain books or stories as part of the treatment of children and adults who are emotionally or mentally disturbed. Trained bibliotherapists can sometimes help such people to come to terms with their problems through reading stories which have a relevance to their problems. In much less dramatic ways most children and adults who can read sufficiently well or who can listen to stories, receive this satisfying and constructive feeling with the 'right' stories. Children and adults who can read continue to do so, voluntarily, because they enjoy it. This enjoyment comes from:

- Seeing oneself vicariously in fictional form
- Taking on another's character in dream or wish fulfilment
- Showing how others tackled situations/problems, good and bad
- The information obtained

Many other benefits occur in the reading process and these are indicated in Chapter Eleven.

There is obviously a strong connection between what children want and need in books and criteria for selecting by librarians and teachers, although reading can mean different things to different people depending upon the reason for which the reading is being undertaken. Reading for pleasure, reading to pass the time, reading for the imaginative experience, reading to obtain information, reading to practise the skill of reading, all these and more mean that a multiplicity of books and kinds of book is needed, from reading schemes for learning to read, through comics and periodicals to story books and information books. There are, in some countries, books for all kinds of reading and reader, catering for the relaxed pleasant time of a good reader to what is often a hard demanding time for the poor reader.

Whatever a child reads, voluntarily, can be helpful to him, despite the belief amongst some children's literature specialists and some teachers, that only 'good' children's literature should be made available to children and young people. But that idea is looked at in more detail in the chapter on selection criteria (Chapter Nine).

Adults' need for children's books

The parents, teachers and librarians also need or want children's books and have reading preferences within children's literature. They want or need children's books for use with children:

- To entertain
- To increase knowledge
- To encourage individual learning and use of books

When parents select books for their children or offer guidance they tend to have two main preferences, to find and share with the child the books of their own youth, which may or may not be relevant to the age, experience, social circumstances or ability of the child, and to provide the child with books that they think will develop him, usually in the 'educational' sense. In some cases parents are seduced by the visual attractions of the cover or the illustrations.

Teachers need books which will complement and supplement their teaching, whether fictional or subject-based themes. They want and prefer children's books which do this clearly, in accordance with whatever standards obtain in their school or teaching field and which fit the particular age and ability of their students, in school matters. Some teachers see that the child is a child first and a school pupil second, and want *for* the child books that have something to say to the whole child.

Librarians' needs and interests in children's literature are much more widespread and varied. What the librarian needs is physical access to stock appropriate for the library's clientele. Most children's librarians are professionally interested in children's literature as a broad genre of writing, the literary, psychological, educational and sociological factors, and most have a personal interest in one or other kind of book for children.

Many other adults in a community or a nation have needs and interests in children's books, either from a literary standpoint or because they are involved with

children and need to know something about the relationship of books to children.

Children's reading interests can be ascertained by means
of surveys, questionnaires, observation and simply by
asking them. But it is important to bear in mind that a need
may be for a book that a child ought to have for his work,
that would enable him to do a better project or essay and
to learn more; or, unidentified by the child but recognized
by an adult as necessary for the child. A want can be
described as what the reader would like to have; evidence
of a desire or an interest; and a demand is what a reader
asks for. So librarians and teachers concerned with
providing books should be aware that children may
demand, or ask for, books that they do not need and need
books that they do not want or ask for.

It makes good sense for anyone involved in promoting
books to children, for whatever purpose, to try to obtain
some indication of interest and need in order to better
carry out the task of evaluating and selecting books for
children, and then making them accessible to children.

Many adults have different preferences to meet differing
purposes for reading and many would find it difficult to say
why they liked or disliked a book. It is noticeable when
talking with children about books that they too may choose
a book to fit the desire of the moment for escapism, but
select a quite different book when a deeper need for
satisfaction is felt.

Adults and children alike may find some parts of interest
rather than the whole and will say 'I like the bit about . . .',
but the whole-hearted response is evident when the reader
says 'Have you any more like this?'

References

1 Whitehead, Frank et al. *Children and Their Books*.

Schools Council Project, Macmillan, 1977

2 Ingham, Jennie. *Books and Reading Development; the Bradford Book Flood experiment*. Heinemann/BNB, 1981

3 Davies, Florence. *Books in the School Curriculum; a compilation and review of research relating to voluntary and intensive reading*. EPC and NBL, 1986

4 J. Bird. *Young Teenage Reading Habits: a study of the Bookmaster Scheme*. British Library, 1982

5 Waltham Forest Libraries and Arts Department. *Teenagers and Libraries; a study in Waltham Forest*. 1986

6 Dunster, June. *Early Teenage Reading; a reading survey of 13, 14, 15 year olds in Ferndown and West Moor*. Dorset County Library, 1984

Further reading

Fasdick, Adele M. *Current Research on the Reading Interests of Young People in North America*. Paper presented to IFLA General Conference, Chicago 1985. Available from IFLA HQ, The Hague, Netherlands

Fry, Donald. *Children Talk About Books; seeing themselves as readers*. Milton Keynes, Open University Press, 1985

Heather, Pauline. *Young People's Reading; a study of the leisure reading of 13–15 year olds*. CRUS Occasional Paper no. 6, Sheffield Centre for Research on User Studies, 1981

Marshall, Margaret R. *Handicapped Children and Books*. BNB, 1986 (Report 20)

Marshall, Margaret R. *Public Library Services to Teenagers in Britain*. British Library LIRD Report no. 5, 1982

Nottinghamshire County Youth Services. *Survey of Reading Material in Youth Clubs*. Nottingham, Notts County Library Services, 1981

Prince, Alison. 'How's Business'. *Books For Your Children*, Spring 1987, pp. 2–3, (writing in schools)
Schlager, Norma. 'Predicting children's choices in literature; a development approach'. *Children's Literature in Education*, vol. 9, 1978

CHAPTER NINE

How to Evaluate Children's Books

Where do I begin?

1 Start with the book.

- Look at its external appearance, size, front cover design, back cover information.
- Read the blurb on the inside cover for the author or publisher's intentions or descriptions.
- Open the book and note your reactions to the size and readability of the print, the ease of reading print and picture as a result of the page layout.
- Read the book.
- Apply the specific criteria relevant to the picture book, fiction or non-fiction content.

2 Consider the purpose for which you are selecting/ evaluating this book. For example: to be given to a known child; to be used by a class of children; to be put into stock in a children's library or a teenage library; to be read by a child with special needs; for assessment for an award.

3 Think about any overall aims or policy framework behind this evaluation. For example: does it fit the stated criteria for the award; will it contribute to the development of the child's mental or imaginative growth; is it within the financial guidelines laid down.

4 Remember that as an evaluator you are exercising your own critical faculties, judgements and preferences, which

may be unconscious. To these must be added the conscious judgements, assessments and objectives required when selecting for others.

What criteria should be applied to the evaluation of fiction?

It is possible to specify in great detail the criteria to be applied but as this book is intended as an introduction to aspects of the very wide range of children's books it is necessary only to touch on some of the more important areas. Aspects such as the place of that book in the total library collection or its format and price are necessary considerations but more difficult is a set of criteria related to the literary content.

This consideration is, of course, paramount when books are being selected for literary awards or studied in literature classes. The same kinds of literary analysis can be applied to children's literature as to any literature and further readings on this are given at the end of this book, and discussed in Chapter 2: What is children's literature?

Bearing in mind that the experience of literature by the evaluator provides a basis for comparison and helps towards the development of an almost intuitive 'feel' for recognizing what is good, consideration should be given to the following features when attempting the literary evaluation of a children's book:

● The subject matter ought to have been chosen by the writer because he has something to say on the theme, something that is original. Although the theme may be commonplace the author's, or his characters', view must be original, stretching the imagination and widening knowledge, clarifying reality and deepening understanding, not necessarily in a complex way. Simplicity may well be the more effective.

231

- The action should carry out the idea, with events and characters progressing, not necessarily logically, but acceptably within the limits set by the theme. There should be no recourse to outside agencies hitherto unrelated to the plot, no solving the problem or alleviating the situation by unrelated intervention, even in fantasy where the willing suspension of disbelief is involved.
- The characters should 'live'. Their strengths, weaknesses, credibility, conviction, interrelation must flow from the picture built up through the narration, conversation, thoughts of others and individual actions, which all contribute to a convincing and integrated portrait of a character, who should develop during the story.
- A sense of time and environment should form the basis whether the story is set in the past, present or future.
- Language, vocabulary, sentence structure make up the components of what is often called style. The style of writing may vary from one book to another, though written by the same author, if he considers that the style is a necessary part of the total impact of the theme. But usually there are individual clues, idiosyncrasies, patterns of thought or of words which can identify the great writers, the prolific writers and the formula writers. Aspects of style include factors such as: how appropriate the style is to the subject matter; the balance of narration and dialogue; natural dialogue; sentence patterns; mood creation, such as mystery, gloom, evil, joy, security.

Complex sentence structure and extended vocabulary may be suitable but consider the ease of reading in terms both of difficulty of language and difficulty of concepts.

- A sense of reality, even in fantasy, makes for a good book, in that there is pleasure not merely from the surface enjoyment of a good read, but the deeper if subconscious, satisfaction of having gone through a vicarious, but at the time of reading, *real* experience. For example, the story may evoke a sense of pity or justice or a laugh or a weep; the responsive reading is important.
- An essential factor also is the style of illustration and its relevance to the theme of the book, complementing, supplementing and extending the writing style.
- The literary value lies not so much in the subject or theme as in how that theme is presented, how it is revealed to the child reader's perceptions.

Literary analysis starts then with asking questions such as: what did the author intend to do? How did he attempt it? Did he achieve it? If not, why not?

Other forms of analysis and evaluation can start from different bases as indicated earlier in the chapter, though all must be taken into account when selecting books for children.

What are the overall considerations involved before selecting information books?

Selecting non-fiction for effective reading means taking into account the following:

- The purpose for which it is being read.
- Recognition of the kinds of non-fiction which will facilitate that purpose.
- Availability of non-fiction works suitable for effecting that purpose.
- Awareness of the physical features of non-fiction which aid effective reading.

● Ensuring that the skills needed for effective use are learned by the children so that they *can* read effectively what you and they have selected.

There are selection criteria and evaluation criteria in addition to these general factors: special criteria applicable to particular subject fields such as science or to particular kinds of reference work such as encyclopaedias or dictionaries. There are also the possibilities in some countries that questions are asked about information books which appear to violate required principles concerning racism, sexism, violence, political or religious stances.

Potential usage

Potential usage of a non-fiction work brings up the need to assess the book for its potential to answer the kinds of questions that might be put to it. This is related to the scope and presentation of the content and to the author's style of writing.

Certain kinds of information need require certain kinds of information book and, on the part of the reader, particular forms of reading skill or strategy.

An information book can be a fact book capable of providing nuggets of information in answer to specific queries such as: What were the dates of the Battle of Gettysburg, the independence of Nigeria, the first Russian spaceship, Captain Cook's landing in Australia, the end of the Second World War? Or how many legs has a spider? What are the colours of the rainbow? What is the chemical symbol for water? All these are straightforward facts requiring the reader simply to locate them in the information book and identify them as the answer to his question. You should, therefore, select the kind of information book that facilitates quick answers to these quick questions.

But the question may be more complex and require an information book capable of providing further information to questions like: What caused the Battle of Gettysburg or How do spiders make webs? To these there are answers which are relatively non-controversial but more detailed · than the previous answers. These would require a more detailed book in which the reader locates the information, identifies it as basically appropriate, sorts it mentally and selects the details which together give the answer.

Still more complex questions can be asked of an information book and a much more complex reading strategy may be required of the reader in finding the answers to questions like: What were the effects of the Battle of Gettysburg compared with those of Custer's Last Stand? Or, what is the role of the spider in the world of nature? Here the reader must select a book which goes much more deeply and analytically into the subject matter, and in addition to locating the information and identifying it as basically applicable, the reader must assimilate the information, analyse it, compare it and contrast it, and *understand* it, before being able to answer the question – because there are few books which provide all sides of every subject. The onus is often on the reader to make the connection.

Thus you may need to ask, in the knowledge of the readers for whom the selection is made. Is this book capable of answering one or more of the types of question my readers will put to it? Can this book provide the answers better pictorially via the illustrations and other visual aids in the book than by text? Pictures can be a visual language, more informative than text, but the two together if well designed can be of maximum aid to children and young people especially those who have a reading problem.

What should I look for in information books?

Detailed features applicable to most information books can be described under the following headings:

Content

- Scope, broad or specific; starting and finishing at what level of knowledge or at what points in the subject matter.
- Accuracy of factual information and illustrative content; evidence of generalizations or bias.
- Sequencing of information in a logical progression.
- Up-to-dateness of information.

Authority

Authority can be assessed by noting the author's experience, qualifications or other credentials in the subject field; often indicated in the blurb, on the title page or in the introduction.

The reputation of the series or publisher may also indicate reliability and authenticity.

Presentation

- Style appropriate to the subject and to intended use in terms of language, for example, technical, simple, popular, descriptive, discursive.
- Appropriate to age in the concepts offered; the layout; the kinds of illustration; the arrangement or organization of the information in terms of chronological, A–Z and so on.
- Use of chapters, headings, references, diagrams, maps and so on.
- Use of primary sources where appropriate.
- Presence of helpful features such as contents, list,

pagination, glossary, further reading list (of books suitable for similar age/level of reader), index.

- Aids to ease of use, such as, arrows pointing from text to relevant illustration; the placing of illustrations.

Illustration

- The importance of visual information, preferably in colour, because colour itself gives information.
- Relevance to the text; much illustration is decorative rather than informative.
- Positioning in the text, to enable the reader to relate what is read to what is seen.
- Style of illustration, for example, representational, abstract, photographic, original source pictorial material.
- Emphasis on the significant where relevant rather than leaving the reader to decide what he should be looking for.

Format

- Size, in terms of handling by intended readership; psychological appeal; wear and tear.
- Binding suitable for intended use, for example, spiral for books to be laid flat; laminated covers for books to be constantly handled in working conditions.
- Quality of paper to ensure clarity, appeal and use. See-through paper impedes legibility.
- Print; legibility, clarity; distinction between headings by the use of italics or bold type for emphasis; avoidance of slabs of print by use of margins, indenting, headings, white space and so on; importance of equal clarity of subsidiary information, captions and index.

Assessment of overall quality in its own right as a readable, comprehensible and informative book, and then in comparison with other works on the same topic; does this book take the subject further; is it easier to read; are the illustrations better; is it a more useful format? Does it cost more?

How can I assess illustration when I know little about art?

Read the chapter on illustration and children's books in which the purposes of illustration are outlined and a checklist of factors involved given.

Bear in mind that in picture books for young children it is important for the child to see all the picture in order to identify the content and understand what is seen. This means no overprinting of text on illustration which spoils both the legibility of the text and full concentration on the picture. There should be no bleeding to the edge of the page, that is, taking the picture right to the edge and beyond, which can take both the eye and the mind off the page, if as in many cases, some bleeding produces half an object or scene. The child may not be able to conjecture from an incomplete view.

Look for a freshness of approach to a hackneyed subject or a reinterpretation of a classic book, individuality allied to the strength of the basic drawing within the illustration.

In non-picture books where small line drawings are often used consider whether they are there to break up the text or are an integral and interrelated part of the book.

What about books for children with special needs?

Detailed criteria are given in the books and guidelines by Margaret Marshall: *Seeing Clear; Books and materials for the partially sighted child; See All, Say All; a selection of books for the language-deprived child; Books for the Mentally Handicapped; criteria for selection,* and *Libraries and the Handicapped Child.*[1] Between them they cover most of the editorial, illustrative and technical requirements in books for children who have impairment of the mind, of hearing or of vision. Overall, such children benefit from books with the following features:

- Binding that opens flat, whether spiral or ring binding or flexible in other ways.
- Paper that is opaque to avoid see-through, and non-glare to prevent reflection.
- Print that is easy on the eye, increased size and weight with an open 'a'.
- Plenty of white space around and between with good inside margins to prevent the eye from going right across the page.
- Short, simple, relevant vocabulary and sentence structure.
- No word play, metaphors or foreign words unless in clear context.
- Simple concepts and familiar settings.
- Representational illustrations or photographs, in colour, and placed relevant to the text in order to give clues to the text.
- A beginning, a middle and an end whether fiction or non-fiction.
- Visually attractive cover.
- Humour, to create the positive feeling that despite the effort required to read, it can be an enjoyable experience.

For children with a disability that affects reading and for the older less-able reader there are also individual books from the range of 'ordinary' books that will fit the bill, and those who select and evaluate should always assess *every* book for its potential suitability for the special child.

The less-able teenage reader now has several hundred books in series catering for the needs if not the interests. The criteria here are as follows:

- An attractive cover.
- A large proportion of illustration to text but not a picture book.
- Medium-sized print, well spaced and with good margins.
- Simple words and short sentences but not to the point of dehydration.
- Storyline and characters close to the readers' chronological age, or adult.
- Maximum amount of humour relevant to the story.
- A worthwhile experience, so that after mastering the words the reader has also gained in knowledge and enjoyment.

When should I reject a children's book?

The reasons for not selecting certain children's books may be three-fold, that they do not meet literary, physical, or ideological standards or any one or combination of these. A book may be superficial, didactic, with caricatures or stereotyped characters or situations, glamorized, lacking some or all of the criteria discussed earlier, or those laid down by an award-making body.

Poor physical quality of book production may also necessitate exclusion, depending upon the intended usage or the stated criteria. The price or estimated value for money is often linked with this, though where there is no alternative it is often necessary to select a book despite its poor physical production.

But a common feature of rejection is that which could be called censorship. This can take the form of pre-censorship, meaning that authors and publishers avoid writing, or publishing, books with a particular theme or content. This varies from country to country depending upon the social/political/religious mores of the country.

However even when there is little pre-censorship, books may be rejected by librarians, teachers and parents because the content is thought to be unsuitable.

Reasons commonly given include the felt need to protect child readers from unpleasant, corrupting or frightening areas of adult or child life, that a child is too young to understand; usually applied to subjects such as sex, death, varieties of philosophical, sociological, opinion or practice.

Then there is the rejection of aspects already looked at in Chapter One – the books with characters or situations which suggest racism or sexism. There is a growing understanding of the ways in which social conditioning affects attitudes both towards people of different sexes and people of differing ethnic backgrounds, and how such attitudes and treatment are reflected in books for children and for adults.

These and any other discriminatory conditions imposed on children's books should take their place beside the other criteria. Censorship is more common in the area of teenage novels than in other kinds of literature for children and young people. The sensitive areas, particularly for USA and Islamic countries, are sex, religion, profanity, violence, drugs and alcohol. But as indicated, 'offensive' passages must be related to their context in the whole work, the reader, whether adult or teenager distinguishing between the pornographic and the lewd treatment, the adolescent ribald vulgarities, and the treatment of sexual relationships as an integral part of the story. Gratuitous violence and its glamorization, and gratuitous profanities, swearing or bad language, would be a cause for concern but the inclusion of violent episodes or of cursing would not of themselves be a reason for rejecting a book.

Crime and violence are enjoyed and coped with by children and teenagers in films, books and magazines. Any suggestion of a co-relation between teenage crime and that kind of reading has been refuted, the high teenage crime rate in many countries being the result of a poor environment, illiteracy and lack of intelligence in most cases.

There are many books in which a 'sensitive' theme is treated responsibly as an integral part of the whole book. Examples include extortion in Robert Cormier's *The Chocolate War*; violence in Bernard Ashley's *Terry on the Fence*, Joan Lingard's *Across the Barricades*, Robert Westall's *The Machine Gunners* and S. E. Hinton's *Rumble Fish*. Drugs are the theme of the latter's *That Was Then This Is Now*, and M. Duke's *Sugarcube Trap*. Sex is part of the theme of Judy Blume's *Forever*, Paul Zindel's *My Darling, My Hamburger*, David Rees's *Quentin's Man* and of Aidan Chambers's *Breaktime*.

Certain physical functions and unpleasant allusions are found in Raymond Briggs's *Father Christmas* and *Fungus the Bogeyman*, both highly successful in many countries and much appreciated by teenagers almost to the point of cultism.

While many writers find a freedom in writing for teenagers that is not possible when writing for children, most do not abuse that freedom, and most are aware that teenagers today know a great deal about sex, violence, war, racial prejudice, wealth and poverty, from television at a superficial level. It can be helpful and enjoyable to read a deep exploration of a theme in story form, where the impact of the theme on individuals and society can be felt through characterization and the plot in a serious yet enjoyable treatment.

What are the broad aims in evaluating and selecting?

Most people assessing books for children work from the belief that reading is a good thing and that books should educate/develop/stretch/enrich the minds of child readers, and are convinced that books exist which will achieve this aim. In many countries the dearth of children's books, or their poor quality, present teachers and librarians with little opportunity for selection. Whatever is obtainable is needed. But in such countries, and in those where there is a wide range of children's literature, the following, which is not in any order of priority, may be a helpful basis when selecting books for children.

Select books that:

- Reflect national, local and individual values, experiences and scenes.
- Introduce children to their own cultural heritage.
- Provide a vicarious experience of a world they do not live in, in terms of time, space and culture.
- Enlarge the mind and the imagination.
- Offer experience in the creative and scientific inquiry process.
- Enable the reader to acquire, or change, knowledge, values and attitudes.
- Encourage an appreciation of beauty and human achievement, motivation and aspiration.
- Allow the discernment of good/bad, right/wrong.

It is also a good thing to remember that there are books that are good for a particular age range, good for satisfying known interests, good for the less-able reader, good for developing the imagination, good for aiding visual perception, good for identifying with emotionally, good for understanding how other people live, good for stimulating aspiration, good for developing reading skills, good for

243

developing literary taste, good for aiding spoken language, good for reading aloud and good for a laugh.

Is selection policy a good idea?

For teachers and librarians a stated policy can be a helpful foundation for library book selection if the contents are not rigid constraints but recommended guidelines. The benefits of such a policy statement include the following:

- It enables everyone to know the basis of selection.
- Responsibilities of individuals concerned with selection are assigned and clarified.
- Criteria indicated will aid the selection process.
- Material selected will be more effective.

A selection policy statement or guideline should cover the objectives or aims. It should define the readership in specific or general terms depending upon the circumstances. For example, it may be defined as including the gifted reader, the able, the less-able, the handicapped, the minority language speaker, the pre-school child or branch library's clientele.

Knowing for whom the selection is made influences what is to be selected and this can also be included in the statement; for example fiction, information books, reference books, periodicals, pamphlets, illustrations, audio-visual materials, hardback and paperback books, according to the local need/finance/space available/policy requirements.

The aids to selection can be indicated, including bibliographies, reviews, critical works, selection panels, schemes for viewing actual material. Any provisos affecting selection should be stated, whether these be cost, language, theme or physical format.

The personnel concerned with selection can be indicated with a clear statement that, though several staff/teachers/

students and so on may be involved in the selection process, the librarian's decision is final.

The selection policy should therefore:

- Refer to objectives
- Define readership
- Outline selection personnel
- Specify materials by type and level
- Identify provisos in terms of quantity, quality criteria, finance, areas of controversy
- Outline methods of and aids to selection

What are the criteria for children's book awards?

The evaluation of children's literature for awards is part of a very complex field where rules, criteria and effects vary considerably from country to country and from one award to another.

It is clear that in those countries where there is a large amount of children's literature there is also a range of children's book awards, as demonstrated in the select list given later in the chapter.

The basic factors that need to be considered when either creating awards or assessing them include the following:

- Rules of entry, for example: eligibility in terms of nationality, date of publication, type of literature, children's age group.
- Terms of award, for example: the best literary book outstanding in any year, best total work, most popular book, outstanding illustration, outstanding information book, new talent, best on a theme, most socially useful, best translation or the outstanding contribution to the world of children's literature.
- Nominations, for example: via publisher, librarian, reader.

- Judges, for example: writers, librarians, publishers, literary critics, graphic experts, children.
- Methods of assessment, for example: procedures, timescale, individual and collective judging.
- Criteria for selection, related to the terms of the award.
- Value of the award, for example: medal, money or prestige.
- Possible effects of awards, for example: raising the standards of writing and illustration, encouraging writers and illustrators, rewarding merit, giving recognition and publicity to the children's book world, providing a basis for quality collections of children's literature.

The list that follows contains examples of national and international awards for children's literature. Their rules, criteria and rewards vary and are too many and too complicated to be included here. Unless otherwise stated the awards are for excellence in children's literature, usually selected from the publications of any one year, and usually from amongst the writers of that country.

Awards in Britain

- *Best Books for Babies*: Annual. For books for children up to four years old. British Book Marketing Council and *Parents* magazine: submitted by publisher. £1000.
- *Carnegie Medal*: Annual. For children's book of outstanding merit in English, first published in UK in the preceding year. Selected by librarians through the Youth Libraries Group of the Library Association. Medal.
- *Children's Book Award*: Annual. For the best work of fiction up to age fourteen selected by adults and

children of the Federation of Children's Book Groups. Certificate.

- *Children's Book Competition*: Annual. For children's story for seven- to eleven-year olds, previously unpublished. Sponsored by Faber, the *Guardian* and the BBC. £2,500.
- *Kate Greenaway Award*: Annual. For the distinguished work of illustration in a children's book. Selected by librarians through the Youth Libraries Group of the Library Association from works published in the preceding year. Medal.
- *Kathleen Fidler Award*: Annual. Manuscript competition open to writers of any nationality who have not previously published a novel for the eight to twelve age group. Sponsored by Blackie and administered by the National Book League, Scotland. £500.
- *Guardian Award for Children's Fiction*: Annual. For outstanding work of fiction by a British or Commonwealth writer, first publication in UK. £250.
- *Geravi Gujerat Book Award for Racial Harmony*: Annual. For children's book promoting racial harmony in Britain's multi-racial society. *Asian News Weekly*, administered by the Book Trust. £100.
- *Kurt Maschler (Emil) Award*: Annual. For work of imagination in the children's book field in which text and illustration are of excellence and so presented that each enhances yet balances the other. Administered by the Book Trust. £1000 and bronze statue of Emil.
- *Mary Vaughan Jones Award*: Every three years. For an outstanding contribution to children's books and literature in the Welsh language over a period of time. Administered by the Welsh National Centre for Children's literature.
- *Mother Goose Award*: Annual. For the most exciting newcomer to British children's book illustration.

Books for Children. Bronze Egg, scroll and £200.

- *Other Award*: Annual. For children's book of literary merit that children enjoy and which balances roles in sex, race and occupation and so on. *Children's Book Bulletin*. Commendation.
- *Signal Poetry Award*: Annual. For excellence in work published in the preceding year in the UK. *Signal*. £100.
- *Smarties Prize*: Annual. For outstanding children's book. Sponsored by Rowntree Mackintosh. £8,000.
- *Times Educational Supplement, Information Book Awards*: Annual. For distinction in content and presentation in information books origination in the UK and Commonwealth. Two sections: junior up to nine and senior, ten to sixteen. *TES*. £150 each winner.
- *Tir na n-og Awards*: Annual. For author of best original children's book published in Welsh and for Anglo-Welsh children's book wherever published with authentic Welsh background. Welsh National Centre for Children's Books. £500 each.
- *Whitbread Awards (children's book category)*: Annual. For outstanding book for children seven-plus published in UK or Republic of Ireland, written by British author or one settled in UK or Ireland for five years. Sponsored by Whitbread, administered by the Booksellers Association of Great Britain and Ireland. £3,000.
- *Young Observer Teenage Fiction Prize*: Annual. For the best full length novel for teenagers published in UK. *Observer*. £600.

Select list of awards in other countries

- Australia: Children's Book of the Year Award (a) for

children's book, (b) for picture book; Clifton Pugh Award for the most visually pleasing entry to the Book Council Awards.

- Austria: State Prize for Young People's Literature; Vienna Children's and Youth's Book Prize.
- Canada: Book of the Year for Children Medal; Canadian Children's Book Award; Canadian Library Association Best French Children's Book.
- Czechoslovakia: Marie Majerova Prizes (a) writer, (b) illustrator, for their life work in children's books.
- Denmark: Danish Prize for Children's and Youth Books.
- France: Enfance du Monde Prize; Fantasia Prize; Grand Prize for Children's Literature; Grand Prize for Youth Literature.
- Germany (GDR): East German Youth Organization Prize.
- Germany (FDR): German Juvenile Book Award.
- Greece: Greek National Prize.
- Israel: Ben-Yitzhak Award (for illustration).
- Japan: Sankei Award; Owl Prize for illustration (chosen by visitors to the children's book exhibition).
- Netherlands: Dutch Prize for the Best Children's Books.
- New Zealand: Russell Clark Award for illustration; Esther Glen Award for children's book.
- Norway: Damm Prize; Children's and Youth Book Award; Norwegian State Prize.
- Poland: Janus Korezak Prize; The Eagle's Feather (awarded by teenagers for their favourite writer).
- Sweden: Nils Holgersson Medal.
- Switzerland: Swiss Teachers' Association Youth Book Prize.
- USA: Newbery Medal; Caldecott Medal (for illustration); Laura Ingalls Wilder Award; National Book

Award for Children's Literature; Mildred Batchelder Award (for translation); National Council for Teachers of English Award (for Excellence in Poetry for Children).

There are other awards for each country and these can be ascertained from the publication *Children's Books: Awards and Prizes*, published by the Children's Book Council, New York.[2]

International awards: select list

IBBY (International Board on Books for Young People) organizes the *Hans Christian Andersen Awards* every two years; one for an author and one for an illustrator whose complete works form an outstanding body of literature.

The *IBBY Honours List* every two years selected from each national section's entries (three per nation). For excellence in writing, illustration and translation, presentation of the best of the country's publications and suitable for worldwide publication.

The *International Jane Addams Children's Book Award* is given by the Women's International League for Peace and Freedom and the Jane Addams Peace Foundation.

International Reading Association Award is given annually to an author showing unusual promise in children's book writing.

Two awards are given at the Bologna Book Fair, an international event. *Critici in Erba Prize* is given for the best illustrated book and is selected by a jury of children. The *Graphis Prize* goes to a children's and young people's book considered best from a technical and graphic viewpoint by a jury of experts.

The *Noma Concours* for children's picture book illustration in Asian–Pacific, Arab–African, and Latin America–Caribbean regions.

Awards for services to the world of children's literature

Examples include the Eleanor Farjeon Award in Britain, the Spanish National Prize in Spain and the Constance Lindsay Skinner Award in the USA. These are awarded to researchers, critics, lecturers, promoters of children's literature in organizations and areas, and who in many cases also write books for or about children and their books.

Whatever form of evaluation or selection of children's books takes place it involves consideration of the objectives, the needs, interests and abilities of child readers, and the literary criteria, graphic quality and production. It requires also an understanding of the place of each book in comparison with others in the world of children's literature, an understanding which develops with knowledge and experience.

References

1 Margaret R. Marshall. *Seeing Clear; books and materials for the partially sighted child.* Swindon, School Library Association, 1985, large print edition
2 Margaret R. Marshall. *See All Say All; a selection of books for the language-deprived child.* IBBY British Section, 1985
  Margaret R. Marshall *et al. Books for the Mentally Handicapped Child and Adult; a guide to selection.* The Hague, IFLA, 1983
  Margaret R. Marshall. *Libraries and the Handicapped Child.* Gower, 1981
3 Children's Book Council. *Children's Books; awards and prizes.* New York, Blond, 1986

Further reading

Barker, Keith. *In the Realms of Gold; the story of the Carnegie Medal*. Julia MacRae Books, 1986
Griffiths, Vivien. *Primer of Book Selection Policy and Practice in Both School and Public Libraries*. Library Association Youth Libraries Group, 1983
Stones, Rosemary. *Pour Out the Cocoa, Janet; sexism in children's books*. Longman/Schools Council, 1983

CHAPTER TEN

Bibliographical Aids to Children's Literature

The world of children's books encompasses many countries, many professions and many needs. One of the needs is for information *about* the books. Bibliographical aid towards deeper knowledge, current news or practical guidance is part of the infrastructure of that world.

The functions of bibliography include identifying, listing, describing, evaluating, comparing, analysing, criticizing, promoting and publicizing and each of these aspects can be found in one or other kind of bibliographical aid concerned with children's books. The bibliography of children's literature is extensive and in many languages, but examples, mostly in the English language, are given in the following categories:

Histories of children's literature and children's book illustration

- *The historical development of books for children* is charted in the foremost work, F. J. Harvey Darton's *Children's Books in England; five centuries of social life.* The third edition revised by Brian Alderson in 1982 for CUP relates the books to life in each period and maintains the high standard of scholarship. Robert Leeson's *Reading and Righting; the past, present and future of fiction for the young* (Collins, 1985) examines development from the social standpoint of the working classes and the common culture and needs; while John

Rowe Townsend's *Written For Children; an outline of English-language children's literature* (2nd rev. edn, Viking Kestrel, 1983) offers a condensed view of the national scene.

A discursive work on major children's writers 1860–1930 is *The Secret Gardens; the Golden Age of children's literature*, by Humphrey Carpenter (Allen & Unwin, 1985); while another slice of history is examined in J. S. Bratton's *The Impact of Victorian Children's Fiction* (Croom Helm, 1981) and in Jonathan Cott's *Pipers at the Gates of Dawn; the wisdom of children's literature* (Viking, 1984); Maurice Saxby's valuable two-volume *History of Australian Children's Literature* (Sydney, Wentworth 1969 and 1984) also shows connections with English children's literature.

A different historical perspective is available in Eric Quayle's *Early Children's Books; a collector's guide* (David & Charles, 1983) and in the Children's Books Historical Society's *Cataloguing of Early Children's Books; a guide for collectors* (Children's Books Historical Society, 1979).

● *The development of illustrated books for children* is described and analysed in Brian Alderson's *Sing a Song For Sixpence; the English picture-book tradition and Randolph Caldecott* (CUP, 1986); while two other works tackle a smaller part of the vast subject, Jonathan Cott's *Victorian Colour Picture Books* (Allen & Unwin, 1984) and John Barr's *Illustrated Children's Books* (British Library, 1986).

The standard history, with an American bias, is *Illustrators of Children's Books*, a multi-volume work. The original volume compiled by Bertha Mahoney covered 1744 to 1945, with subsequent volumes 1946–56 by Ruth Hill Viguers and 1957–66, 1967–76 by Lee Kingman, published by Hornbook.

- *Studies of particular genre form another grouping*, exemplified by Gillian Avery's *Childhood's Pattern; a study of the heroes and heroines of children's fiction, 1770–1950*, (Hodder & Stoughton, 1975); Mary Cadogan and Patricia Craig's *You're a Brick Angela; the girls' school story 1839–1985*, (Gollancz, 1986); and Isabel Quigley's *The Heirs of Tom Brown; the English school story* (OUP, 1984).

  The background to prize-winning books since 1933 is outlined by Keith Barker in *In the Realms of Gold; the story of the Carnegie Medal* (Julia MacRae Books/Youth Libraries Group, 1986).

  In addition to complete books on the theme there are hundreds of references to the historical development of children's books, texts and illustrations, in books about children's literature and hundreds of articles on many aspects of writers and books throughout the ages in journals connected with art, literature and education. Such articles can be located through periodical indexing and abstracting media.

Critical works

The amount of critical description and analysis has risen sharply in the last ten years, largely in the periodical literature, but major works in book form can be categorized thus:

- *Selections of articles or papers collected into book form*; as in Margaret Meek's *The Cool Web; the pattern of children's reading* (Bodley Head, 1977); Virginia Haviland's *Children's Literature; views and reviews* (Bodley Head, 1973); Nancy Chambers's *The Signal Approach to Children's Books* (Kestrel, 1980); Sheila Egoff's *Only Connect; readings on children's literature* (OUP, 1980); and the volumes of *Children's Literature; annals of the Modern Language Association Division of Children's Literature and the Children's Literature Association* (Yale University, 1980 to date).

Collections of conference papers can provide useful and interesting viewpoints as in *Through Folklore to Literature*; papers presented at the Australian National Section of IBBY Conference on Children's Literature in Sydney in 1978 and edited by Australia's well-known children's literature historian, Maurice Saxby (IBBY Australia Publications, 1979).

Seen from the angle of educationalists, Geoff Fox's compilation *Writers, Critics and Children*; articles from *Children's Literature in Education* (Heinemann, 1976) offers studies and opinions from a range of writers, teachers and lecturers.

- *Collections of critical comment* by an individual are exemplified by Aidan Chambers's *Booktalk*: occasional writing on literature for children (Bodley Head, 1985); and Elaine Moss's *Part of the Pattern* (Bodley Head, 1986), which additionally provides an almost autobiographical picture of her own noteworthy part in the development of the children's book world.

- *Critical works on particular aspects of children's literature* are required reading for many students and the following offer a variety of themes and viewpoints such as Bruno Bettelheim, *The Uses of Enchantment; the meaning and importance of fairy tales* (Penguin, 1978). Ann Swinfen, *In Defence of Fantasy; a study of the genre in English and American literature since 1945* (Routledge & Kegan Paul, 1984) analyses amongst others, Hoban's *The Mouse and His Child*, C. S. Lewis's *Narnia*, Le Guin's *Earthsea* and Tolkien, plus many other adult and children's fantasy novels.

Malcolm Edwards and Robert Holdstock, *Realms of Fantasy* (Doubleday, 1983) is a large, beautifully illustrated description of the fantasy lands, such as, Tolkien's Middle Earth, Doyle's Lost Worlds, Moorcock's Melnibone, Donaldson's Land of Thomas Covenant, Mervyn Peake's Gormenghast, Howard's Hyborea and Le Guin's Earthsea.

Margery Fisher, *The Bright Face of Danger* (Hodder & Stoughton, 1986) describes and evaluates adventure stories for adults and children over the years. Margery Fisher, *Classics for Children and Young People* (Stroud, Thimble Press, 1986) is an analytical guide to this oft-disputed subject.

John Quirke, *Disability in modern children's fiction* (Croom Helm, 1984) looks at the ways in which children with a disability are portrayed in a range of children's books. Jacqueline Rose's *The Case of Peter Pan; the impossibility of children's fiction* (Macmillan, 1984), investigates the elements of Peter Pan and other books which border on the impossible.

● *Controversial issues* are looked at in Jack Zipes's *Don't Bet on The Prince; contemporary feminist fairy tales in North America and England* (Gower, 1986). Nicholas Tucker edited *Suitable for Children?; controversies in children's literature* (Sussex University Press, 1976); Gillian Klein researched *Reading into Racism; bias in children's literature and learning materials* (Routledge, 1985), and E. M. Sheridan discusses *Sex Stereotypes and Reading Research Strategies* (Newark, Delaware, International Reading Association, 1982).

● *Comment on individual writers, and artists* is made in a wide range of books but the following exemplify the category; Sheila Ray, *The Blyton Phenomenon; the controversy surrounding the world's most successful children's writer* (Deutsch, 1982); Neil Philip, *A Fine*

Anger; a critical introduction to the work of Alan Garner (Collins, 1981); Selma Lanes, *The Art of Maurice Sendak* (Bodley Head, 1981).

- *Comment on books for categories of reader* is represented by the following which tend to be descriptive and recommendatory: Dorothy Butler, *Babies Need Books* (Penguin, 1980), *Five to Eight; the vital years of reading* (Bodley Head, 1986); Robert Carlsen, *Books and the Teenage Reader* (Harper and Row, 1980); Margaret R. Marshall, *Libraries and Literature for Teenagers* (Gower, 1975). Numerous English language journal articles analyse and comment on the broad scene, on particular genres and on individual authors and illustrators.

Biographies and autobiographies of authors, illustrators and other children's book people

These vary from short monographs to full-length biographies and from the discursive style to quick-reference treatment.

- *Autobiographies* such as Rosemary Sutcliff's *Blue Remembered Hills* (Bodley Head, 1983) in her typical style of writing; Roald Dahl's exuberant account of his early life in *Boy* (Cape, 1984) and Enid Blyton's *The Story of My Life* (Grafton, 1986) in her chatty style.
- *Biographies* such as Barbara Stoney's account in *Enid Blyton, a Biography* (Hodder & Stoughton, 1986) is different in style from Hugh Brogan's *The Life of Arthur Ransome* (Cape, 1984) and Angela Bull's *Noel Streatfeild* (Collins, 1984). The title *By Jove, Biggles; the life of Captain W. E. Johns*, by Peter Ellis and Piers Williams (W. H. Allen 1981) fits the subject as does *Beyond the Wild Wood; the world of Kenneth Grahame* (Webb and Bower, 1982).

Two major and quite different biographies of Beatrix Potter are available. An early work by Margaret Lane, *The Tale of Beatrix Potter* was issued in a revised edition (Warne, 1985) and Judy Taylor's highly praised work *Beatrix Potter, Artist, Storyteller and Countrywoman* was published in 1986 by Warne.

● *Substantial reference works of biographical information* include the revised *Twentieth Century Children's Writers* (Macmillan, 1984) edited by D. L. Kirkpatrick with annotated biographies of hundreds of writers and illustrators. The massive and costly *Something About the Author* edited by Anne Commire (Detroit, Gale Research Co, 1986) has cumulative indexes and is illustrated with photographs, book illustrations and film stills.

Most journals concerned with children's books include biographical and autobiographical articles, for example, the regular feature Authorgraph, in *Books For Keeps* and, Author Portrait, in *Bookbird*.

Bibliographies and indexes

The task of locating and bringing together the vast array of published information into one bibliography of children's literature is yet to be undertaken in Britain, and in many other countries. The most comprehensive book listing is usually the national bibliography. Britain lags behind, in that though the *British National Bibliography* (BNB) includes children's books there is not a separate section from which all items identified as relevant to children's literature could be extracted quickly for use.

BNB cumulates from weekly issues to annual volumes but children's literature is identified only at Dewey number 823.9J. Non-fiction, poetry, drama and works about children's literature are all in the main Dewey non-fiction sequence and cannot be identified as for children without prior knowledge. Other lists exist on a commercial basis, for example, in UK, Whitaker's *Children's Books in Print*, the most recent volume 1987, with about 25,000 in-print titles and information about publishers' series.

In the USA, Bowker's *Children's Books in Print* is an annual publication, while Marcie Muir's *Bibliography of Australian Children's Books* (Deutsch 1970, 1976) provides a record of publications to that date.

Indexes to particular forms of literature include Margaret Smyth's *Picture Book Index*, a thematics index (AAL Publications, 1987) and its American counterpart *A–Zoo: Subject Access to Children's Picture Books* compiled by Caroline W. Lima (Bowker, 2nd rev. ed., 1985). Nicholas Chandler's *The Pauper's Poetry Index; a thematic index to cheaper poetry books*, published by Knowsley Leisure Services Libraries Division in England, is a useful tool as is Helen Morris's *The New Where's That Poem?* (Blackwell, 1986).

The dearth of comprehensive bibliographies and specific indexes may be relieved as the use of computers opens up the possibilities for such compilations.

Catalogues

Allied to the listing in the previous section are the published catalogues of a number of institutions, for example:

- *Libraries*: such as the *British Library Catalogue* in which books are not listed separately for children, and the *Library of Congress Catalogue* in which there is ease of access to children's books. In the UK the National Library for the Handicapped Child published its 700-page *Catalogue of Library Holdings 1984–1986* in easy-to-read typeface and with each entry in catalogue-card layout with enriched information in coded form.

- *Special collections*: such as that of the Osborne Collection in Boys and Girls House in Toronto, Canada, and the collection of children's books in the Rare Books Division of the Library of Congress. The five-volume catalogue of the *Childhood in Poetry* collection in the Library of the Florida State University was compiled by John Mackay Shaw.
- *Exhibitions*: such as *The Children's Books of Yesterday; a survey of 200 years of children's reading*, compiled in 1985 by J. Scragg for the John Rylands Library, University of Manchester, produce catalogues to accompany the exhibitions.
- *Publishers*: who introduce new publications and indicate the backlist for intending purchasers by means of annual and/or seasonal catalogues.
- *Booksellers*: particularly second-hand and rare book-shops which often sell early children's books by mail via a catalogue or duplicated list.
- *Library suppliers*: whose stock catalogues enable would-be purchasers to see what is available and/or to order from the catalogue.
- *Specialist catalogues*: such as Hans-Jorg Uther's *Katalog zur Volkserzählung* in two volumes (Saur, 1987), with 1,135 pages of entries for books of folk literature.

Guides to the literature

In many countries there is a large quantity of such guides which are produced by libraries, by organizations and by individuals. Most national libraries, children's literature research centres, librarianship organizations, public library children's departments and school libraries compile guides for parents, researchers, librarians, teachers and for the children themselves. The content, style of entry and annotative evaluative or descriptive information in the guide will be determined by which of these groups is the intended readership.

- Some countries produce annual lists of the best of the year's publications, as in *Children's Books of the Year*, selected by, in the past, Elaine Moss, Barbara Sherrard-Smith and, currently, by Julia Eccleshare for the National Book League in the UK. In the USA the Children's Services Division of the American Library Association compiles annually *Notable Children's Books 19—*. In the Netherlands the Netherlands Books and Library Centre (NBLC) makes an annual recommendations list.
- In the UK, library and children's book organizations such as the Youth Libraries Group, the School Library Association and the National Book League (now the Children's Book Foundation of the Book Trust) have a publications programme which includes for example: Janet Newman, *Sex Education; a practical evaluation of materials* (YLG, 1983); Children's Services Team, Birmingham Public Libraries, *Peace At Last; books for the pre-school child*, (YLG, 1986); Margaret R. Marshall, *Seeing Clear; books and materials suitable for the partially sighted child*, (revised ed., in large print, SLA, 1985); Anthea Raddon, *Exploring cultural diversity; an annotated fiction list*, (SLA, 1985), Jessica Yates, *Teenager to Young Adult; recent paperback fiction for 17–19 years*. (SLA, 1987), Rachel Redford, *Hear to Read; guide to children's audio-cassettes*, (NBL, 1986).
- Public library guides are numerous and usually aimed at parents or children. The following English public

library authorities' lists are offered as good examples: Nottinghamshire County Libraries, Hertfordshire County Libraries, Bradford Metropolitan District Libraries, Waltham Forest London Borough libraries.

Most American and Australian city library services have excellent publication and publicity departments, providing a wide range of book lists.

• Commercial guides include examples such as *The Good Book Guide to Children's Books*, edited by Bing Taylor and Peter Braithwaite (editorial adviser Elaine Moss (4th edn, Penguin, 1987), is designed for parents and children, contains advice on learning to read, guiding readers, and succinct reviews of about six hundred books, providing a balanced selection of good reading, old and new, fiction and non-fiction. Others are:

The Books For Keeps Guide to Children's Books for a Multi-Cultural Society, 0–7, (*Books for Keeps*, 1986) compiled by Judith Elkin; Baker Book Services, *Reading for Enjoyment; lists for various age groups*, and the Adult Literacy and Basic Skills Unit's, *Resources: a guide to materials* (ALBSU, 1986), which lists books and pamphlets suitable for the less-able teenager and adult.

• Miscellaneous examples indicate the wide range of available guides: *The White Ravens*; *a selection of international children's and youth literature* (Munich, International Youth Library, 1986) an annotated list of books in English with 350 recent titles from forty countries. *Das Buch den Jugend* is an annual list of books recommended as basic stock for school libraries or children's departments of public libraries by the Arbeitkreis für Jugendliteratur, in West Germany. *Notes for a Different Drummer* and its sequel *More Notes*, a guide to juvenile fiction portraying the handicapped (USA, American Library Association, 1984) was compiled by Barbara Baskin.

In general, guides to the literature must be up-to-date to be useful, a difficult task when many children's books go out of print quickly and when the guides may not be acquired until some time after publication.

Resources related to educational aspects of reading and children's books

There is a vast amount of prescriptive literature about the *teaching* of reading, the use of reading schemes and the testing of readability. These topics are not included in this section, though they are indeed part of the children's book world. The books listed here are more concerned with *reading* rather than learning to read, and emphasize children's books rather than reading schemes.

- *Early reading*: examples of the variety of books include: Dorothy Butler and Marie Clay, *Reading Begins At Home* (Heinemann, 1979) a fluent and passionate plea to parents; Liz Waterland, *Read with Me; an apprenticeship approach to reading* (Stroud, Thimble Press, 1985), short and succinct with the emphasis on 'real' books; Carol Baker, *Reading Through Play; the easy way to teach your child* (Macdonald, 1980), describes the kinds of pre-reading play that help a young child towards reading; Margaret Meek, *Learning to Read*, (Bodley Head, 1982), a very readable, wise and comprehensive account with explanations and advice for parents and other interested adults, placing the emphasis on the child rather than on the technique.
- *Reading at school is the next step*: Cliff Moon and

Bridie Rabam, *A Question of Reading* (Macmillan, 1980) is aimed at teachers and concentrates on strategies of learning to read but bears in mind individualized reading also. Vera Southgate's Planning for Reading series is in three volumes: (1) *Children Who Do Read*, (2) *Reading: teaching for learning*, (3) *Reading for Information* (Macmillan Ed, 1984) which are aimed at teachers and students, pressing the point that they are not only teaching children to read but are attempting to make the children into *readers* by technique, motivation and enjoyment.

● *Promoting and sharing reading*: Helen Arnold, *Listening to Children Reading* (Hodder & Stoughton, 1986) promotes the importance of reading, while Elizabeth Wilson's *The Thoughtful Reader in the Primary School* (Hodder & Stoughton, 1983) and Ann D. Carlson's *Early Childhood Literature Sharing Programmes in Libraries* (Hampden, Conn. Shoestring Press, 1985) are concerned with widening and deepening the reading experience.

Roger Morgan's *Helping Children Read; the paired reading handbook* (Methuen, 1986) describes the formalized linking of a child with an adult whether teacher or parent, to provide the one-to-one help which many children do not get at home.

Jim Trelease in his eminently readable *The Read-Aloud Handbook* (Penguin 1984), makes the case for shared reading in a more natural state, while Nancy Polette and M. Hamilton look at *Exploring Books With Gifted Children* (New York, Libraries Unlimited, 1980).

● *Research into books and reading in school*: is brought into focus in Florence Davies's *Books in the School Curriculum; a compilation and review of research relating to voluntary and intensive reading*, (EPC and

NBL, 1986), with 433 pages of interesting and useful information. Similarly, Jennie Ingham's report on the Bradford Book Flood Experiment in *Books and Reading Development* (Heinemann/BNB, 1981) provides a mass of detailed findings.

- *Research into minority group needs*: is exemplified by Pirkko Elliott's report number 6, *Library Needs of Children Attending Self-Help Mother-Tongue Schools in London* (London School of Librarianship, Polytechnic of North London, 1981) which despite the title, is more concerned with book needs.

  The background to the Reading Materials for Minority Groups Project at Middlesex Polytechnic is shown in video and pamphlet in Jennie Ingham's *Telling Tales Together* (Cadmean Trust, 1986).

- *Miscellaneous works related to children's books in education include*: Vivien Griffiths, *Primer of Book Selection Policy and Practice in Both School and Public Libraries* (Library Association Youth Libraries Group 1983).

  Peter Kennerly, *Running a School Bookshop; theory and practice* (Ward Lock Educational, 1978); Donald Fry, *Children Talk About Books; seeing themselves as readers* (Milton Keynes, Open University, 1985); Peggy Heeks, *Choosing and Using Books in the First School* (Macmillan Educational, 1984); Eileen Colwell, *Storytelling* (Bodley Head, 1980) from the pen of the world-famous exponent of storytelling.

Periodicals

Most countries have at least one vehicle for publishing views or reviews of children's books and those who work with children and books are usually avid readers of such journals. Periodical publications can be divided into the following sections:

- *Literary journals*: such as *Signal, approaches to children's books*, edited by Nancy Chambers, quarterly from Thimble Press, and *Children's Literature in Education*, an international quarterly with an Anglo-American editorial board, from IBIS Information Services Ltd.
- *Journals with critical articles and review sections*: such as *Hornbook Magazine* edited bi-monthly from Boston Massachusetts; *Top of the News*, produced monthly by the Children's Services Division of the American Library Association in Chicago, Illinois; the international journal *Bookbird* issued by the International Board on Books for Young People (IBBY) and the International Institute for Children's Literature and Reading Research in Vienna, Austria, quarterly and edited by Dr Lucia Binder; *The Children's Literature Association Quarterly* edited by Dr Ruth McDonald at the Department of English, Northeastern University, Boston Mass.

  Dragon's Tale, a journal about Welsh children's literature from the University of Aberystwyth in Wales and *Bookquest* from the Literacy Centre of the Faculty of Educational Studies at Brighton Polytechnic are further British examples; while two Australian journals in this category are *Orana* quarterly from Riverwood New South Wales and *Reading Time*, the major children's literature journal.
- *Journals covering children's literature and librarianship or education*: such as *The International Review of Children's Literature and Librarianship*, issued three times a year, edited by Margaret Kinnell and published by Taylor Graham Publishing, London; the American journal *School Library Journal*, issued monthly; Britain's *School Librarian*, issued quarterly by the School Library Association; the Australian *Review*,

issued quarterly by the School Libraries Branch of the Education Department of South Australia; *Books for Keeps*, issued six times a year by the School Bookshop Association in London; *The Use of English*, a quarterly journal; *Reading*, the quarterly journal of the International Reading Association; and the *Emergency Librarian*, from Dyad Services in Ontario, Canada.

● *Review journals specifically concerned with reviewing children's books*: English-language examples include *Growing Point*, edited by Margarey Fisher in nine issues a year; *Junior Bookshelf* in six issues a year; *Books For Your Children*, a magazine for parents, published quarterly. *The Bulletin of the Center for Children's Books* is a monthly publication from Chicago; *Children's Books* is under the auspices of the British Council's *British Book News* and publishes quarterly a useful journal with a large quantity of reviews and review articles.

● *Book supplements*: are exemplified in the quarterly supplements on children's books in the *Times Literary Supplement* and the regular reviews in the *Times Educational Supplement*. National newspapers in many countries have regular or occasional sections on children's books, as do women's magazines and general periodicals.

● *Individual libraries, schools and organizations*: also produce their own journals or review media, usually for local use.

● *Journals in non-English language countries*: for example *Barn och Kultur* in Sweden, *Buch und Bibliothek* in West Germany, *Detskaya Literatura*, in the USSR, *Parapara* in Venezuela, and *En Nu Over Jeugdliteratuur* from The Hague, Netherlands.

Abstracts

These can take several forms and cover general or specific aspects of the children's book world. Perhaps the most specific internationally is *Children's Literature Abstracts* edited by Colin Ray for IFLA quarterly, and covering books, pamphlets and journal articles, with an annual index, accessing about seventy journals from many countries.

Two American works abstract reviews of children's books, *Book Review Digest*, published by Wilson ten times a year, containing reviews of books published in the USA and reviewed in the past one-and-a-half years, and *Children's Literature Review* published by Gale of Detroit twice a year, containing excerpts from reviews and critical commentary.

Of the several general abstracting works which include in their coverage aspects of children's literature and reading, three examples are: *Library and Information Science Abstracts* (LISA) provided by Library Association Publishing in Britain; *Library Literature*, provided by H. W. Wilson in the USA, both of which cover a wide variety of the world's professional librarianship periodical literature; and the more general abstract *British Humanities Index*, published by the Library Association in the UK in which articles are abstracted from a wide range of general, educational and literary journals.

Theses and surveys

The considerable amount of research being undertaken by students of children's literature at all levels in many countries is not well documented nor as available as it should be, so that any evidence of its existence is welcome.

In addition to general works such as the annual *Index to Theses* (London, ASLIB) there are specialist sources such as *Radials Bulletin*, research and development, information and library science, published twice a year by Library Association Publishing; Peter Hunt's *Children's Book Research in Britain*, research in British institutions of higher education on children's books and related subjects (Cardiff, UWIST); *Phaedrus*, an international journal of children's literature research, edited by James Fraser in Marblehead, Mass.

Individuals working in schools or libraries often survey the reading needs and interests of the children and such small-scale local identification is valuable. On a larger scale, surveys indicate the commonality of much of children's reading across national boundaries in terms of genre and age grouping, though titles within the genres may differ between countries. Some examples of published surveys now follow:

Bird, Jean, *Young Teenage Reading Habits; a study of the Bookmaster Scheme*, (The British Library, 1982).

Camden Libraries and Arts Department, *Report of the Working Group on Library Provision for Teenagers*, (London Borough of Camden, 1983).

Dunster, June, *Early Teenage Reading; a reading survey of 13, 14 and 15 year olds*, (Dorset County Library, 1984).

Fasick, Adele M. *Current Research on the Reading Interests of Young People in North America*, (IFLA, 1984).

Ingham, Jennie, *Books and Reading Development; the Bradford Book Flood Experiment*, (Heinemann, 1981).

Whitehead, Frank, *Children and Their Books; a national survey*, (Macmillan, 1977).

Reference works

From the mass of reference books that can be used to dip into for specific information only a sample can be included here:

Carpenter, Humphrey and Prichard, Mairi, *The Oxford Companion to Children's Literature*, (OUP, 1984), is a useful start despite the many omissions.

Kirkpatrick, D. L., ed., *Twentieth Century Children's Writers* (Macmillan, 1984), contains signed articles with bibliographies for each entry.

Children's Book Council, *Children's Books; awards and prizes*, (N. Y. Children's Book Council, 1986), lists the world's awards.

Maissen, Lena, ed., *International Directory of Children's Literature Specialists* (Saur, 1986) which does not include British specialists.

Morris, Helen, *The New Where's That Poem?*, (Blackwell, 1986), a useful guide to identifying the source of an anthologized poem.

Chandler, Nicholas, *The Pauper's Poetry Index; thematic index to cheaper poetry books*, (Knowlsley Leisure Services Libraries Division), with a junior and senior division of poems.

Smyth, Margaret, *Picture Book Index*, (AAL Publishing, 1987), for locating illustrations by subject content.

Lima, Carolyn W., *A–Zoo: Subject Access to Children's Picture Books* (Bowker, 2nd rev. ed., 1985) a much larger work.

Sequels, vol. 2, Junior Books, (AAL Publishing, 7th ed., 1987).

Periodical List, a list of about sixty periodicals concerned with children's books, (Centre for Children's Books, The Book Trust, 1986).

Miscellaneous

There are many such items throughout the world – papers presented at conferences, reports, surveys, lists, publicity leaflets, guides to libraries and institutions concerned with children and a wide range of children's and youth books in school and society. Guides to using books in class projects; aids to book selection for the gifted through to the handicapped, information for teachers, parents and librarians – all too numerous to be listed in this book. Much is only of local use, some is ephemeral, but their presence is indicated here as a part of the mass of material that can be labelled 'bibliographical sources'.

CHAPTER ELEVEN

Promoting Children's Books

Publicity, public relations, promotions, advertising, exhibiting, display, marketing strategies, are all words used to describe the means by which those who have children's books attempt to get them to the knowledge of, and into the hands of, children and adults.

Apart from the obvious commercial considerations the need to promote children's books raises at least two questions: why promote children's literature and how can children's literature be promoted?

Benefit to the child reader

- The child is exposed through reading, to the possibility of development of the following: the thought processes, the imagination, the intellect, vocabulary, language, social and emotional stimulation, knowledge, mental and visual perception.
- Through books the child has access to society's thoughts and experiences, and through the skills of reading the child can take part in the practical demands placed on a member of a literate society, for example, reading notices, instructions, official forms. Both aspects set firm foundations for the future adult.
- Children are unlikely to see the full range of children's books unless it is brought to their attention by one means or another, and unlikely to find the particular books required unless help is available.

Benefit to the adult users of children's books

Promotion is necessary to inform adults who need children's books for their own purposes or for use with children. The majority of adults are parents selecting with or on behalf of their children, and teachers selecting for library purposes or for class use. Children's book people needing books for study and research purposes are frequent users of various kinds of library or collection. But within a community there are many adults and organizations concerned with children, and the promotion of children's books to them can be of benefit to the children they serve.

It often comes as a surprise to individuals and organizations who have a particular professional or commercial concern for children, that there are large numbers of other individuals and organizations who are involved with the use of children's books in their particular specialism, thus a list of the kinds of groups or places in the community in which children's books *are* involved may be helpful to publishers, booksellers, librarians, teachers and others who work with or on behalf of children and young people:

Public Libraries
Schools and colleges of further education
Playgroups and nursery schools
Guides, scouts, brownies and so on
Women's organizations
Probation offices (for delinquent youth)
Toy libraries
Societies for handicapped children
Community relations groups
Family reading schemes
Adult and baby clubs and clinics
Hospital and home tutors
Hospitals: patient service and therapy

Prisons and detention centres
Field study centres
Tufty clubs (road safety for children)
Nursery nurses' courses
Child assessment centres
Colleges of education
Colleges of librarianship
Social services' departments
Residential care associations
Bookshops
Youth clubs
Adventure playground supervisors
Youth workers
Pressure groups
Careers officers
Summer play schemes
Local children's book groups
Teachers centres
Local history societies
Museum services
Ethnic language schools
Various educational bodies such as curriculum development centres, school library associations, teaching trade unions and parent/teacher associations

Promotion to, and by, each of these is obviously a major possibility and needs to be exploited.

Promotion via libraries

Where the library is a public library, a school library or a specialist collection, it is wasteful if the books are on the shelves unused or little used. Highlighting kinds of book by one means or another will bring them to the attention of those in the library. Promotion outside the library will

275

inform the wider community. This is likely to make the books cost-effective and will, therefore, indicate to those who provide the book funds that the money is well spent and that more money or at least a continuation of funds, is worthwhile.

The library *is* display; the way it is arranged, the categorization of books on the shelves, the shelf labels and tier guides. Some public and school libraries (and book-shops) display the children's books stock by broad age category, for example: babies and pre-school, picture books, beginning reader, younger reader, older reader, teenage, young adult. Others use the main fiction genres such as animal stories, contemporary themes, fairy tales, myths and legends, family, fantasy and magic, ghost and horror stories, humour, mystery and adventure, school stories, science fiction, short stories, stories of the past, teenage and young adult. Yet others arrange children's fiction alphabetically by author, some also adding a pictogram sticker to each book to identify the broad genre content.

Non-fiction is similarly a form of display, exhibiting the range of subjects in some kind of order, normally in Dewey classification order, but sometimes colour-coded or arranged by broad subject theme. Many also differentiate between hardback and paperback format.

Although front facing display is the best and most attractive, space often precludes more than a small proportion of stock being exhibited in this way. Teenage libraries and displays of picture book 'flats' are most often able to use this method.

Librarians are aware of the need to promote and to offer a wide range of activities and events. The following list gives examples of some methods employed:

● Display of books, periodicals, pictures, toys, games

and other materials extracted from the stock in order to publicize its existence or to back up a topical event or a study theme.

- Library guiding by shelf labels, tier guides, location guides, wall charts, posters, use of the catalogue, notices and so on to facilitate ease of access to the books.
- Booklists of new acquisitions, for age or interest groups and for school projects, to enable children (or adults) to know what is available in the library in those areas.
- Library instruction on what is in the library, how to find it, how to use it and how to get the most out of books now and in the future.
- Children's library magazine, to provide a vehicle for children's own creative writing and to give book and library news.
- Storytelling, to introduce to the children books, excerpts, poems and pictures that they might not otherwise read or see; to whet the appetite for reading; to provide a stimulus for developing the skill of listening; adding to vocabulary, imaginative experience and knowledge; aiding identification; offering a valuable group experience of books.
- Library reading clubs, some provide lists of books to be read, towards a badge or star or other reward; some are family schemes where parents and children and librarian read a specific book together and discuss it; some are aimed at particular kinds of books as with the Science Fiction Club or the Poetry Club organized by some libraries.
- Activities in the library, such as art hobby groups, talks by specialists, brains trusts and quizzes, film shows, handicraft hours, concerts and music sessions, puppet groups, competitions, are all designed to

277

interest the reader on a wider scale.

- Visits to the local library by classes of school children from local schools, both to introduce them to the library service and to choose books.
- Parent/child clubs, in which pre-school children and their parents, or ethnic groups read and talk and play.
- Paperback and swap shops, whereby children bring their own finished or unwanted books and exchange (or swap) them for something different, from the shelf set aside for this purpose.
- A school bookshop or other bookselling agency.
- Parents' bookshelf in school or public library.
- Time in school to read for pleasure.
- Reading week in which authors, publishers, printers, booksellers and so on describe their work, and reading is encouraged.
- Holiday programmes in the library and outside.
- Advice to individual children and adults.

Specific promotion activities in the community

- Through liaison with all organizations and groups concerned with children, by publicity, public relations and provision of books and advice.
- Talking about books to children in school, in youth clubs and other organizations where children and young people are.
- Talking about books to adults in their organizations and their conferences and courses.
- Storytelling in public places, possibly using bus, boat, or train for book activities, where appropriate, and mobile libraries with generators for film shows.
- Organizing displays of books at local festivals, fairs and shows.
- Using the local press, radio and television and any

other communication media locally to promote books and libraries.

Some library services take part in the National Children's Book Week activities for which the Book Trust produces a *Children's Book Week Handbook*, about fifty pages of ideas on publicity, fund-raising, bookselling and author visits.

Many hold regular promotional events such as Hertfordshire's Sixth-Form Reading Festivals and its Fiction Weeks (for adult and children's fiction).

Some have personnel dedicated to promotion such as Bradford's Children's Book Promotions Librarians, Hampshire's Challenge Team (going into schools) and the publicity/promotions/publications teams in many library authorities in Britain.

School library services employ a variety of means to promote books in schools and a recent example is the launch of a secondary schools mobile book exhibition in Hampshire which visits schools throughout the country, in addition to the normal schools library service.

Promotion of children's books in libraries is important because the very existence of the library is vital. It provides:

- A link with the whole of human knowledge and experience
- An opportunity for self-education or to complement school education
- Availability of choice
- A place and a time to read voluntarily
- A loan facility
- A community focal point
- Enjoyment and therefore motivation to read more

Librarians must meet with teachers, writers, publishers,

booksellers and educationalists to give the widest possible publicity to the need for books and related materials for children and the need for bibliographic help for those attempting to provide a book service for children.

Between them they can point to the need for national coordination and promotion of children's book services and to the importance of coordination at all levels within a country.

Such meetings can be arranged in the form of conferences, one-day schools, workshops, committees, or informal invitations to discussion. They should not only be the opportunity to share views and information and experiences but also an occasion for creating or reinforcing a policy, planning a course of action, encouraging translation and the creation of indigenous children's books.

They can be sponsored by local members of international groups such as the International Federation of Library Associations (IFLA) or the International Board on Books for Young People (IBBY), or the Regional Book Development Centres of Unesco, or the British Council.

Meetings can be arranged by national groups such as the Library Association or the School Library Association or national book organizations; or by educational institutions such as schools of librarianship or schools of education for teachers. Training officers in individual library systems or educational authorities can include courses on children's books in their in-service programmes. Enthusiastic individuals in the world of children's books may call together interested people.

Promotion of books in schools

The study of *Books in the School Curriculum*[1] compiled by Florence Davies for the Educational Publishers Council indicated that much more was needed in schools in the way of promoting books 'as an intrinsic source of enjoyment and pleasure' and as 'a resource for learning', encouraging 'extensive and voluntary reading' of fiction and special interest books while cultivating 'effective, intensive reading'.

Promotion by allowing children to *read* is in its infancy in schools, more time being spent on learning *how* to read in the primary school and in analysing books for study in the secondary school.

The use of book boxes, pre-selected by experts is common, for example: Scholastic's picture books for early readers and fiction for five to seven-year-olds. Books for Students Kaleidoscope boxes selected by Cliff Moon, Judith Elkin, and others, and the Puffin Story Corner with four infant collections.

The acronym USSR, uninterrupted sustained silent reading, is gathering support, evidenced in one project in Australia entitled DEAR, drop everything and read.

School library promotion to pupils and staff is vital and most books on school librarianship teach this subject. The advantages of school bookshops are made clear in Peter Kennerley's discussion on teenage reading and school bookshops in his book *The School Bookshop*[2] and in the section on bookselling here.

Bookselling

Although the Booksellers' Association and the Book Marketing Council have a brief that includes promotion of children's books, the average bookseller is faced with considerable difficulty in doing more than window display and general advertising. Shortage of space for the necessary bookstock and for the customer, limited window display space, few staff and fewer with knowledge of children's books, means that only the specialist children's book shops can promote by display, by posters, competitions, events and advice, on a regular basis.

As the majority of children are either not living anywhere near a bookshop, or are but never go into it, promotion is the only way to improve the low percentage of booksales of children's books, by better shelving, shelf labelling, stock arrangement, market research, liaison with local schools and public libraries, presence at fairs and markets, parents' events and organization's meetings. The problem of time, staff and appropriate stock are part of the general need for improvement in British bookselling.

An example of the Book Marketing Council's efforts is the annual Readathon, a sponsored reading event not only to promote reading but also to aid a selected charity. Other campaigns have included Teen Read and Best Books For Babies.

Bookshops in schools are an answer to the dearth of bookshops in the community and many teachers or librarians in primary and secondary schools administer what is usually a lockable bookcase of paperback fiction and non-fiction in one or other of several schemes available. The School Bookshop Association, a national organization, offers advice and help, publication and the magazine *Books For Keeps*. The little brochure answers the questions 'Why School Bookshops?' thus:

> School bookshops can play a vital role in getting children into the habit of buying books – essential if they are to become regular readers: they help to break through the 'book barrier' – the idea that many children have that books are solemn objects associated with school subjects; they introduce children to the pleasure of choosing, buying and owning their own books; they bring children into contact with a wide range of books they would not normally encounter; they have an advantage over the ordinary bookshop (even if there is one in the area) in that they can be

precisely geared to the needs of children; and finally they can do much to foster home/school relationships and offer a practical way to involve parents in school life.

Some schools use purchase schemes from Bookwise or Bookworm, others have a sale or return arrangement with a local bookshop. Others have slotted into the W. H. Smith school bookshop scheme while yet others prefer the Scholastic scheme, choosing from a catalogue.

The mail-order bookclubs are mentioned in the chapter on publishing and bookselling, as is bookselling in public libraries.

In publishing, library supply bookselling and retail bookselling the production and distribution of catalogues is common, promoting mainly to people who are already committed to books and reading. More needs to be done to catch the unaware.

Home libraries

In some countries there has been a system of small libraries often in the absence of a widespread system of public libraries. Known as Home Libraries in, for example Zimbabwe (see Chapter Four) and bunko in Japan (originally for children who had returned to Japan after living abroad with their parents, and who could read only in their foreign language), they are intended to draw together adults and children in a community, share communally a stock of children's books, and promote them by activities, storytelling, drama and talks. The getting together of parents and teachers in a community is seen in Britain in the number of organizations concerned with children and books.

Organizations and their exhibitions

The Federation of Children's Book Groups, the School Library Association, the Youth Libraries Group, the School Libraries Group, the Children's Book Circle, the Children's Book Section and numerous other associations of people interested in children's books make efforts to promote them and to keep themselves informed. Along with publishers' exhibitions and those of the many organizations, children's books are promoted at festivals, fairs, book weeks, conferences and seminars, courses and trade fairs, to both children and adults.

Promotion starts with parents in the home and continues through school, through the organizations to which the child belongs, through the facilities in the community, whether they be self-help organizations, public libraries or commercial bookselling outlets.

These efforts must be underpinned by the promotional work of the book trade and its official associations, to form a cooperative network involved in general and specific activities, national and local, for example:

- Meetings of all interested in children and books
- Exhibitions of children's books, illustrations and related materials, general, thematic, or for the needs of special ages, conditions or groups of children
- Creation of children's libraries in public libraries, schools, playgroups, community centres, or book box services or travelling libraries
- Establishment of regional and national libraries of children's books, and national centres of study and research into children's books
- Liaison with organizations and individuals for the specific furtherance of knowledge and services
- Translation of children's books into national or local vernacular

- Use of radio, television and press for publicity and information about children's books
- Organization of national book weeks

All the suggestions listed are activities that are carried out in many countries but a decision on which to employ for most effective promotion of books rests on a number of factors, such as the nature of the local community, geographical distribution of the population, transport facilities, availability of electricity and equipment, the age range of children in the locality, school and organization links. These factors would be taken into consideration in the forward planning along with time, space, bookstock, personnel and cost factors.

The basic requirements without which promotion cannot take place, are an adequate range and number of books, and enthusiastic and knowledgeable book people.

These factors express the whole concept of the children's book world: encouragement to writers and artists to create children's books, encouragement to make the books available, and encouragement to children to read and enjoy.

References

1 Florence Davies, *Books in the School Curriculum*. Educational Publishers Council and National Book League, 1986
2 Peter Kennerley. *Running a School Bookshop; theory and practice*. Ward Lock Ed. 1978

Further reading

Aitken, David and Kearney, Anthony. 'Children's books in teacher education: at St. Martin's College, Lancaster'.

Signal, 49, Jan. 1986, pp. 44–51

Arnold, Helen. *Listening to Children Reading*. Hodder & Stoughton, 1986

Butler, Dorothy. *Babies Need Books*. Bodley Head, 1980

Butler, Dorothy and Clay, Marie. *Reading Begins at Home*. Heinemann Educational, 1979

Carlson, Ann D. *Early Childhood Literature Sharing Programs in Libraries*. Hamden, Conn. Shoestring Press, 1985

Chambers, Aidan. *Introducing Books to Children*, Heinemann, 1983, 2nd edn

Colwell, Eileen. *Storytelling*. Bodley Head, 1980

Gawith, Gwen. *Library Alive; promoting reading and research in the school library*. A & C Black, 1987

Hall, Nigel. *The Emergence of Literacy*. Hodder & Stoughton, 1987

Marshall, Margaret R. 'Library services to young adults'. *IFLA Journal*, July 1986, no.2, pp. 5–25

Marshall, Margaret R. *Public Library Services to Teenagers in Britain*. British Library, 1982

Neumayer, Peter F. 'Children's literature as it is taught in university English Departments in USA'. *Bookbird*, 4, 1985, pp. 4–11

Polette, Nancy and Hamlin, Marjorie. *Exploring Books with Gifted Children*. New York, Libraries Unlimited, 1980

Trelease, Jim. *The Read-Aloud Handbook*. Penguin, 1984

Wertheimer, Leonard (ed.), 'Library services to ethno-cultural minorities'. *Library Trends*, Fall 29 (2), 1980, whole issue.

Wilson, Elizabeth. *The Thoughtful Reader in the Primary School*. Hodder & Stoughton, 1983

Bibliography

List of Books Referred to in the Text

Adult Literacy and Basic Skills Unit. *Resources; a guide to materials in adult literacy and basic skills*. ALBSU, 1986, 0 906509696

Aiken, Joan. *The way to write for children*. Elm Tree Books, 1982, 0241 10746 6

Alderson, Brian. *Sing a song for sixpence; the English picture book tradition and Randolph Caldecott*. C.U.P., 1986, 0 521 33179 X, pb 0521 33760 7

Aliki. *How a book is made*. Bodley Head, 1986, 0 370 310039

Arnold, Helen. *Listening to children reading*. Hodder & Stoughton, 1986, 0 340 26298 2

Avery, Gillian. *Childhood's pattern; a study of the heroes and heroines of children's fiction 1770–1950*. Hodder & Stoughton, 1975, 0 340 16945 1

Baker, Carol. *Reading through play; the easy way to teach your child*. Macdonald, 1980, 0 356 07048 4

Barker, Keith. *In the realms of gold; the story of the Carnegie Medal*. Julia MacRae Books/Youth Libraries Group, 1986, 086203 260 1

Barr, John. *Illustrated children's books*. British Library, 1986, 0 7123 0098 8

Bettelheim, Bruno. *The uses of enchantment; the meaning and importance of fairy tales*. Penguin, 1978, 0 14 0 55135 2

Bienstock, June K. and Anolik, Ruth B. *Careers in fact and fiction*. Chicago, American Library Association, 1985, 0 8389 04246

Bird, Jean. *Young teenage reading habits; a study of the*

Bookmaster scheme. British Library, 1982, 0 71233007 0

Blyton, Enid. *The story of my life*. Grafton, 1986,
0 246 12795 3

Bratton, J. S. *The impact of Victorian children's fiction*.
Croom Helm, 1981, 0 85664 777 2

Brogan, Hugh. *The Life of Arthur Ransome*. Cape, 1984,
0 224 02010 2

Bull, Angela. *Noel Streatfeild; a biography*. Collins, 1984,
0 00 195044 4

Butler, Dorothy. *Babies need books*. Bodley Head, 1980,
0 370 30151 X and Penguin, 1980, 014 02 2434 3

— *Five to eight; the vital years of reading*. Bodley Head,
1986, 0 370 30672 4

Butler, Dorothy and Clay, Marie. *Reading begins at home*.
Heinemann Educational, 1979, 0 86863 2678

Butler, Francella, *et al.*, ed. *Children's literature*; annual of
the Modern Language Association Division on Children's
Literature and the Children's Literature Association.
Yale University Press, 1980 to date.

Cadogan, Mary and Craig, Patricia. *You're a brick, Angela;
the girls' story 1839–1985*. Gollancz, 1986, 0 575 03825 X

Carlsen, Robert. *Books and the teenage reader*. Harper &
Row, 1980, 0 06 010626 3

Carlson, Ann D. *Early childhood literature sharing
programs in libraries*. Hamden, Conn., Shoestring Press,
1985, 0 208 02068 3

Carpenter, Humphrey. *Secret Gardens; the Golden Age of
children's literature*. Allen & Unwin, 1985

Carpenter, Humphrey and Prichard, Mari. *The Oxford
companion to children's literature*. O.U.P., 1984,
019211582 0

Cass, Joan. *Literature and the young child*. Longman, 2nd.
ed., 1984, 0 582 362121

Chambers, Aidan. *Booktalk; occasional writing on literature
and children*. Bodley Head, 1985, 0 370 308581

— *Introducing books to children*. Heinemann, 2nd. ed.,
1973, 0 435 89805

— *Plays for young people to read and perform*. Stroud,

Thimble Press, 1982, 0 903355 10 8 (Signal Bookguide)

Chambers, Nancy, ed. *The Signal approach to children's books*. Kestrel, 1980, 0 7226 5641 6

Chandler, Nicholas. *The pauper's poetry index: thematic index to cheaper poetry books*. Knowsley Leisure Services Libraries Division, 1986

Children's Book Council. *Children's books: awards and prizes*. New York, CBC, 8th ed., 1986, 0 933 63300 9

Children's Books' Historical Society. *Cataloguing of early children's books; a guide for collectors*. Children's Books Historical Society, 1979, 0 9507038 0 X

Colwell, Eileen. *Storytelling*. Bodley Head, 1980, 0 370 30228 1

Commire, Anne, ed. *Something about the author; autobiography series*. Vol.2, Detroit, Gale Research, 1986, 0 8103 44505

Cott, Jonathan. *Pipers at the gates of dawn; the wisdom of children's literature*. Viking, 1984, 0 670 80003 1

Cott, Jonathan, ed. *Victorian color picture books*. Allen Lane, 1984, 0 7139 1703 2

Creative writing and publishing for children in Africa today; proceedings of the seminar held in Sierra Leone, 1983. Gloria Dillsworth, Sierra Leone Library Board, Freetown, Sierra Leone, 1984

Dahl, Roald. *Boy*. Cape, 1984, 0 224 02985 1

Darton, F. J. Harvey. *Children's books in England; five centuries of social life*. 3rd edn, revised by Brian Alderson, C.U.P., 1982, 0 521 24020 4

Davies, Anne Marie and Hedge, Ann. *Racism in children's books*. Writers and Readers, 1985, 0 86316 091 3

Davies, Florence. *Books in the school curriculum; a compilation and review of research relating to voluntary and intensive reading*. Educational Publishers Council and National Book League, 1986, 0 85386 111 0

Dunster, June. *Early teenage reading; a reading survey of 13, 14 and 15 year olds in Ferndown and West Moors*. England, Dorset County Library, 1984, 0 85216 3606

Educational Publishers Council. *Sex stereotyping in school and children's books*. EPC, 1981, 6pp., 0 85386074 2

Educational Publishers Council. *Publishing for a multi-cultural society* EPC, 1983, 0 853 86077 7

Edwards, Malcolm and Holdstock, Robert. *Realms of fantasy*. Doubleday, 1983, 0 385 18888 9

Egoff, Sheila. *Only connect; readings on children's literature*. O.U.P., 2nd edn, 1980, 0 19 540309 6

Elkin, Judith (comp.). *The Books for Keeps guide to children's books for a multi-cultural society; 0–7*. Books For Keeps, 1986, 0 269 7785

Elliott, Pirkko. *Library needs of children attending self-help mother-tongue schools in London*. School of Librarianship, Polytechnic of North London, 1981, 0 900639 19 9 (Research Report no. 6)

Ellis, Alec. *A history of children's reading and literature*. Pergamon, 1968, 008 012 586 7

Ellis, Peter and Williams, Piers. *By Jove, Biggles. The Life of Captain W. E. Johns*. W. H. Allen, 1981, 0 491 02755 3

Fasdick, Adele M. *Current research on the reading interests of young people in North America*. Paper presented to the International Federation of Library Associations General Conference, Chicago, 1985.

Fisher, Margery. *The bright face of danger; an exploration of the adventure story*. Hodder & Stoughton, 1986, 0 340 229934

— *Classics for children and young people*. Stroud, Thimble Press, 1986, 0 903355 20 5 (Signal Bookguide)

— *Intent upon reading; a critical appraisal of modern fiction for children*. Brockhampton, 1964 (O/P)

Fox, Geoff *et al*. *Writers, critics and children; articles from Children's Literature in Education*. Heinemann Educational, 1976, 0 435 18303 6

Fry, Donald. *Children talk about books; seeing themselves as readers*. Milton Keynes, Open University Press, 1985, 0 335 15032 2

Gawith, Gwen. *Library alive; promoting reading and research in the school library*. A. and C. Black, 1987, 0 7136 2900 2

Goldsmith, Evelyn. *Research into illustration; approach and review*. C.U.P. 1984, 0 521 25674 7

Green, Peter. *Beyond the wild wood; the world of Kenneth Grahame: author of the Wind in the Willows*. Webb & Bower, 1982, 0 906671 44 2

Griffiths, Vivien. *Primer of book selection policy and practice in both school and public libraries*. Library Association/Youth Libraries Group, 1983, 0 946581 01 0

Hall, Nigel. *The emergence of literacy*. Hodder & Stoughton/ UKRA, 1987, 0 340 402164

Hasan, Abul. *The book in multilingual countries*. Unesco, 1978, 92 3 101573 7 (Report no. 82 in Reports and Papers on Mass Communication)

Haviland, Virginia, ed. *Children's literature; views and reviews*. Bodley Head, 1973, 0370 01595 9

Heather, Pauline. *Young people's reading; a study of the leisure reading of 13–15 year olds*. Sheffield, Centre for Research on User Studies, 1981 (CRUS Occasional Paper, no. 6)

Heeks, Peggy. *Choosing and using books in the first school*. Macmillan Educational, 1981, 0 333 32645 8

Hiner, Mark. *Paper engineering for pop-up books and cards*. Tarquin Publications, 1985

ILEA, Learning Resources Branch. *Anti-sexist resources guide*. Inner London Education Authority, 1984

Ingham, Jennie. *Books and reading development; the Bradford Book Flood Experiment*. Heinemann/BNB, 1981, 0435 10450 0

Ingham, Jennie and Brown, Valerie. *The state of reading; a report of the research carried out for the Educational Publishers Council*. EPC/NBL, 1986, 0 85386 112 9

International Institute for Children's Literature, Osaka. *International co-operation and networking*; the proceedings of the international conference on children's literature in Osaka 1986.

International Youth Library. *The white ravens; a selection of international children's and youth literature; annotated*

list of 350 recent children's books from 40 countries.
Munich, IYL, 1986

Kennerley, Peter. *Running a school bookshop; theory and
practice.* Ward Lock ed., 1978, 0 7062 37625

Kennerley, Peter. *Teenage reading.* Ward Lock edn, 1979,
0 7062 3889 3

Kirkpatrick, D. L., ed. *Twentieth century children's writers.*
Macmillan, 1984, 0333 247434

Klein, Gillian. *Reading into racism; bias in children's
literature and learning materials.* Routledge, 1985,
0 7102 01605

Lane, Margaret. *The tale of Beatrix Potter; a biography.*
Warne, rev. edn, 1985, 0 7232 32660

Lanes, Selma G. *The art of Maurice Sendak.* Bodley Head,
1981, 0 370 30386 5

Leeson, Robert. *Children's books and class society, past
and present.* Writers and Readers Publishing Co-operative,
1977, 0 904613 37 2

— *Reading and righting; the past, present and future of
fiction for the young.* Collins, 1985, 0 00 184413 X

Lima, Carolyn W. *A–Zoo: Subject access to children's
picture books.* Bowker, 2nd rev. edn, 1985, 08352 2134 2

McDowell, Myles. 'Fiction for children and adults; some
essential differences', in Fox, Geoff *et al.*, *Writers, critics
and children*, pp. 140–56

Mahoney, Bertha E. *Illustrators of children's books;
1744–1945.* Hornbook, 1947, later volumes edited by R.
Viguers and Lee Kingman

Marshall, Margaret R. 'Categorization in children's books'.
Unpublished research report for Children's Book Action
Group (BA/PA/LA), 1986

— *Handicapped children and books.* British National
Bibliography, 1986, 0 7123 3067 4 (Report no. 20)

— *Libraries and literature for teenagers.* Gower, 1975,
0 233 966048

— *Libraries and the handicapped child.* Gower, 1981,
0 23397299 4

— *Public library services to teenagers in Britain.* British

Library, 1982, 0 7123 3006 2 (Library and Information
Research Report no. 5)
— *Seeing clear; books and materials for the partially-
sighted child*. School Library Association, rev. edn, in
large print, 1985, 0 900641 45 2
— *See all, say all: a selection of books for the language-
deprived child*. IBBY British Section, 1985, 0 9508515 15
— *The Right Stuff*: books for the Young Adult
Collection. Library Association/Youth Libraries Group,
1987, 0 946 58106 1
Marshall, Margaret R., Simonis-Rupert, S. and Holst, S.
*Books for the mentally handicapped child and adult; a
guide to selection*. The Hague, International Federation of
Library Associations, 1983, 90 70916 010
Meek, Margaret. *The cool web; the pattern of children's
reading*. Bodley Head, 1977, 0 370 301447
— *Learning to read*. Bodley Head, 1982, 0 370 301 544
Michel, Andrée. *Down with stereotypes; eliminating sexism
from children's literature and school textbooks*. Unesco,
1986, English edn, 92 31023802
Milne, Christopher. *The enchanted places*. Eyre Methuen,
1974, 0 413 31710 2
Moon, Cliff and Raban, Bridie. *A question of reading*.
Macmillan Educational, rev. edn, 1980, 0 333 30429 2
Morgan, Roger. *Helping children read: the paired reading
handbook*. Methuen, 1986, 0 416 96540 7
Morris, Helen. *The new where's that poem?* Blackwell, 1986,
0631 139427
Morse, Brian. 'Poetry, children and Ted Hughes', in
Chambers, N. *Signal Approach to Children's Books*, pp.
109–25
Moss, Elaine. *Part of the pattern*. Bodley Head, 1986,
0 370 30 860 3
— *Picture books for young people 9–13*. Stroud, Thimble
Press, 1981, 0 90335515 9 (Signal Bookguide)
National Library for the Handicapped Child. *Catalogue of
library holdings 1986*. NLHC, 1986, 0 948664 00 2
Nottinghamshire County Youth Services. *Survey of reading*

material in youth clubs. Nottingham, Nottingham County Library, 1981

Orjasaeter, Tordis (comp.). *Books for language-retarded children; an annotated bibliography.* Unesco/IBBY, 1985, (Studies on Books and Reading No.20).

Patel, Bhadra and Allen, Jane. *A visible presence; black people living and working in Britain today.* National Book League, 1985, 0 85353 394 6

Philip, Neil. *A fine anger; a critical introduction to the work of Alan Garner.* Collins, 1981, 0 00 195043 6

Polette, Nancy and Hamilton, M. *Exploring books with gifted children.* New York, Libraries Unlimited, 1980, 0 87287 216 5

Quayle, Eric. *Early children's books; a collector's guide.* David & Charles, 1983, 0 7153 83078

Quicke, John. *Disability in modern children's fiction.* Croom Helm, 1984, 0 7099 2102 0

Quigley, Isabel. *The heirs of Tom Brown; the English school story.* O.U.P., 1984, 0 19 281404 4

Raddon, A. *Exploring cultural diversity; an annotated fiction list.* School Library Association, 1985, 0 900 641 444

Ray, Sheila. *The Blyton phenomenon; the controversy surrounding the world's most successful children's writer.* Deutsch, 1982, 0 233 97441 5

Redford, Rachel. *Hear to read; annotated list of audio-books.* NBL, 1986, 0 85353 4039

Rose, Jacqueline. *The case of Peter Pan: or the impossibility of children's fiction.* Macmillan, 1984, 0 333 31975 3

Salway, Lance. *Reading about children's books; an introductory guide to books about children's literature.* NBL, 1986, 0 85353 404 7

Saxby, Maurice. *A history of Australian children's literature.* 2 vols., Sydney, Wentworth, 1969

Saxby, Maurice, ed. *Through folklore to literature; papers presented at the Australian National Section of IBBY Conference on Children's Literature, Sydney, 1978.* IBBY Australia Publications, 1979, 0 90821 00 5

Scherf, Walter. *Lexikon der Zaubermarchen*. Stuttgart, Alfred Kroner Verlag, 1985

— *Die Herausfordering des Dämons: form und funktion grausiger Kindermärchen*. Saur, 1986, 3 598 10664 5

Scragg, J., ed. *Children's books of yesterday; a survey of 200 years of children's reading*; exhibition catalogue. Manchester, Rylands Library, University of Manchester, 1985, 0 86373 039 6

Shaw, John Mackay. *Childhood in poetry*. Florida State University Library, 5 vol. catalogue

Sheridan, E.M. *Sex stereotypes and reading: research strategies*. Newark, Delaware, International Reading Association, 1982

Shulevitz, Uri. *Writing with pictures; how to write and illustrate children's books*. New York, Watson-Guptill Publications, 1985, 0 8230 5940 5 (UK distributor: Phaidon).

Smyth, Margaret. *Picture book index*. A.A.L. Publishing, 1987, 0 900092 65 3

Southgate, Vera. *Reading; teaching for learning*. Macmillan Educational, 1984, 0 333 34696 3

Stones, Rosemary. *Miss Muffet fights back*. Penguin, 1983

Stones, Rosemary (comp.). *More to life than Mr. Right; stories for young feminists*. Piccadilly Press, 1985, 0 948826 61 7

Stones, Rosemary. *Pour out the cocoa, Janet; sexism in children's books*. Longman/Schools Council, 1983, 0 582 38895 3

Stoney, Barbara. *Enid Blyton; a biography*. Hodder & Stoughton, 1986, 0 340 39216 9

Sumsion, John. 'Public Lending Right in the UK', in *Writers and artists year book*. A. and C. Black, 1987 (and annually), pp. 431–7

— *Setting up public lending rights; a report to the Advisory Committee*. Stockton-on-Tees, Registrar of Public Lending Rights, 1984, 0 9509825 04

Sutcliff, Rosemary. *Blue remembered hills*. Bodley Head, 1983, 0 370 30940 5

Swinfen, Ann. *In defence of fantasy; a study of the genre in English and American literature since 1945*. Routledge & Kegan Paul, 1984, 0 7100 9525 2

Taylor, Bing and Braithwaite, Peter. *The good book guide to children's books*. Penguin, annually (eg. 1987) 0 14009750 3

Taylor, Judy. *Beatrix Potter; artist, storyteller and countrywoman*. Warne, 1986, 0 72323314 4

Townsend, John Rowe. 'Standards of criticism for children's literature', in Chambers, N. *The Signal approach to children's books*, pp. 193–207

— *A sounding of storytellers*. Kestrel, 1979, 0 7226 5599 1

— *Written for children; an outline of English language children's literature*. Viking Kestrel, 2nd rev. edn. 1983, 0 722 65466 9

Trease, Geoffrey. 'The historical novelist at work', in Fox, Geoff *et al.*, *Writers, critics and children*, pp. 39–51

Trelease, Jim. *The read-aloud handbook*. Penguin, 1984, 0 14.00 7049 4

Tucker, Nicholas. 'Books that frighten', in Haviland, V. *Children and literature*, pp. 104–9

— *Suitable for children? Controversies in children's literature*. Sussex University Press, 1976, 0 85621 048 X

— *The child and the book*. C.U.P., 1982, 0 521 27048 0

Unesco. *Statistical yearbook*. Annual

Uther, Hans-Jorg. *Katalog zur Volkserzahlung*. Saur, 1987, 3598 10669 6 2 vols. p. 1135

Waltham Forest Libraries and Arts Department. *Teenagers and libraries – a study in Waltham Forest*; Report of a working party. London, Waltham Forest, 1986

Waterland, Liz. *Read with me; an apprenticeship approach to reading*. Stroud, Thimble Press, 1985, 0 903355 175

Whitehead, Frank, ed. *Children and their books; a survey of children's reading interests*. Schools Council Project, Macmillan, 1977, 0 423 891200

Wilson, Elizabeth. *The thoughtful reader in the primary school*. Hodder & Stoughton, 1983, 0 340 26295 8

Wrightson, Patricia. When cultures meet; a writer's response, in Saxby, M. *Through folklore to literature*, pp. 187–202

Yates, Jessica. *Teenager to young adult; recent paperback fiction for 13 to 19 years*. SLA, 1986, 0 9 00641 47 9

Young Writers; annual compilation of winning entries to W. H. Smith Young Writers' competition

Zipes, Jack, ed. *Don't bet on the prince; contemporary feminist fairy tales in North America and England*. Gower, 1986, 0 566 00913 7

Periodical articles referred to in the text

Aiken, Joan. Interpreting the past, *Children's Literature in Education*, Summer 1985, pp. 67–83

Aiken, David and Kearney, Anthony. Children's books in teacher education at St. Martin's College, Lancaster, *Signal*, 49, Jan. 1986, pp. 44–51

Alderman, Belle. Australian research and studies in children's literature, *Reading Time*, 100, July 1986, pp. 27–9

Ashley, Bernard. TV reality – the dangers and the opportunities, *Books For Keeps*, March 1987, no. 43, pp. 16–17

Bagnall, Peter. Narnia revisited; The future of children's books and of the book trade, *The Bookseller*, no. 4194, 10 May 1986, pp. 1864–71

Bell, Anthea. Translating humour for children, *Bookbird*, 2, 1985, pp. 8–13

Byars, Betsy. Spinning straw into gold, *The School Librarian*, vol. 34, no. 1, March 1986, pp. 6–13

Carrington, Bruce and Short, Geoff. Comics: a medium for racism, *English in Education*, 18 (2), Summer 1984, pp. 10–14

Cianciolo, Patricia J. Internationalism of children's literature; trends in translation and dissemination, *Bookbird*, 1, 1984, pp. 5–14

Costanzo, W. Reading interactive fiction; implications of a new literary genre, *Educational Technology*, June 1986, pp. 31–6

Dickinson, Peter. Fantasy; the need for realism, *Children's Literature in Education*, 17 (1), 1986, pp. 39–51

Donelson, Ken. Almost thirteen years of book protests – now what?, *School Library Journal*, 31 (7), 1985, pp. 93–8

Epstein, Connie. A publisher's perspective, *Hornbook Magazine*, 62 (4), 1986, pp. 490–3

Giles, Alan. The new market for children's books; a closed shop for booksellers?, *The Bookseller*, 26 July 1986, pp. 354, 355, 357–8

Hannabus, Stuart. The child's eye; a literary viewpoint, *International Review of Children's Literature and Librarianship*, vol. 1, no. 3, Winter 1986, pp. 103–14

Harranth, Wolf. Some reflections on the criticism of translations, *Bookbird*, 2, 1985, pp. 4–8

Harrison, James. Reader/listener response to humor in children's books, *Canadian Children's Literature*, 44, 1986, pp. 25–32

Hazareesingh, Sandip. Racism and cultural identity; an Indian perspective, *Dragon's Teeth*, 24, 1986, pp. 4–10

Hodgkin, Marni. A personal philosophy of publishing for children, *Signal*, 46, Jan. 1985, pp. 44–59

Hughes, Shirley. Grand designs, *Books for Keeps*, 38, 1986, pp. 6–7

Hunt, Peter. Childist criticism, *Signal*, no. 43, Jan. 1984, pp. 42–58

Kalisa, B. G. An interview with noted African children's writer Remi Adedeji, *Bookbird*, 1, 1984, pp. 17–21

Macleod, Anne Scott. Censorship in children's literature, *Library Quarterly*, 53 (1), Jan. 1983, pp. 26–38

Marshall, Margaret R. Library services to young adults, *IFLA Journal*, July 1986, pp. 15–25

Meek, Margaret. Review, *International Review of Children's Literature and Librarianship*, vol. 1, no. 3, Winter 1986, pp. 118–19

Moss, Elaine. Picture books then and now, *Books For Keeps*, 38, 1986, pp. 4–5

Nettell, Stephanie. Bringing a sense of joy; an interview with Errol Le Cain, *Children's Books* (BBN), Sept. 1986, pp. 2–5

— Crossing barriers; an interview with Brian Wildsmith, *Children's Books* (BBN), March 1987, pp. 2–5

— Rehabilitating that rabbit, *Books For Keeps*, no. 44, May 1987, pp. 12–13

Neumayer, Peter F. Children's literature as it is taught in university English Departments in USA, *Bookbird*, 4, 1985, pp. 4–11

Newsround, *Library Association Record*, 89 (8), Aug. 1987, pp. 437–40

Nöstlinger, Christine. Acceptance speech for the 1984 Andersen Writer's Medal, *Bookbird*, 4, 1984, pp. 8–11

Prince, Alison. How's business, *Books for Your Children*, vol. 22, no. 1, Spring 1987, pp. 2–3

Reeder, Stephanie Owen. Sound the drums and clash the symbols, *Reading Time*, 97, Oct. 1985, pp. 14–23

Roll, Dusan. A preview of the Tenth Biennial of Illustration Bratislava-BIB 85, *Bookbird*, 1, 1985, pp. 53–6

Saxby, Maurice. The art of Patricia Wrightson and the illustrations of Robert Ingpen, *Bookbird*, 2, 1986, pp. 4–8

Schlager, Norma. Predicting children's choices in literature; a development approach, *Children's Literature in Education*, vol. 9, 1978, pp. 371–6

Schulz, Marianne. The role of illustration in children's literature, *Bookbird*, 3, 1985, pp. 15–17

Self, David. Queen Puffin. (Kaye Webb), *Times Educational Supplement*, 14 Nov. 1986, pp. 37 and 38

Southall, Ivan. Coat of many colours, *Reading Time*, 100, July 1986, pp. 38–40

Stops, Sue. How to bring children to books, *Books For Keeps*, 30 Jan. 1986, p. 8

Svensen, Asfrid. Opening windows on to unreality; some elements of the fantastic in Scandinavian children's literature, *International Review of Children's Literature and Librarianship*, vol. 2, no. 1, Spring 1987, pp. 1–9

Thomson, Pat. Anthologies; past, present and future, *Books For Keeps*, 37, 1986, pp. 4–9

Totemeyer, Andree-Jeanne. Social criticism in South African children's and youth literature, *Bookbird*, 2, 1986, pp. 9–21

Townsend, John Rowe. Children's author and surviving, *Books for Your Children*, 20 (3), 1985, pp. 8–9

Tucker, Nicholas. Games-books; the best-sellers, *New Society*, 23 May 1986, pp. 10–12

— Trends in school stories, *Children's Literature in Education*, no. 45, Summer 1982, pp. 79–83

Viewpoints on criticism; international perspectives, *Bookbird*, 3, 1984, pp. 8–18

Walsh, J. P. and Townsend, J. R. Writers and critics, *Hornbook Magazine*, Oct. 1982, 28 (1), pp. 498–504

Watson, James. Challenging assumptions; ideology and teenage fiction in today's global village, *International Review of Children's Literature and Librarianship*, vol. 1, no. 3, Winter 1986, pp. 65–71

Werner, Craig. A blind child's view of children's literature, *Children's Literature in Education*, 12, 1984, pp. 209–16

Wertheimer, Leonard, ed. Library services to ethno-cultural minorities, *Library Trends*, 29 (2), Autumn 1980, whole issue

Wettern, Arnold. International understanding through children's literature, *Bookbird*, 1, 1985, pp. 32–35

Whalley, Irene. The Cinderella story 1724–1919, *Signal*

Approach to Children's Books, pp. 14–155
Also
Books For Keeps, March 1981, no. 7: issue on humour
Books For Keeps, May 1986, no. 38, and May 1987, no. 44:
  issues on picture books
Reading Time, 100th issue, July 1986: devoted to the
  development of children's literature in Australia.

List of children's books referred to in the text

Adams, Douglas. *The Hitchhiker's Guide to the Galaxy*.
  Pan, 1979, 0330 25844 8
Adams, Pam. *A Book of Ghosts*. Child's Play, 1978,
  08595 3 028 0
Adams, Richard. *Watership Down*. Puffin, 1973,
  0 14 030601
Aesop's fables ed. Patricia Crampton. Dent, 1980,
  04606058 9
Agard, John. *Say it again Granny*. Bodley Head, 1986,
  0 370 30676 7
Ahlberg, Allan and Janet. *Each Peach Pear Plum*. Viking
  Kestrel, 1978, 0 670 28750 9
Ahlberg, Allan. *Mrs. Plug the Plumber*. Kestrel, 1980,
  0 7226 5659 9
Ahlberg, Janet and Ahlberg, Allan. *The Jolly Postman*.
  Heinemann, 1986, 0 434 92515 2
— *The Old Joke Book*. Viking Kestrel, 1978, 0 670 52273 2
— *Peepo!* Picture Puffin, 1983, 014 050384 6
Aiken, Joan. *The Kingdom Under the Sea*. Cape, 1971,
  0 224 61882 2
— *A Whisper in the Night*. Gollancz, 1982, 0 575 031050
— *The Wolves of Willoughby Chase*. Penguin, 1971,
  0 14 0303103
Alcock, Vivien. *The Cuckoo Sister*. Methuen, 1985,
  0 416 52210 6

Alcock, Vivien. *The Haunting of Cassie Palmer*.
  Methuen, 1980, 0146 89250 7
Alcott, L. M. *Little Women*. Collins, 1983, 0 00 690348 7
Alderson, Brian trans. *The Brothers Grimm; popular folk
  tales*. Gollancz, 1986, 0 575 0 2446 1
Alexander, Lloyd. *Book of three*. Collins, 1973,
  0 00 670592 8 (Prydain cycle)
Aliki. *How a Book is Made*. Bodley Head, 1986,
  0 370 310039
Allen, Pamela. *Who Sank the Boat?* Hamish Hamilton,
  1982, 0 241 11802 6
Anno, Mitsumasa. *Anno's Alphabet*. Bodley Head, 1974,
  0 370 012755
Ashley, Bernard. *Dinner Ladies Don't Count*. Julia MacRae,
  1981, 0 86203 017 X
— *Running Scared*. Puffin Plus, 1986, 014 032079 2
— *Terry on the Fence*. OUP, 1975, 019 271377 9
— *The Trouble with Donovan Croft*. Penguin, 1977,
  014 030974 8
Awdry, Rev. W. *Thomas the Tank Engine and the Tractor
  Pop-up Book*. Kaye & Webb, 1984, 0 7182 0854 4
Bagnold, Enid. *National Velvet*. Piccolo, 1985,
  0 330 28632 3
Bailey, John, McLeish, Kenneth and Spearman, David.
  *Gods and Men; myths and legends from the world's
  religions*. OUP, 1981, 019 278020 4
Baines, Talbot. *Fifth Form at St. Dominic's*. O/P
Bang, Mollie. *Ten Nine Eight*. Julia MacRae, 1983,
  0 86203 139 7
Barber, Richard. *A Companion to World Mythology*.
  Viking Kestrel, 1979, 0 7226 6251 3
Barrie, J. M. *Peter Pan*. Hodder, 1981, 0 340 26430 6
Bawden, Nina. *The Witch's Daughter*. Gollancz, 1966,
  0 575 00177 1
Beckmann, Gunnel. *Mia*. Bodley Head, 1974, O/P

Beresford, Elizabeth. *The Wombles*. Puffin, 1975, 014 030794 X

Berridge, Celia. *On My Way to School*. Deutsch, 1976, 0 233 96748 6

Blake, Quentin. *Nursery Rhyme Book*. Armada, 1985, 0 00662461 8

— *Mr. Magnolia*. Cape, 1980, 0 224 01612 1

Blishen, Edward. *Oxford Book of Poetry for Children*. OUP, 1963, 0 19 276031 9

Blishen, Edward and Garfield, Leon. *God Beneath the Sea*. Longman, 1970, O/P

Bloom, Freddie. *The Boy Who Couldn't Hear*. Bodley Head, 1977, 0 370 01811 7

Blume, Judy. *Forever*. Piccolo, 1984, 0 330 28533 5

Blyton, Enid. *Five on a Treasure Island*. Hodder, 1983, 0 340 33018 X

— *The Naughtiest Girl in the School*. Hamlyn, 1979, 0600 38414 4

— *Noddy and the Aeroplane*. Purnell, 1984, 0 361 00424 9

Bold, Alan, Owen, Gareth and O'Callaghan, Julie. *Bright Lights Blaze Out*. OUP, 1986, 019 276059 9

Bond, Michael. *Paddington Bear*. Collins, 1972, 0 00 182 112 1

Bosche, Susanne. *Jenny Lives with Eric and Martin*. Gay Men's Press, 1983, 0 907040 225

Boston, Lucy M. *The Children of Green Knowe*. Faber, 1954, 0 571 064604

— *The Sea-egg*. Puffin, 1978, 0 14 031087 8

Boynton, Sandra. *Moo, Baa, La Lala*. Methuen, 1983, 0 416 45490 9

Briggs, Raymond. *The Fairy Tale Treasury*. Young Puffin, 1974, 0 14 050 103 7

— *Father Christmas*. Hamish Hamilton, 1973, 0 241 022606

— *Fungus the Bogeyman*. Hamish Hamilton, 1977, 0 341 89553 7

Briggs, Raymond. *The Mother Goose Treasury*. Puffin, 1973, 014 005088 X

— *The Snowman*. Hamish Hamilton, 1978, 0 241 10004 6

— *When the Wind Blows*. Penguin, 1983, 014 00 66063

Brinsmead, Hesba. *Pastures of the Blue Crane*. Penguin, 1978, 014 031014 2

Brown, Ruth. *Our Puppy's Holiday*. Andersen, 1987, 0 86264 145 4

Browne, Anthony. *A Walk in the Park*. Hamish Hamilton, 1967, 0 241 89397 6

— *Through the Magic Mirror*. Hamish Hamilton, 1976, 0 241 89307 0

Buckeridge, Anthony. *Jennings Goes to School*. J. Goodchild, 1984, 0 86391 015 7

Burke, Susan. *Alexander in Trouble*. Bodley Head, 1979, 0 370 30143 9

Burningham, John. *Mr. Gumpy's Outing*. Cape, 1973, 0 224 61909 8

Burnford, Sheila. *The Incredible Journey*. Hodder, 1975, O/P

Butler, Bill. *The Spying Machines*. Hodder, 1985, 0 340 36532 3

Byars, Betsy. *The Eighteenth Emergency*. Bodley Head, 1974, 0370 10924 4

— *The Night Swimmers*. Bodley Head, 1980, 0 3770 3017 2

Campbell, Joanne. *Caitlin Trilogy*. Bantam, 1986, 0 553170767, 0 5531 7794X, 0553 20601 X

Carle, Eric. *1, 2, 3 to the Zoo*. Hamish Hamilton, 1986, 0 241 12360 7

— *The Very Hungry Caterpillar*. Picture Puffin, 1974, 0 14 050087 1

Carroll, Lewis. *Alice in Wonderland*. Gollancz, 1984, 0 575 03263 4

Carter, Angela. *Sleeping Beauty and Other Favourite Fairy Tales*. Gollancz, 1982, 0 575 03194 8

Causley, Charles. *Early in the Morning*. Viking Kestrel, 1987, 0 670 80810 5

— *The Tail of the Trinosaur*. Hamlyn, 1976, 0 600 38738 0

Chambers Children's Colour Dictionary, ed. by E. M. Kirkpatrick. Chambers, 1981, 0 550 10623 5

Chambers, Aidan. *Aidan Chambers' Book of Ghosts and Hauntings*. Kestrel, n.e. 1980, 0 7226 5210 0

— *Breaktime*. Bodley Head, 1978, 0 370 30122 6

— *Dance on My Grave*. Bodley Head, 1982, 0 370 30366 0

Child's Play. *There Was an Old Lady*. Child's Play, 1973, 0 85953 021 3

Cleary, Beverly. *Fifteen*. Puffin, 1977, 0 14 0309489

Cole, Babette. *Princess Smartypants*. Hamish Hamilton, 1986, 0 241 11885 9

Cooper, Susan. *The Dark is Rising*. Bodley Head, 1984, 0 370 30815 8

Cormier, Robert. *Beyond the Chocolate War*. Gollancz, 1985, 0 575 03711 3

Cousins, Jane. *Make it Happy*. Penguin, rev. ed. 1986, 014 054278

Cresswell, Helen. *The Bagthorpes Abroad*. Faber, 1984, 0571 13350 9

— *Lizzie Dripping*. Puffin, 1985, 0 14 0317511

Crompton, Richmal. *Just William*. Macmillan, 1983, 0337 358481

Crowther, Robert. *The Most Amazing Hide and Seek Alphabet Book*. Viking Kestrel, 1977, 0 7226 5314 X

Dahl, Roald. *Charlie and the Chocolate Factory*. Allen & Unwin, 1967, 0 048823077 4

— *The Witches*. Cape, 1983, 0224 02165 6

Danziger, Paula. *There's a Bat in Bunk Five*. Heinemann, 1987, 0 434 934135

Darke, Marjorie. *Comeback*. Puffin Plus, 1983, 014 031405 9

Davies, Andrew. *Marmalade at Work*. Blackie, 1984, 0 200 72827 X

— *Marmalade Atkins' Dreadful Deeds*. Magnet, 1982, 0 423 00560 X

Davies, Hunter. *Flossie Teacakes Fur Coat*. Armada, 1984,
0 00672178 8

Dejong, Meindert. *The House of Sixty Fathers*. Puffin,
1971, 014 030276 X

De la Mare, Walter. *The Voice; a sequence of poems*.
Faber, 1986, 0 571 13973 6

Dickinson, Peter. *Weathermonger*. Gollancz, 1984,
0 575 03475 0

Digby, Anne. *The First Term at Trebizon*. Granada, 1980,
024611419 3

Doherty, Berlie. *Children of Winter*. Methuen. 1985,
0 416 51130 9

Dunbar, Joyce. *Mundo and the Weather-child*. Heinemann,
1985, 0 434 93590 5

Duncan, Lois. *Stranger with My Face*. Pan Horizon, 1986,
0 33029255 2

Dyer, Elinor Brent. *The Chalet School and Barbara*.
Collins, 1982, 0 00 690375 4

Edwards, Dorothy. *My Naughty Little Sister Stories*.
Magnet, 1984, 0 416 22000 2

Eliot, T. S. *Old Possum's Book of Practical Cats*. Faber,
1962, 0 571 04578 2

Elliott, Michelle. *The Willow Street Kids*. Marilyn Malin
Books, 1986, 0 233 97954 9

Endersby, Frank. *Jasmine's Bed Time*. Child's Play, 1984,
0 85953 186 4

Enright, Elizabeth. *The Saturdays*. Puffin, 1970,
0 14 0302131

Fairweather, Eileen. *French Letters; the life and loves of
Miss Maxime Harrison, Form 4C*. The Women's Press,
1987, 0 7043 4903 5 (Livewires)

Fine, Anne. *Madame Doubtfire*. Hamish Hamilton, 1987,
0 241 12001 2

Fisk, Nicholas. *Mindbenders*. Viking Kestrel, 1987,
0 670 812447

Fitzhugh, Louise. *Nobody's Family is Going to Change*. Armada, 1978, 0 00 671351 3

Foreman, Michael. *All the King's Horses*. Hamish Hamilton, 1976, 0241 89291 0

Fortune, J. J. *Revenge in the Silent Tomb*. Armada, 1984, 0 00 692419 0

Fowler, Richard. *Let's Make it Go from Side to Side*. Ventura, 1985, (for Marks and Spencer) 0 90628434 1

Fox, Paula. *How Many Miles to Babylon?* Macmillan, 1962, O/P

French, Fiona. *Future Story*. OUP, 1983, 019 279778 6

— *Snow White in New York*. OUP, 1986, 019 271543 7

Gag, Wanda. *Millions of Cats*. Faber, 1929, 0 571 05361 0

Galdone, Paul. *The Three Billy Goats Gruff*. Worlds Work, 1974, 0 437 42513 4

Gallico, Paul. *The Snow Goose*. Penguin, 1982, 014 0026819

Gardam, Jane. *Bilgewater*. Hamish Hamilton, 1976, 0 241 89398 4

— *Summer After the Funeral*. Puffin, 1983, 014 031500 4

Garfield, Leon. *Jack Holborn*. Kestrel, 1984, 0 7226 5088 4

Garfield, Leon and Blishen, Edward. *The God Beneath the Sea*. Corgi, 1980, 0552 98012 9

Garner, Alan. *The Owl Service*. Collins, 1967, 0 00 184603 5

— *The Stone Book Quartet*. Collins, 1983, 0 00 184289 7

Godden, Rumer. *A Kindle of Kittens*. Macmillan, 1982, 0 333 32964 3

Goodall, John. *Paddy Goes Travelling*. Macmillan, 1982, 0 333 33188 5

Goscinny and Uderzo. *The Adventures of Asterix Omnibus*. Hodder, 1985, 0 340 37245 1

Gower, Mick. *Swings and Roundabouts*. Collins, 1981, 0 001 845 27 6

Graham, Amanda. *Arthur*. Spindlewood, 1986, 0 907 349 06 4

Grahame, Kenneth. *The Wind in the Willows*. Methuen, 1908, 0 416 39360 8

Gregory, Susan. *Kill-a-Louse-a-Week*. Viking Kestrel, 1986, 0670 81005 3

Gretz, Susanna. *Teddybears 1–10*. Collins, 1973, 0 00660647 4
— *Teddybears ABC*. Collins, 1979, 0 00661649 6

Guy, Rosa. *Edith Jackson*. Gollancz, 1979, 0 575 026073

Hallworth, Grace. *Mouth Open, Story Jump Out*. Methuen, 1984, 0 416 23550 6

Hamilton, Virginia. *The People Would Fly; American black tales*. Knopf, 1985

Hargreaves, Roger. *Mr. Men's Sports Day*. Thurman, 1977, 0859850641

Harris, Geraldine. *Children of the Wind*. Macmillan, 1986, 033332850 7

Hastings, Selina. *Sir Gawain and the Loathly Lady*. Walker, 1986, 0 7445 02950

Haugaard, Erik. *Hans Andersen; classic fairy tales*. Gollancz, 1985, 0 575 03558 7

Haviland, Virginia. *The Faber Book of North American Legends*. Faber, 1979, 0 571 11038 X

Hay, Dean. *Things in the Kitchen*. Collins, 1976, 0 00 195811 9

Heaney, Seamus and Hughes, Ted, ed. *The Rattle Bag*. Faber, 1982, 0571 11966 2

Heaslip, Peter. *My Dad*. Methuen Educational, 1984, 0 423 50470 3

Henri, Adrian and McGough, Roger. *The Mersey Sound*. Penguin, 0 14 058534 6

Hentoff, Nat. *This School is Driving me Crazy*. Pan, 1980, 0 330 25941 5

Herge. *Tintin and the Picaros*. Methuen, 1976, 0 416 57660 5

Hill, Douglas. *Warriors of the Wasteland*. Piccolo, 1984, 0 330 284525

Hill, Eric. *Little Spot Board Book; colours*. Heinemann, 1985, 0 434 942677

— *Where's Spot?* Heinemann, 1980, 0 434 94288 X

— *Where's Spot?* (sign language edition) National Deaf Children's Society, 1986, 0 904691 306

Hines, Barry. *Kestrel for a Knave*. Penguin, 1985, 014 0029524

Hinton, Nigel. *Buddy*. Dent, 1982, 0 460 06089 9

Hinton, S. E. *Rumble Fish*. Gollancz, 1980, 0 575 02710 X; Armada, 1977, 0 00671210 X

— *Tex*. Gollancz, 1980, 0 575 02710 X

— *That Was Then This Is Now*. Armada, 1975, 0 00670944 3

Hoban, Russell. *The Mouse and His Child*. Faber, 1969, 0 571 0844 9

Hollick, Helen. *Come and Tell Me*. Dinosaur, 1986, 0 8122 661 2

Holm, Anne. *I am David*. Methuen, 1965, 0 416 23340 6

Howker, Jannie. *Badger on the Barge and Other Stories*. Julia MacRae, 1984, 0 86203194 X

Howker, Jannie. *The Nature of the Beast*. Julia MacRae, 1985, 0 86203194 X

Hughes, Shirley. *Chips and Jessie*. Bodley Head, 1986, 0 370 30666 X

— *It's Too Frightening for Me*. Penguin, 1980, 0 14 031158 0

— *Lucy and Tom's ABC*. Gollancz, 1984, 0 575 0 33983

Hughes, Ted. *The Iron Man*. Faber, 1968, 0 571 08247 5

— *Moonbells and Other Poems*. Bodley Head, 1986, 0 370 30762 3

Hughes, Thomas. *Tom Brown's Schooldays*. Puffin, 1983, 0 14 035022 5

Hunter, Mollie. *The Stronghold*. Hamish Hamilton, 1974, 0 241 89026 8

Ingham, Jennie. *The Tiger and the Woodpecker*. Luzac, 1986, 090 4804356 (Hindi edn.)

Innocenti, Roberto. *Rose Blanche*. Cape, 1985,
0 22462841 3

Ireson, Barbara. *In a Class of Their Own; school stories*.
Faber, 1985, 0 571 13474 2

Jackson, Steve and Livingstone, Ian. *Fighting Fantasy*.
Puffin, 1984, 014 031709 0

Jaffrey, Madhur. *Seasons of Splendour*. Pavilion, 1985,
0 907516 0

Jansson, Tove. *Finn Family Moonintroll*. Puffin, 1970,
0 14 030150 X

Jensen, Virginia Allen and Haller, D. W. *What's That?*
Collins, 1979, 0 00 19635 8

Jessell, Camilla. *Mark's Wheelchair Adventures*. Methuen,
1975, 0 416 8070 8

Johns, W. E. *Biggles Works it Out*. Hodder, 1984,
0 340 34839 9

Johnson, Audean. *Soft as a Kitten*. Random House, 1983,
0 394 85517 5

Jonas, Ann. *The Trek*. Julia MacRae, 1986, 0 86203 244 X

Jones, Diana Wynne. *The Ogre Downstairs*. Macmillan,
1974, 0 333 15917 9

Junior Pears Encyclopaedia, ed. Edward Blishen. Pelham
Books, 1984, 0 720 71524 5

Juster, Norton. *The Phantom Tollbooth*. Collins, 1974,
0 00 670799 8

Kastner, Erich. *Lotte and Lisa*. Puffin, 1975, 0 14 030167 4

Keats, Ezra Jack. *Peter's Chair*. Bodley Head, 1968,
0370 00790 5

— *The Snowy Day*. Bodley Head, English/Turkish
edn 1980, 0 370 30242 7

Keeping, Charles. *Joseph's Yard*. OUP, 1969,
0 19 279651 8

— *Railway Passage*. OUP, 1974, 0 19 279700 X

Kemp, Gene. *The Clock Tower Ghost*. Faber, 1981,
0 571 11767 8

— *Jason Bodger and the Priory Ghost*. Faber, 1985,
0571 136451

— *The Turbulent Term of Tyke Tiler*. Puffin, 1979,
0 14031135 1

Kennemore, Tim. *The Wall of Words*. Puffin, 1984,
0 14 031596 6

Kingsley, Charles. *The Water Babies*. Pan, 1973,
0 330 23832 9

Kipling, Rudyard. *The Cat that Walked by Himself*.
Picturemac, 1986, 0 333 38717 1

Klein, Norma. *Breaking Up*. Pan Horizon, 1986,
0 33029293 5

Lang, Andrew. *The Blue Fairy Book*. Kestrel, 1975,
0 7226 5064 7

Lavelle, Sheila. *Holiday with the Fiend*. Hamish Hamilton,
1986, 0 241 11857 3

Lawrence, Louise. *Children of the Dust*. Bodley Head,
1985, 0370 30679 1

— *The Warriors of Taan*. Bodley Head, 1985,
0 370 30715 1

Lear, Edward. *Complete Nonsense*. Faber, 1947,
0 571 06440 X

Leeson, Robert. *Grange Hill Rules – OK?* Armada, 1979,
0 00671658 X

— *It's My Life*. Armada, 1981, 0 00671783 7

— *Maroon Boy*. Armada, 1982, 0 00672097 8

— *The Third Class Genie*. Hamish Hamilton, 1981,
0 241 10623 0

— *The Time Rope*. Longman, 1986, 0582 250889

Le Guin, Ursula. *A Wizard of Earthsea*. Gollancz, 1971,
0 575 00717 6

Lester, Julius. *The Tales of Uncle Remus; the adventures of
Brer Rabbit*. Bodley Head, 1987, 0 370 31089 6

Lewis, C. S. *The Lion, the Witch and the Wardrobe*.
Collins, 1974, 0 00 183140 2

Lewis, Naomi. *The Snow Queen*. Kestrel, 1979, 07226 5487 1

Lindsay, Norman. *The Magic Pudding*. Angus & Robertson, 1976, 0 20713278 X

Lindgren, Astrid. *Pippi Longstocking*. OUP, 1954, 0 19271097 4

Lingard, Joan. *Across the Barricades*. Hamish Hamilton, 1972, 0 241 02167 7

— *The Clearance*. Hamish Hamilton, 1974, 0 241 89021 7

Lively, Penelope. *The Ghost of Thomas Kempe*. Heinemann, 1973, 0 43494894 2

Lobel, Arnold. *Frog and Toad All Year*. Worlds Work, 1977, 0 437 901092

Lodge, Bernard and Roffey, Maureen. *The Grand Old Duke of York*. Bodley Head, 1975, 0 370 010761 6

Lofting, Hugh. *The Story of Dr. Dolittle*. Cape, 1966, 0 22460437 6

Loup, Jean Jacques. *The Architect*. Cape, 1977, 0 224 01398 X

MacDonald, George. *At the Back of the North Wind*. Penguin, 1984, 014 035030 6

McEvoy, Seth. *Batteries Not Included*. Grafton, 1986, 0583 30982 8

McGibbon, Jean. *Hal*. Heinemann, 1974, 0 434 94986 8

McGough, Roger. *Sky in the Pie*. Kestrel, 1983, 07226 5830 3

Maclachan, Patricia. *Sarah, Plain and Tall*. Julia MacRae, 1986, 0 86203 247 4

Macmillan's Children's Encyclopaedia. Macmillan, 1984, 0333 27393 1 (2 vol. ed.)

Magorian, Michelle. *Goodnight Mr. Tom*. Kestrel, 1981, 07226 57013

Mahy, Margaret. *The Changeover*. Dent, 1984, 0 460 06153 4

— *The Downhill Crocodile Whizz and Other Stories*. Dent, 1986, 0 460 06237 9

— *The Haunting*. Dent, 1982, 0 460 06097 X

— *A Lion in the Meadow*. Picture Puffin, 1972,
0 14 05043 X

Maris, Ron. *Better Move on Frog*. Julia MacRae, 1982,
0 86203083 8

— *Is Anyone Home?* Julia MacRae, 1985, 0 86203 217 2

Marryat, Frederick. *Children of the New Forest*. Dent, ·
1955, 0 460 05032 X

Marshall, James Vance. *Walkabout*. Puffin, 1980,
0 14 031292 7

Marshall, Ray and Bradley, John. *Watch It Work: The Car*.
Viking Kestrel, 1986, 0722 659601

Marshall, Ray and Korky, Paul. *Humpty Dumpty Pop-Up
Book*. Kestrel, 1983, 0 7226 5862 1

Masefield, John. *Box of Delights*. Fontana, 1984,
0 00672415 9

Mathias, Beverley comp. *The Hippo Book of Funny Verse*.
Hippo, 1987, 0590 70677 2

Mayne, William. *Cathedral Wednesday*. Hodder, 1972,
0 34015202 8

Milne, A. A. *Winnie the Pooh*. Methuen, 1973,
0 416 16860 4

Montgomery, L. M. *Anne of Green Gables*. Puffin, 1977,
0 14 030 945 4

Moore, Patrick. *The Space Shuttle Action Book*. Arum
Press, 1983, 0906053 366

Mordillo, Guillermo. *Mordillo's Football*. Hutchinson,
1979, 0 09 138830 9

Murphy, Jill. *The Worst Witch*. Puffin, 1981, 0 140 31348 6

Nesbit, E. M. *The Phoenix and the Carpet*. Penguin, 1984,
014 035062 4

— *The Railway Children*. Armada, 1978, 0 00 691476 6

Nimmo, Jenny. *The Snow Spider*. Methuen, 1986,
0 416 54530 0

Norton, Mary. *Bedknob and Broomstick*. Dent, 1957,
0460 05655 7

Norton, Mary. *The Borrowers*. Dent, 1975, 0 400 05104 0

Nöstlinger, Christine. *Conrad*. Andersen, 1976,
0 90547803 7

— *Fly Away Home*. Andersen, 1985, 086264 090 3

Oakley, Graham. *The Church Mouse*. Macmillan, 1972,
0 333 13259 9

O'Brien, Robert C. *Mrs. Frisby and the Rats of Nimh*.
Gollancz, 1972, 0 575 01552 7

O'Brien, Robert. *Z for Zachariah*. Gollancz, 1984,
0 57503378 9

Opie, Iona and Peter. *The Oxford Dictionary of Nursery
Rhymes*. O.U.P., 1951, 019 869111 4

Ormerod, Jan. *Sunshine*. Puffin, 1983, 014 050362 5

Ormerod, Jan and Lloyd David. *Reading*. Walker, 1985,
0 7445 02594

Orwell, George. *Animal Farm*. Penguin, 1978, 014 000 314

O'Shea, Pat. *The Hounds of the Morrigan*. O.U.P., 1985,
0 19 271506 2

Owen, Annie. *Annie's ABC*. Orchard Books, 1987,
1 85213 013 X

Oxenbury, Helen. *The Helen Oxenbury Nursery Rhyme
Book*. ed. Brian Alderson. Heinemann, 1986,
0 434 95604 X

— *Helping*. Methuen/Walker, 1982, 0416 06080 3

— *Shopping*. Methuen/Walker, 1982, 0416 06060 9

Pascal, Francine. *Malibu Summer*. Bantam, 1986,
0553 26050 2 (Sweet Valley High)

Patten, Brian. *Grave Gossip*. Unwin, 1986, 0 04821041 2

Pearce, Philippa. *A Dog So Small*. Kestrel, 1975,
0 7226 5261 5

— *Tom's Midnight Garden*. O.U.P., 1958, 0 19 721128 8

Pienkowski, Jan. *The Haunted House Pop-up Book*.
Heinemann, 1979, 0 434 95635 X

Pierce, Tamora. *In the Land of the Goddess*. O.U.P., 1986,
0 19721551 8

Pithers, David and Greene, Sarah. *We Can Say No*. Hutchinson, 1986, 0 09 167160 4

Potter, Beatrix. *The Tale of Mrs Tiggywinkle*. Warne, 1950, 07232 0597 3

Powling, Chris. *The Daredevils and Scaredycats*. Abelard-Schuman, 1979, 0 200 72623 4

— *The Phantom Carwash*. Heinemann, 1986, 0 434 93034 2

Price, Willard. *The Underwater Adventure*. Cape, 1935, 0 224 61180 1

Prince, Alison. *The Ghost Within*. Methuen, 1984, 0 416 467709

— *The Doubting Kind*. Longman/Topliner, 1986, 0 333 22321 7

Proysen, Alf. *Little Old Mrs. Pepperpot*. Hutchinson, 1958, 0 09 051290 1

Purnell. Bath Books, eg *Animals*. Purnell, 1985, 0 361 06760 7

Ransome, Arthur. *Swallows and Amazons*. Cape, 1930, 0224 60631 X

Rawlings, M. *The Yearling*. Piccolo, 1976, 0 330 24761 1

Rayner, Mary. *Mr and Mrs Pig's Evening Out*. Macmillan, 1976, 032 19371 7

Read, Herbert ed. *This Way Delight*. Faber, O/P

Richards, Frank. *Billy Bunter of Greyfriars School*. Granada, 1983, 0 583 30524 5

Rippon, Angela. *Victoria Plum's Garden*. Purnell, 1985, 0 361 06715 1

Rodgers, Mary. *Freaky Friday*. Puffin, 1976, 0 14 0307516

Rosen, Michael. *Don't Put Mustard in the Custard*. Deutsch, 1985, 0 233 977848

— *When Did You Last Wash Your Feet?* Deutsch, 1986, 0 00672 676 3

Ruskin, John. *King of the Golden River*. Dover, 1975, 0486 20066 3

Saint-Exupery, Antoine de. *The Little Prince*. Heinemann, 1945, 0434 961604

Salkey, Andrew. *Hurricane*. O.U.P., 1979, 019 277087 X

Sallis, Susan. *Sweet Frannie*. Heinemann, 1983, 0 434 961655

Sendak, Maurice. *In the Night Kitchen*. Bodley Head, 1971, 0 370 015495

— *Where the Wild Things Are*. Bodley Head, 1967, 0 370 00772 7

Serraillier, Ian. *The Silver Sword*. Cape, 1956, 0224 60677 8

Sewell, Anna. *Black Beauty*. Puffin, 1971, 0 14 030064 3

Shakespeare, William. *Romeo and Juliet*. illus. by Von. Michael Joseph, 1981, 0 7181 2357 3

Shyer, Marlene Fanta. *Welcome Home Jellybean*. Granada, 1982, 0 583 30496 6

Smallman, Claire, *Outside-In:* a Lift-the-flap Body Book. Macdonald, 1986 0 356 11819 3

Smith, Dick King. *The Fox Busters*. Gollancz, 1978, 0 575 02444 5

— *Saddle Bottom*. Gollancz, 1986, 0575 03715 6

Southall, Ivan. *The Long Night Watch*. Methuen, 1983, 0 416 44610 8

— *To the Wild Sky*. Angus & Robertson, 1967, 0 207 94634 5

Spence, Eleanor. *The October Child*. O.U.P., 1976, 0 19 271384 1

Sperry, Armstrong. *The Boy Who Was Afraid*. Bodley Head, 1963, 0 370 00910 X

Stevenson, R. L. *A Child's Garden of Verses*. Gollancz, 1985, 0 575 03727 X

— *Treasure Island*. Gollancz, 1982, 0 575 03149 2

Stobbs, William. *A Widemouthed, Gaping, Waddling Frog*. Pelham, 1973, 07207 08494

Stones, Rosemary ed. *Mother Goose Comes to Cable Street*. Kestrel, 1977, 07226 52771

Stones, S. and Dickinson, H. *Mitthu the Parrot*. Luzac Storytellers, 1986, (Urdu/English) 0 7109 101 2 5

Storr, Catherine. *Great Tales From Long Ago: Richard the Lionheart*. Methuen, 1987, 0 416 63970 4

— *Ruth's Story*. Watts, 1986, 086313 347 9

Strachan, Ian. *Journey of 1000 Miles*. Magnet, 1985, 0 416 51880 X

Styles, Morag. *You'll Love This Stuff; poems from many cultures*. CUP, 1987, 0 521 31275 2

Sutcliff, Rosemary. *The Light Beyond the Forest*. Bodley Head, 1979, 0 370 30191 9

Taylor, Mildred. *Roll of Thunder, Hear My Cry*. Gollancz, 1977, 0 575 0 2384 8

Tennyson, Alfred. *The Lady of Shalott*. O.U.P., 1986, 019 276057 2, illus. Charles Keeping

Thiele, Colin. *Chadwick's Chimney*. Methuen, 1980, 0 416 86670 0

— *Fire in the Stone*. Puffin, 1981, 0 14 031360 5

Thomas, Gwyn and Crossley-Holland, Kevin. *Tales from the Mabinogian*. Gollancz, 1984, 0 575 035315

Tolkien, J. J. R. *The Hobbit*. Allen & Unwin, 1984, 0 04 823273 4

— *The Lord of the Rings*. Allen & Unwin, 1979, 004 8232009

Townsend, Sue. *The Growing Pains of Adrian Mole*. Methuen, 1984, large print ed. ISIS, 1984 1 85089 038 2

Townsend, John. *Gumble's Yard*. Viking Kestrel, 1984, 0 670 80081 3

Townson, Hazel. *The Siege at Cobb Street School*. Andersen, 1983, 026264 0415

Treece, Henry. *The Viking's Dawn*. Penguin, 1967, 0 14 030320 0

Turner, Ethel. *Seven Little Australians*. Ward Lock, 1894, O/P

Twain, Mark. *The Adventures of Huckleberry Finn*. Puffin, 1970, 0 14 030080 5

317

Untermeyer, Louis. *The Golden Treasury of Poetry*. Collins, 1961, 0 00 106124 0

Verne, Jules. *Journey to the Centre of the Earth*. Blackie, 1979, 0216 88506 X

— *20,000 Leagues Under the Sea*. Bantam, 1983, 0553 21063 7

Vincent, Gabrielle. *Bravo Ernest and Celestine!* Julia MacRae, 1982, 0 86203 074 9

Vipont, Elfrida. *The Elephant and the Bad Baby*. Hamish Hamilton, 1969, 0 241 01639 8

Voigt, Cynthia. *The Homecoming*. Collins, 1983, 0 00 1841475

Wachter, Oralee. *No More Secrets for Me*. Viking Kestrel, 1986, 0 670 00719 2

Walsh, Jill Paton. *The Dolphin Crossing*. Macmillan, 1967, 0 373 09096 9

— *The Emperor's Winding Sheet*. Puffin, 1976, 0 14 0308334

— *A Parcel of Patterns*. Kestrel, 1983, 0 7226 5898 2

Watanabe, Shigeo. *How Do I Put It On?* Bodley Head, 1979, 0 370 30 20 6 0

Waters, Fiona. *Golden Apples; poems for children*. Heinemann, 1986, 0 434 97163 4

Watson, James. *The Freedom Tree*. Gollancz, 1986, 0 575 03779 2

— *Talking in Whispers*. Gollancz, 1983, 0 575 03272 3

Wayland's Atlas of the World. Wayland, 1985, 0 85078 702 5

Webb, Kaye ed. *I Like This Poem*. Puffin, 1979, 014031295 1

West, Colin. *It's Funny When You Look at It*. Heinemann, 1984, 0 09 158480 9

Westall, Robert. *The Cats of Seroster*. Macmillan, 1984, 0 33 37549 1

— *Futuretrak 5*. Kestrel, 1983, 0 7226 5880 X

— *The Machine Gunners*. Macmillan, 1975, 0 333 18644 3

— *The Scarecrows*. Bodley Head, 1984, 0 370 30844 1

Wheels go Round. Methuen, 1981, 0 416 20840 1

White, E. B. *Charlotte's Web*. Hamish Hamilton, 1952, 0 241 90098 0

Wilde, Oscar. *The Fairy Stories of Oscar Wilde*. Gollancz, 1976, 0 575 02170 5

Wilder, Laura Ingalls. *The Little House on the Prairie*. Methuen, 1970, 0 416 07140 6

Wildsmith, Brian. *ABC*. OUP, 1981, 0 19 272122 4

Willard, Barbara. *Spell Me a Witch*. Hamish Hamilton, 1979, 024110084 4

Williams, Jay. *The Practical Princess and Other Liberating Fairy Tales*. Bodley Head, 1985, 0 370 030819 0

Williamson, Henry. *Tarka the Otter*. Puffin, 1971, 0 14 030060 0

Wilson, Bob. *Stanley Bagshaw and the Fourteen Foot Wheel*. Hamish Hamilton, 1981, 0 241 10634 6

Wood, John Norris. *Nature Hide and Seek; oceans*. Methuen, 1985, 0 416 51410 3

Woodford, Peggy ed. *Misfits*. Bodley Head, 1984, 0 370 30824 7

Wrightson, Patricia. *The Rocks of Honey*. Puffin, 1966, 0 14 030269 7

Yeatman, Linda. *Pickles*. Piccadilly Press, 1986, 0946 826 37 4

Zindel, Paul. *The Pigman*. Bodley Head, 1967, 0 370 010 34 5

Zion, Gene and Bloy, Margaret. *Henry the Dirty Dog*. Bodley Head, 1960, 0 370 00696 8

Play series mentioned in the text
Dramaworld, C.U.P.
Junior Drama series, Macmillan

BIBLIOGRAPHY

Playmakers, C.U.P.
Playreaders, Macmillan
Plays Plus Readers, Holt Rinehart
Scene Scripts, Longman
Six Plays for Today, Murray
Spirals, Hutchinson
Star Plays, Longman
Take Part, Ward Lock Ed.
Young Drama, Methuen.

Index

323

326